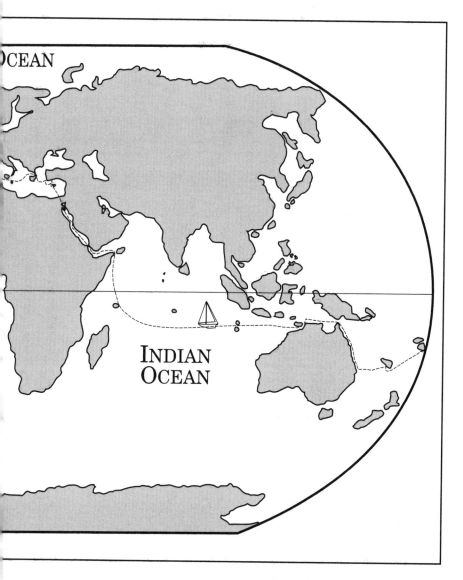

OCEAN

INDIAN
OCEAN

**Nautical
Miles**

D0841363

With The Wind

TO SAIL THE WORLD

With The Wind

TO SAIL THE WORLD

by NICK ELLISON

Kilo Publishing Co.
Newport, Kentucky

To Pat, John, Katie, Andy and Sam

Copyright © 1996 by Nicholas C. Ellison

Publisher's Cataloging in Publication
    (Prepared by Quality Books Inc.)

Ellison, Nick
    With the wind: to sail the world/by Nick Ellison.
    P. Cm.
    Includes bibliographical references.
    ISBN 0-9651825-0-9

    1. Ellison, Nick C.—Voyages. 2. Lusty Wind II (Boat)
    3. Voyages around the world. I. Title.

G440.E55E55 1996   910.4'1
                                                    QBI96-20264
    LCCN 96-94276

Published by   Kilo Publishing Co.
                144 Ridgewood Place
                Newport, Kentucky 41075-1616
                U.S.A.
                Tel: (606) 441-4059
                          (888) 545-6782 (Toll Free)
                FAX: (606) 441-8517
                Email: Kilopub@aol.com

Cover design by Design Phase, Inc.
Cover copy by Environmental Technologies and Communications Inc.
Book design by Katherine Kremer Pennington
Typesetting and graphics by TypeCraft! Inc.
Color separation by PrePress Inc.
Photographs by author unless otherwise noted.
Printed in The United States of America by Steinhauser, Inc.

First Edition

I wish to express my deep appreciation
to John Deering and Peggy Kreimer
whose assistance and suggestions
plus their persistent faith in *With the Wind*
was critical in bringing about its completion.

CONTENTS

CHARTS AND ILLUSTRATIONS

FORE

Ft. Thomas, Kentucky

April 1, 1996

My business card says I am a real estate developer. But I am a sailor. I love the sea and all that it means. I love a boat and all that it means. For me, from November 1991 to March 1994, our boat, *Lusty Wind II*, meant literally everything – my family, my time and my dream – as we sailed around the world.

We did it in shifts, leaving the boat in safe ports with new crews of family and friends flying in and out of the adventure. This book is your invitation to join our crew. If you're a sailor, you won't have to be asked twice. If you're not, I'd like to think you will be by the time we reach the magically beautiful mountains of Fatu Hiva, or certainly by the time we face down the gun boat of the Saudi Navy in the Red Sea.

Did I say gun boat? Don't let that dissuade you. You might miss meeting the real Big Bahama Mama, calling the bluff of a phalanx of fishing trawlers off the deadly reefs of Australia, lunching with spies at the Seychelles Yacht Club, hiking to the pinnacle of a mountain monastery in the Aegean, and sailing through the Pillars of Hercules.

When I finally returned from the sea, the most frequently asked question was "What did the trip cost?"

As I said, I'm a real estate developer and the year of intense planning and two-and-a-half years of being away most of the time happened to be poor years for real estate. That allows me to say "I probably saved a couple hundred thousand dollars a year, because if I had been home I would have been foundering with some suburban office building." The truth is, I don't know the cost. Whatever it was, it was worth it.

The second most frequent question: "When you are taking your boat across the ocean, where do you park it at night?"

It's difficult to know where to start with this one. First, of course, she's not an it.

My favorite homecoming exchange came in a conversation with a clerk at a Northern Kentucky shop.

Clerk: "We haven't seen you in a long time."
Me: "I've been away for two-and-a-half years."
Clerk: "Where have you been?"
Me: "I sailed around the world."
Clerk: "Oh, is that right. I've got a cousin who went to Cancún."

Well, I don't know if this trip can compare with Cancún. But I've done my best to stuff these pages with the people, the seas, the lands and the history that prove that half the fun IS in getting there.

There are times during the story that I will take a side trip into details of history, geography, geology and navigation techniques that some readers may want to forego. Those sections are set aside. It makes them easy to savor or easy to navigate around − sort of like literary coral reefs. Enjoy them or avoid them as you will.

Sailors today, with all their safety gear and creature comforts, are following in the wake of giants who sailed uncharted waters. Part of the foundation of our civilization is based on the feats of these courageous seamen. Today's sailors are safer and more comfortable but the wind blows just as hard and the ocean water is just as far over our heads as it ever was.

Our family's adventure was not just the adventure of wind and wave, navigating and sailing. It contained in a small way the spirit of Columbus, de Gama, Magellan, Cook, and Slocum. If you don't know all the names now, you will. We took pride in touching on their adventures and accomplishments.

And now, a short primer to the terminology you will find in this book:

In the spelling of geographic names, I have followed the convention of the National Geographic Society which assumes a traveler would buy a plane ticket to say Greece, in their home language, but once there board a ferry to Ródhos, utilizing the local language (in this case spelled phonetically). Similarly we refer to the country of Panama and the city of Panamá (local use puts the accent mark on the second "a"). International bodies of water are in our home language which explains why we sail across the Gulf of Aden to the Port of Adan.

Navigators use nautical miles (6,076 feet) instead of statute miles (5,280 feet). Sailors often refer to statute miles as land miles. Nautical miles are one minute of a degree of the circumference of the earth, thus 1/21,600th (360 X 60) of the earth's circumference. As the earth is a little lumpy, the length of the nautical mile is by international agreement. Navigators use this dimension because it relates to the charts of most nations and to celestial navigation. Readers need only to consider that the nautical mile is 15% longer than the statute mile. Also if a boat is traveling at 7 knots she is going 8 land miles per hour.

Although sailing today is not a reckless endeavor, any reader planning a blue-water voyage surely knows that sailing does have its dangers. This book and the charts and diagrams herein, are an account of my family's experiences. I do not claim to be a master mariner and this book or the charts herein are not intended nor should they be used for navigation.

And now, welcome aboard. We're sailing around the world and like life itself, "we must sail sometimes with the wind and sometimes against it."

"I find the great thing in this world is not so much where we stand, as in what direction we are moving: To reach the port of heaven, we must sail sometimes with the wind and sometimes against it, – but we must sail, and not drift, nor lie at anchor."

The Autocrat of the Breakfast-Table
Oliver Wendall Holmes

Out At Sea

The man who craves an open sea
Is more a man than most could be.
Be guided by an unknown hand,
Heading for an alien land.

It's not the land he wants to reach
Or anchor off a lonely beach.
It's the dare and do of sailing
Not a cause of human failing.

To feel the winds that catch the sails,
Be battered by the winds and gales,
Or battle dangers on the deep
As courage takes a quantum leap.

Often it's not rife with danger,
There are times just to ponder
About the past life's intent,
And wonder how the time was spent.

There are dreams about each notion,
A dream to sail the ocean
With the family or a friend
Aboard the boat, the *Lusty Wind*.

Frank B. Menefee
December 25, 1993

With The Wind

TO SAIL THE WORLD

1

CHAPTER ONE

Bound Around the World

November 11, 1991 – November 15, 1991

Man-O-War Cay, Bahamas – Ft. Lauderdale, FL

It is a quiet start after forty-three years of dreaming. After all, during any month, several boats leave Man-O-War, in the Bahamas, for Florida; and it is likely no one really believes we are bound around the world. It is eight o'clock in the morning. The tide is right to get out of the harbor and we are on our way. George Malone, the manager of Man-O-War Marina, is at the dock to help with our mooring lines and reminds me *Lusty Wind II* has her usual slip reserved for April 1994 – three years away.

I've done this first passage at least 20 times, but I can't let the familiarity lull me into believing we are in for easy times. I remember my first sailboat trip to the Bahamas and the trials that new waters can bring.

I grew up in a home where the *National Geographic Magazine* was a part of my life. As early as I can remember, I grabbed the *National Geographic* as soon as it hit the mailbox. However, my mind was not always on geography; it frequently was on pictures of scantily clad girls who just happened to be in remote parts of the world. The January 1949 issue had the first of two articles by Irving and Electa Johnson about their voyage around the world – this one of seven was aboard *Yankee*. These articles were my first exposure to the concept of circumnavigation of the world. I studied the articles over and over and resolved to sail my own boat around the world someday.

I traced the trip on countless maps. As I got older, I'd go to the library and read every book I could find on sailboats, circumnavigation, or long ocean voyages, including *Sailing Around the World Alone* by Joshua Slocum. I spent weeks reading and re-reading these books.

During the ensuing years my dreams were overshadowed by cars, girls, college, marriage, career, and babies. Through everything, any picture of or reference to a sailboat triggered the old longing.

At age 21 I was diagnosed as diabetic and was given a draft status of 4F. In those days, the medical profession gave a diabetic 20 years of life. At that time it didn't look like anyone really lived after 40 anyway; so this wasn't too alarming. My first job interview was with a bank in Cincinnati. When I told them my draft status, I thought they would consider me a prize package. Instead, they abruptly ended the interview saying they didn't hire diabetics since diabetics couldn't travel and that might occasionally be necessary for a bank officer. The revelation angered me and rekindled my desire to sail around the world.

Today with easy blood glucose monitoring and magnificent antibiotics, diabetics can take on great adventures that wouldn't have been feasible just a few years ago.

By 1970, my wife Pat and I began chartering boats in the Virgin Islands, the Bahamas, and the Chesapeake Bay. We learned to sail as we bounced off docks and shoals. No one imagined my real intention was to sail around the world.

In 1980, we purchased our first boat – *Lusty Wind*, a Mason 43. We had her commissioned in Ft. Lauderdale, and sailed her for six years in the Bahamas, the Florida Keys, the Florida Gulf coast, and as far away as Hilton Head, South Carolina – still bouncing off docks and shoals. By now, the entire family was hooked on sailing and still no one knew of my plan.

As our four children, John, Katie, Andy, and Sam, began to get older, it became obvious 43 feet would not accommodate six full size people on the voyage I envisioned. When the opportunity came to have a Mason 53 built to our order, we reluctantly parted with *Lusty Wind* and began our warm and respectful relationship with *Lusty Wind II*.

The name of our boats comes from an epic poem *Conspiracy of Charles, Duke of Byron* written in 1608 by George Chapman. One stanza seemed to symbolize what our boats mean to us:

> "Give me a spirit that on this life's rough sea
> Love's t'have his sails fill'd with a lusty wind.
> Even till his sail-yards tremble, his masts crack,
> and his rapt ship runs on her side so low that she
> drinks water, and her keel plows air."

As they say today, "Go for it." Our family was about to learn just how far we would go.

In June 1987, after our son John had graduated from high school, John, some friends and I embarked on the big test of the boat and our resolve. We departed Ft. Lauderdale for Bermuda, the Azores, Gibraltar, and Puerto Bañus, Spain. The rest of the family flew to Puerto Bañus and joined us for a drive through Europe. We flew home, and in January, 1988, I flew back to Spain with some friends. We sailed *Lusty Wind II* home through Gibraltar, Morocco, the Canary Islands, and Antigua.

Relief crews flew in and out at strategic stops. John crewed from St. Kitts to St. Martin and the Virgin Islands. Son Andy crewed from the Virgin Islands to the Turks and Caicos and Man-O-War. We had our share of minor emergencies, but we handled all of them. It is interesting to look back at my pre-departure anxiety. In Ft. Lauderdale, just before our first departure, I ran to the chancellery to get more fuses and then decided I needed another spare pump. I was afraid we'd run out of salt and pepper; so I ran to the grocery for more. By the time we left the Azores for Gibraltar and Spain we weren't running anymore. We looked at one another and said "Are we ready to go? – Yeah" – and we went. Well almost.

With the test run over, the detailed planning for a trip around the world was about to begin. First, I had to convince Pat it was the right thing to do. This step continued until her plane landed at Nuku Hiva in a remote corner of the South Pacific without a return ticket.

An important part of the plan was the age of our children. We wanted to take the trip before John began his career and would not be able to consider such an undertaking and after Sam was old enough both to take care of himself and appreciate the trip. We wanted the best legs of the trip to be in June, July, and August when school is out and all of the family could be aboard.

We spent hours studying pilot books and pilot charts to learn the trade wind system and the best times to avoid major storms in all oceans of the world. After accounting for nature's hazards, we combed sailing magazines to determine areas of the world that mankind has made unsafe.

* * *

The "trade" systems of wind which in turn massage currents rotate clockwise over oceans of the Northern Hemisphere and counterclockwise in oceans of the Southern Hemisphere. The Intertropical Conversion Zone, an area of very little wind and current, lies between these revolving systems along the equator. In the centers of the wind systems are variable winds. Local high and low pressures can cause the wind to blow across these systems for short periods of time. These winds, for their short periods, do not usually affect the currents. Thus, just north and just south of the equator, but out of the ITCZ, the system – and thus the easiest and most pleasant way for a sailboat to travel – is westbound. The system – and the easiest way to travel eastbound – is in the southern high latitudes (closer to the South Pole). Land masses block the route in the northern high latitudes. With the Panama and Suez Canals, it is now not necessary for westbound voyagers to get into the southern high latitudes with their frequently dangerous weather.

Unfortunately, the tropics are where tropical storms with winds over 64 knots present a major threat. In our part of the world, these are hurricanes; in western North Pacific waters, they're typhoons. North of Australia, they're willy-willys; and in the South Pacific and Indian Oceans, cyclones. In all cases, they generate extremely strong winds and monstrous seas that can overwhelm boats much larger than *Lusty Wind II*.

These dangerous storms breed in the Intertropical Convergence Zone and grow as they cross the oceans westbound in the system. They

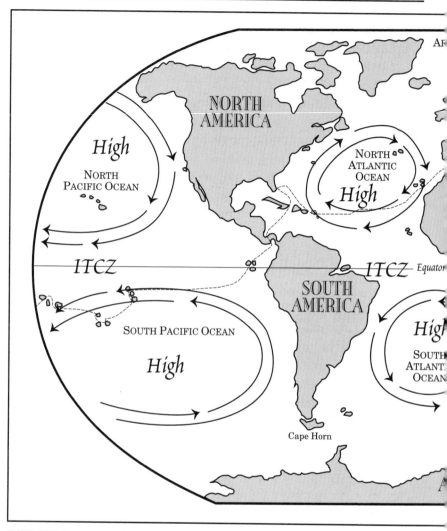

METEOROLOGICAL SYSTEMS The meteorological "systems" of wind which in turn massage currents rotate clockwise over oceans in the Northern Hemisphere and counterclockwise in oceans in the Southern Hemisphere. The Intertropical Conversion Zone, an area of very little

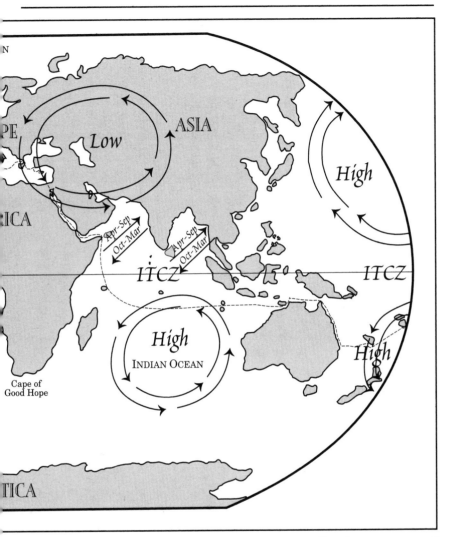

wind and current, lies along the equator. In the centers of the wind systems are variable winds. Local high and low pressures can cause the wind to blow across or against these "systems" for short periods of time. These winds, for their short periods, do not usually effect the currents.

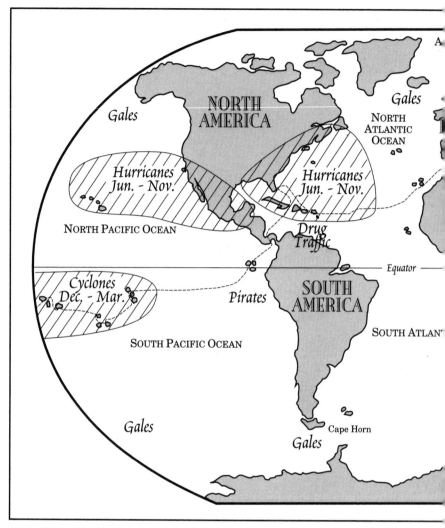

DANGER AREAS Tropical storms are quite predictable as to the area and times of the year. These areas can be avoided by cruising sailboats by waiting out the times of

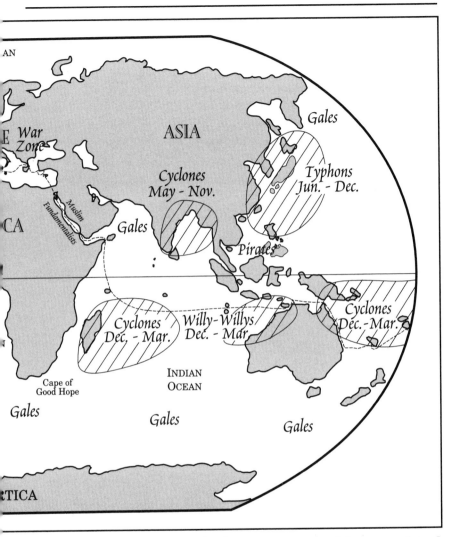

the storms. Areas with dangers caused by mankind change over time but are dangerous all year.

are therefore, most frequent on the Eastern shores of the continents.

The good news is that tropical storms are seasonal and easy to avoid by knowing the following:

- In the North Atlantic and Caribbean the tropical storm season is June – November.
- In the South Pacific, from French Polynesia to the Australian coast, the storm season is December – March.
- In the eastern Indian Ocean, south of Indonesia and northwest of Australia, the storm season is December – March.
- In the western South Indian Ocean, east and north of Madagascar, the storm season is December – April.
- In the Bay of Bengal, east of India, the storm season is May – November.
- In the Gulf of Arabia, west of India, the storm season is both May – June and October – November.

Gales, 32 to 63 knots of wind, are found occasionally in all oceans year round. However, they are more frequent and severe in higher latitudes, both north and south. In short, the closer one gets to the poles, the more likely gales will be encountered.

El Niño, an interannual (occurring every two to six years) warming of the tropical Pacific Ocean, can interrupt or reverse the trade winds and currents in the South Pacific. These of course affect blue-water sailors. If a person is sailing 3,200 nautical miles with fuel for 1,000, a reversal of the system is a real concern. When El Niño occurs it is strongest from October through April. Studies of soil layers along the Nile and tree rings in

California suggest that El Niño has far reaching effects. El Niño disturbs fishing along the west coast of South America as the currents reverse and cold water becomes warm; El Niño reaches its peak at Christmas-time, which is why fisherman named the occurrence after the Christ child. Meteorologists expect soon to be able to predict these seasons.

Besides weaving in and out of storm centers, an around-the-world sailor must consider areas which have been made dangerous by mankind. It is wise to avoid war zones and areas that are politically unstable. Since these areas are now predominantly in Africa and the Middle East, the use of the Suez Canal exposes crews to this danger. Muslim fundamentalists in the Arab world pose another real threat. In the entire Caribbean, sailors must be on guard for smugglers associated with the drug traffic. The most dangerous area is the coast of Columbia, but it's difficult to give this coast much leeway if crews intend to use the Panama Canal. Areas of reported piracy are the Strait of Malacca, most of the waters of the Philippines and the South China Sea, and the Gulf of Guinea on the West Coast of Africa. People often ask if I worry about pirates. "Yes," I reply, "because now they all own boatyards." But, pirates are a real concern, not to be taken lightly.

* * *

Our sailing plan includes leaving the boat at various spots around the globe while we make trips home. So we need to find places to leave the boat that will not have destructive storms but will have low crime rates and reliably staffed marinas to look after the boat. These requirements pretty well limit our choices to New Zealand, Australia from Brisbane south, Singapore, Cyprus, Turkey, Malta, Southern Spain, and seasonally, some islands of the Caribbean. We will time trips home to wait out tropical storm seasons.

In charting our route we looked for four things: beautiful places, interesting places, excellent weather, and good places to provision. The first beautiful place is our starting point at Man-O-War.

From Man-O-War, we have a glorious four-day sail to Ft. Lauderdale with stops at Green Turtle Cay and Allens-Pensacola Cay. It is downwind until we turn southwest in the Gulf Stream for a pleasant beam reach. The only difficult part of this passage is getting up after a big night on Green Turtle Cay. My crew is Ray "River" Wandstrat, a friend from Cincinnati. Our voyage is near the peak of the hurricane season; however, it is a short trip and weather forecasting in this region is excellent.

Our plan is to leave Ft. Lauderdale toward the end of January 1992; so organizing the needed work is critical. The jobs include purchasing and storing of mechanical parts, installing extra fuel cans on deck, and servicing the engine, generator, life raft, bilge pumps, furling systems, and electronics. We install a second GPS navigation system, change our propane stove to a safe new electric stove, buy and stow medical supplies, and buy and stow provisions to last for the two and a half months we anticipate the trip will take before reaching Tahiti, the next major provisioning stop.

In early December I arrive at the boat to organize these efforts. I'm greeted by a plate-sized stain near the middle of the mattress in the aft stateroom. I am furious. It appears someone has used this cabin for some unauthorized activity and has not even had the courtesy to put down a towel or something to avoid the resulting mess. Disgusted, I turn the mattress over. There is a second spot on the other side, in exactly the same position. Now I'm furious. I study the situation and determine that the perpetrators must have been short people to have made those spots in those locations. Rich Gopfert, the Mason Dealer in Ft. Lauderdale who commissioned the boat and has been supervising the current work, is the only person I can think of who is short enough and has access to the boat. The next morning, after waking up in the salon, I go in to study the situation again before confronting Rich. There is still a spot on both sides. I look up at the gimbaled compass on the deckhead above the Captain's bunk, primarily because one of my scheduled tasks today is compensating all the compasses on the boat. I happen to notice an unusual glistening around the edge of the compass. Reaching up, I discover damping oil is leaking between the glass and brass rim on this upside-down compass – Rich is exonerated. Not my last mistake.

Between Christmas and the start of school, son John and I drive to Florida to do some major provisioning. We purchase and fill six 15 gallon deck fuel tanks. In the process of moving and securing them, I'm having chest pains. I sit down, rest, have a beer, and the pain goes away.

We start working again and the chest pains come back. I hope my fears aren't on my face. I don't want to deal with unknown doctors and hospitals far from home; so I make some excuses, and we drive home.

Stress tests indicate serious problems. An angiogram is scheduled. My doctor is talking about potential by-pass surgery.

I cancel the January departure.

The angiogram results are in. If everybody had a heart like mine, my cardiologist would be out of business. When he writes a letter to Pat, he assures her there are many dangers in sailing around the world but, in my case, a heart attack is not one of them.

We're on our way again, with a departure goal of late February. John Coldiron, a friend and frequent crew member, is building a new house and I stop to visit. But I don't stop soon enough. There's a half inch of snow on the drive and I slide toward a pile of stacked plywood, jump the stack and accelerate, hitting a curb and somersaulting into the newly planted shrubs. I have fractured my tibia and fibula about an inch and a half above my ankle; not a good thing – not good timing. If the heart doesn't stop me, this might.

Weeks of follow-up X-rays and wedges in the cast to straighten the growth pay off. John Bever, my friend and doctor, finally admits to a chance I will be ready to go by the last of April.

If we don't leave this spring we may never go. Son John is graduating from college and now happy to be engaged. If we delay much longer, he will be beginning his career and marriage and he will not be able to dedicate the kind of time necessary to be part of the trip.

Everybody says the same thing: "Don't you think someone is trying to tell you something?"

My answer is, "Definitely. I should get to sea before anything else can happen."

Early April, Dr. Bever is reluctant but I'm determined. Against his better judgment he agrees that if I wear my "ski boot" cast and have a check-up X-ray in Panama, I can go. I have been diabetic for 32 years and resulting poor circulation in my feet adds to his concern. He makes me promise that if there is any bending of the leg, I will come home immediately. I, of course, agree unconditionally and arrive again in Ft. Lauderdale with Ken Wandstrat, Ray's son, to complete all last minute details, including dry-cleaning the aft stateroom mattress cover.

2
CHAPTER TWO

Who the Hell is Enrique Malacca?

The sea is a mighty classroom. And blue-water sailors learn by doing. Before we set out around the world, our family had taken countless trips together on both boats. I have learned mechanics by hanging over experts working on the boat, changing oil and filters myself, reading diesel maintenance books, and spending hours with service manuals. I learned electronic navigation skills by using the equipment we have on board, listening to instructions from the installer, and reading over and over the manuals supplied with the equipment. I have learned weather forecasting from books and hours of studying "The Weather Channel."

Planning and equipping a boat for long ocean passages takes more than a boat show visit. Blue-water cruisers must consider hull type, sail plan, sleeping accommodations, fuel capacity, water capacity, refrigerator and freezer capacity, navigation equipment, radios, safety equipment, *ad infinitum*. In selecting makes of equipment, it is important to consider not only the reputation of the manufacturer but which one has the largest worldwide service network.

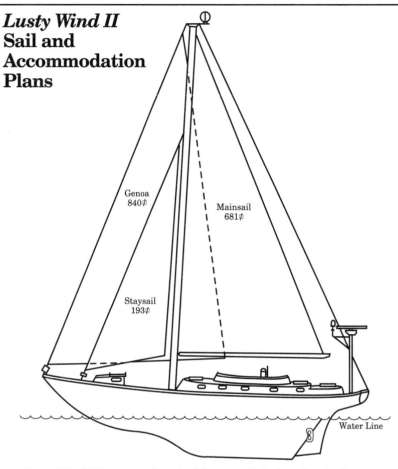

Lusty Wind II Sail and Accommodation Plans

Genoa
840₵

Mainsail
681₵

Staysail
193₵

Water Line

Lusty Wind II is cutter rigged with two sails before the single mast and one aft. Her hull design is a modified full keel with the propeller in an aperture, the rudder affixed both top and bottom, and ample fore and aft reserve buoyancy are provided.

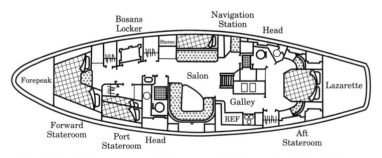

Bosans Locker

Navigation Station

Head

Stereo

Forepeak

Salon

Galley

REF

Lazarette

Forward Stateroom

Port Stateroom

Head

Aft Stateroom

The below deck accommodations provide for up to eight while near shore cruising and four for blue-water.

Unquestionably, the most important single consideration and the premier piece of safety equipment is the design and construction of the hull. The hull of *Lusty Wind II* is hand-laid fiberglass 1-1/2 inches thick below the waterline. This construction is heavy and expensive, but strong. The design is a modified full keel with the propeller in an aperture and the rudder affixed top and bottom. There is no skeg or centerboard susceptible to being damaged in a collision with flotsam or jetsam, a grounding, or a reef encounter. The design has ample reserve buoyancy fore and aft for blue-water cruising. Reserve buoyancy is created by an overhanging bow and stern. Almost all sailboats have an overhanging bow since this is the way sailboats are supposed to look, but all do not have an overhanging stern. Considering the narrowness of the bow, this first feature does not consume much space. But sterns are wide. They can provide reserve buoyancy by angling out of the water, but this angling reduces interior space, including the number of bunks, and thus reduces sales appeal. However, aft reserve buoyancy is a vital safety concern in heavy following seas which tradewind sailors will certainly experience.

Lusty Wind II is cutter rigged, which means there is one mast with two sails before and one after. Her mast is shorter than normal, but she has a longer boom to give equivalent sail area. The lowered center of the sail allows the boom to hold more sail out downwind and reduces roll; both are important on a tradewind passage. The staysail is heavy sailcloth and is used as a storm sail. It is strong, brings the center of effort lower and closer to the center of the boat which gives the boat a less violent ride in heavy weather.

As Richard Henry Dana warns us in *Two Years Before the Mast*, sleeping accommodations at sea are untenable forward of the mast and best closest to the center of the boat. *Lusty Wind II* sleeps eight comfortably at dock or in a pleasant anchorage, but only four or maybe five on blue-water passages.

For passage planning I use 150 nautical miles per day plus one day per passage or two for a long one. We average 163 nautical miles per day (185 statute mile) thus usually arriving a day or so ahead of schedule.

Capacities of fuel tanks, water tanks, and refrigeration and freezer need to accommodate at least 133% of the maximum planned passage. In our case, the maximum is 3,200 nautical miles, or 23 days. With four on board, we use 12 gallons of water per day. With our watermaker, which makes 17 gallons per hour, we can have daily showers, wash the cockpit and deck, and still have all we need. Watermakers are, however, susceptible to failure so water tankage remains important. For fuel calculations, we must consider that in the trade winds at least two-thirds of the time we will be under sail; therefore, a 1,100 mile range is sufficient. At cruising speed we burn two gallons of diesel fuel per hour.

Lusty Wind II was designed by Al Mason, a highly respected naval architect. Mason worked for Philip Rhodes, John Alden, Sparkman and Stevens and he designed PT boats for the U.S. Navy during World War II. Mason sailboats, thus, resemble the classic Philip Rhodes motor-sailors of the 1950's. She was built in Taiwan by Ta Shing Yacht Building Co., Ltd. Ta Shing builds with exceptional craftsmanship. There is some minor difficulty with translation; for example, some seacocks are labeled C WATER IN. Mason sailboats are imported and marketed by Pacific Asian Enterprises Inc. in Dana Point, California. PAE is quite flexible and allowed me to lay out the accommodations plan and specify most equipment.

Fortunately, an accurate and reliable electronic navigation system, GPS (Global Positioning System), is now available for yachts at reasonable cost. The electronics aboard *Lusty Wind II* include GPS; Loran; EPIRB

(Emergency Position Indicating Radio Beacon); radar; radio direction finder; VHF radio (short range); single sideband radio (long range); weatherfax; depth, speed and wind instruments; and autopilot.

We've come a long way from the days when mankind first circled the globe in the late tenth century, as Norse explorers came in contact with Eskimos of Labrador who were of Asian origin. Some believe St. Brendan, an Irish priest, sailed to Newfoundland and to the coast of South America in about 550 A.D. St. Brendan would have contacted people of Asian origin on such a voyage.

Ferdinand Magellan, the first and most famous of all circumnavigators, circled the globe in two trips of half way each. The first was a return from Indonesia to Portugal aboard several Portuguese vessels in 1511 and 1512. The second, a voyage from Spain westbound to the Philippines aboard the Spanish ship *Trinidad* in 1519-1521. Magellan, a Portuguese, was unable to get a commission in Portugal but finally convinced Charles V of Spain that it was worthwhile to finance a voyage around the world to establish Spain's position in the western Pacific. Natives killed Magellan in the Philippines. Although his voyages overlapped east to west by 360 nautical miles, his two voyages left a north to south gap of 900 nautical miles.

Shortly after Magellan had begun his return from the Philippines to Portugal, on the first part of his circum-navigation, he acquired a young male slave in the Strait of Malacca. Magellan named his slave Enrique (Henry) and the man was known in the Western World as Enrique de Malacca. Magellan and his servant became friends. Enrique traveled to Portugal and eventually to Spain to accompany Magellan on his trip from Spain back to the Philippines. At the death of Magellan, Enrique assumed he would be freed, but instead he was claimed by the new captain of the ship. Having had his fill of Spanish justice,

Enrique bided his time until the returning vessel came near the Strait of Malacca at which time he jumped ship and, we may assume, returned to his native land. Therefore, Magellan was 900 nautical miles short and Enrique de Malacca was probably the first man to sail all the way around the world. Enrique's lack of fame is a certain result of his being a slave rather than the captain of a vessel.

Late in the 19th century, yachtsmen of the world began taking around-the-world trips for the same reason mountain climbers were considering Mount Everest: because it was there! The world is there; so let's sail around it. Certainly one of the earliest yachts to circumnavigate was the British brigantine, *Sunbeam*, in 1876-1878, with 11 passengers and 32 crewman, including a nurse, a ladies' maid, and a stewardess. The owner was Thomas Brassey, Esq., M.P., millionaire and liberal member of Parliament.

The first man to circumnavigate the globe alone was Joshua Slocum from 1895 to 1898 aboard *Spray*. In 1895, the Suez Canal was completed and the Panama Canal was an abandoned French construction project. Slocum began his trip eastbound from Fairhaven, Massachusetts and headed for the Mediterranean and the new Suez Canal to eventually go around Cape Horn eastbound. In Gibraltar, at a dinner held in his honor, the English Governor convinced him that westbound through the Strait of Magellan and around the Cape of Good Hope was the better route because of pirates in the Red Sea and the world weather systems; Slocum nonchalantly changed his program and started south to the Strait of Magellan on his westbound passage.

After a hiatus during World War II, yachtsmen again began around-the-world cruises. One of the earliest was the voyage of Irving and Electa Johnson aboard *Yankee*. By the late 1980's and early 1990's, estimates are that

300 yachts a year circumnavigate the world, almost all westbound. Satellite navigation, emergency position indicating radio beacons (EPIRB), single sideband radios, reliable life rafts, and worldwide rescue organizations make sailing around the world a relatively safe endeavor. It is anticipated that the number of circumnavigations, barring wars, will double in the next few years and probably double again soon after that.

Every year some unbelievably courageous yachtsmen circumnavigate eastbound in the southern high latitudes. These include those in the Whitbread Around the World Race, the BOC Challenge, and solo sailors such as Sir Francis Chichester on *Gypsy Moth*, Sir Alec Rose on *My Lively Lady*, and (Sir to me) Dodge Morgan on *American Promise*.

3

CHAPTER THREE

Let's Get Going

April 19, 1992 – May 2, 1991

Ft. Lauderdale – Colón, Panama

I am now ready for leg two, the first big one, of our circumnavigation. We have the boat ready, crew assembled, and three months of provisions aboard.

So much dreaming, so much planning, and so much can yet go wrong. The weather is not at all favorable for a Gulf Stream crossing. My left leg is in a removable cast. We face dangerous weather in the Windward Pass, drug smugglers in the Southern Caribbean, transiting the Panama Canal, crew members arriving on schedule, our arriving on schedule, and, of course, I am still diabetic and, if I had listened to some, not supposed to be doing this. On the bright side, *Lusty Wind II* is a proven bluewater sailor and equipped for the voyage.

I have planned for provisions to last until we get to Tahiti in early July. I estimate we will be at sea 30 days; so I plan for 40 days of provisions on board. We will "top off" the stores in Panama to have at least 28 meals on board for our anticipated 21-day trip from the Galápagos to the Marquesas. For some parts of the trip we will have three crew members and some times five, but four will be the mode. In port, we will usually eat out or replenish supplies accordingly.

Of our planned meals, chicken breasts, steaks, hamburgers, and ground beef for spaghetti all need refrigeration; the remaining dinners are canned. A loss of our refrigeration system or the necessity to go to the life raft will, of course, require food that does not need cooking, much less refrigeration. Twenty-one of the planned dinners meet these criteria, if one can accept unheated, meatless, spaghetti sauce.

Canned vegetables, potatoes, fruit, low sodium soup, tuna, chicken, plus low sodium peanut butter, and low sodium V-8 juice are good emergency foods and, on every blue-water cruise, we pack some of each – and a can opener – in a special locker to take on the life raft. Most contain moisture, are low in sodium, and are nourishing; all need no cooking or refrigeration. Of them all, low sodium V8 Juice is probably the best.

Some of the foods must be very (and I mean very) easy to prepare during rough weather when nobody wants to be down below with many ingredients sliding around. In bad weather, we serve canned stew, canned chicken chow mein, soup and sandwiches, and Dixie Chili (a hometown brand). All are one pot heat and serve. Some specific foods are ideal for blue-water sailing. Pringles potato chips do not mash to dust like those in bags; Ivory Soap makes suds in salt water; Sam's Wholesale Club skinless, boneless, individually frozen chicken breasts are easy to remove from the freezer in any quantity; canned macaroni and cheese is also easy to prepare; small canned hams are simple to grate for a very welcome ham salad in the middle of any sea; and Crystal Light is great if the water supply starts to taste bad.

As a diabetic, I must, of course, watch sugar intake to help control blood sugar and salt intake to control blood pressure which reduces long term kidney problems; so some of our foods are dietetic and as many as possible are low sodium. Low sodium is, of course, also best on the life raft or if water becomes scarce. Candy bars are for insulin reactions, and not for crew consumption. I also carry awful tasting sugar pills in case the candy bars are used up, and additional hard candy is packed in the life raft.

Before leaving each port, we stock up on milk, orange juice, grapefruit juice, fresh potatoes, fresh vegetables for salad, fresh fruit, butter, tomatoes, onions, 6 or 7 loaves of bread, eggs, bacon, ice cream, local cheese, beer, and wine. Potatoes keep longer unwashed with some mud left on. On average, every fourth day we catch a fish suitable for dinner. These were usually dolphin (Mahi Mahi – not Flipper) or yellowfin tuna.

I have a number of food consumption rules while off shore. As captain I take out of the freezer and lockers what the cook is to use. This gives me the chance to monitor the use of supplies and help plan the method of cooking. The method is important for safety on an unstable platform like a boat when grease comes close to cooking heat. We open quickly perishable foods such as cereal, bread, crackers, and snacks one at a time. The opened cereal or snack becomes our favorite until used up; then our favorite changes. Salt air turns these foods stale very quickly and they are then shunned until thrown away. Snacks have a tremendous natural inclination to spill. Since a sailboat is not a level, steady platform, spilling multiplies geometrically by the number of open containers.

The crew from Ft. Lauderdale to Panama is Dan Fay of Northern Kentucky, Ted Blackwood of Ft. Lauderdale, and Ken Wandstrat.

We go to dinner and I give the crew pre-departure work orders. Meanwhile I head off to return our rental car to the airport. Stopping to fill the car's tank, I am standing on one crutch pumping gas when a man comes out of the shadows asking for my wallet and my crutch, which I give him. He then flees, leaving me with one crutch which is still on the boat. This shouldn't surprise me; in eight years, *Lusty Wind II* and I have been to Europe and back, through the Caribbean, and around the world. In this period of time, she has been burglarized three times and I have been robbed once; all four events were in Ft. Lauderdale.

We are up at five the next morning making last minute preparations for our intended departure at six. Just before departure two friends, Evie Wandstrat, crew member Ken's mother, and Ted Richardson, from Northern Kentucky, arrive in a runabout to escort us out of the harbor. For the record, Ted is also a friend of Ray "River" Wandstrat, Evie's husband and Ken's father. The runabout escorts us almost to the outer marker; at which point, Evie and Ted get a complete drenching from the weather we are beginning to encounter and turn to run back. The wind is 25 knots out of the East and we are going east. We're glad the wind is not opposite the northerly flow of the Gulf Stream and not creating severe seas; however, the going is choppy, wet, and slow.

This morning we pass the first big test of circum-navigators. We leave port.

We are making our passage to Panama in the ideal season, excepting that prevailing winds in the Bahamas are from Northeast to Southeast. Unfortunately, not "with the wind" for us. Strong Northeasters, which would make a crossing of the Gulf Stream dangerous are forecast several days in advance. This is only a one-day portion of the voyage. In the Caribbean Sea, late April and May are well before the hurricane season and just

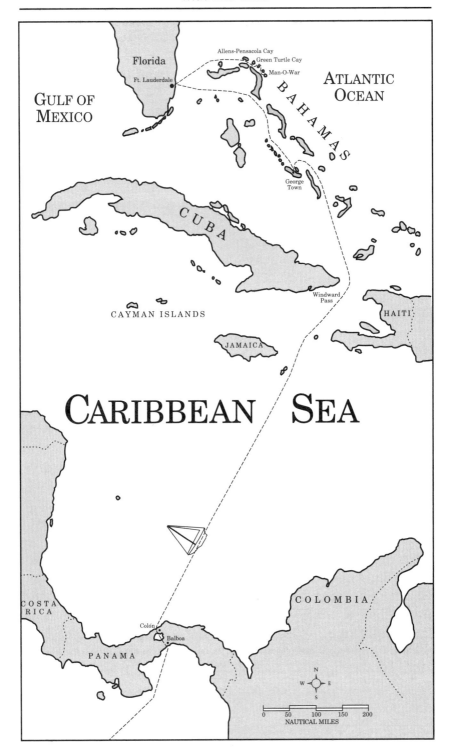

after the boisterous sailing conditions during January through mid-April when the trade winds are at their strongest. The prevailing winds are from the east – ideal for a sail to Panama.

Our first gear problem – our davits hold the inflated dinghy nearly vertical. This design keeps the weight of the dinghy from being too far aft. Weight too far forward or aft can cause a boat to "hobby-horse" in heavy seas, which reduces speed and adds to an uncomfortable ride. But motoring into 25 knots of wind with the dinghy stowed vertically is like pulling a parachute. This problem will be difficult to correct, I can only hope that we will gain an advantage using the dinghy as a sail on most of the rest of this trade wind voyage. We'll discover soon that on upwind passages it is better to deflate the dinghy and stow her on deck.

In the Gulf Stream, Dan Fay, a noted Northern Kentucky gourmand, cooks an excellent chicken dinner. He serves three elegantly prepared plates complete with fresh parsley and buttered garlic bread. We ask him where his dinner is and he makes a mad dash up the companionway to toss his cookies to Davy Jones. The next day we find a fowl smelling surprise – Dan has also thrown a calling card or two in the galley garbage can. Dan won't regain his color until we reach port.

At midnight we pass the Great Isaac Light and enter the Northwest Providence Channel. We have to motor into the wind all the way to Fleeming Channel where we turn south for a hard driving beam reach to George Town on Great Exhuma Island in the Bahamas.

The approach to George Town is a bit complicated with a number of bearings to follow and turns to make to stay in the channel. We are following a coastal freight boat which is a confirmation that we are on the right course. We come to a turn described by the pilot book and the freight boat doesn't change course. When I turn, my crew nearly mutiny. They insist I should respect local knowledge and follow the course of the freight boat. I admit it is a temptation; but not liking "lowly crew members" to question my judgment, I continue on my course. My crew is still watching and yapping when the coastal freighter goes aground. Local knowledge is probably that the tide is rising and after a few beers and a snooze, they may go on. The lesson – beware – local knowledge may be a *Flying Dutchman*.

Our second gear problem – on approaching George Town, our VHF radio stops transmitting. Fortunately it is just a bad microphone and it is easy to have the installer air ship a new one to George Town. The new microphone lasts only a few weeks and the problem plagues us for most of the remainder of the trip. We have a portable VHF that becomes our primary VHF radio for most of the trip.

The marina in George Town is full and the anchorage very crowded because The Family Island Regatta is in progress. We need fuel after our slow motoring against the wind, we approach the fuel dock. After fueling and clearing customs and immigration, I hop to the marina office on my remaining crutch to pay the fuel bill before going back to the anchorage. The woman in charge takes pity on me and my temporary handicap and shuffles several boats around making space for *Lusty Wind II*, a courtesy which we greatly appreciate.

After getting the boat situated, I start to hobble into George Town. Between us and shore, there is a large and elegant power boat with a boarding ladder that completely crosses the dock. To pass this boarding ladder requires sitting on it, swinging my legs and crutches around, and getting back up on the other side. My sailor's conception of the powerboater's mentality of "to hell with everybody else" fuels my annoyance. On my second trip to town, at my required sitting on the boarding ladder, I intentionally sit with all the force I could muster hoping to break it off its mounts and permanently scar her topsides. I do not accomplish my mission, but I do make enough noise to bring out a plump, very pleasant looking, well-dressed, more than middle-aged black woman, absolutely horrified to see my predicament. "That is terrible. Let me get the men and get that ramp moved." I feel a little sheepish, get up, and apologize for the noise. My new friend tells me that when I return, if the ramp is still there, I should let her know immediately. "Well, whom do I ask for?" "You just ask for the Big Bahama Mama," she laughingly replies. When I return a few hours later, the ramp has been properly placed. The next morning a very dignified, gray templed, more than middle-aged man, sitting at a table at the stern of the boat, sees me, jumps up, and apologizes for the prior day's problem. He kindly asks me to take care of my leg and myself. When I get to the marina office, I am surprised to find out who these people are; the gentleman who had just inquired about my leg is Prime Minister Pinling and "The Big Bahama Mama" is indeed "The Big Bahama Mama."

A second large and elegant power boat is docked across from *Lusty Wind II*. The almost elderly owner is joined by a voluptuous girl proudly sporting a string bikini. We asked one of the power boat's crew members if that is the owner's daughter. The answer is, "Well, the 'er' is correct."

After several days of rest, swimming on nearby Direction Island, and watching the regatta, we depart. *Abaco Rage*, Man-0-War's usual entry and winner of the regatta, has taken a pass this particular year so we are at a loss to know whom to cheer.

Our southeast course is in waters protected from strong northwest flowing currents by the Great Bahama Bank. Seventy-five miles east we would be set northwest in the Atlantic current; and just north of Cuba, we would be in strong northwest currents of the Old Bahama Channel.

We are now crossing the Tropic of Cancer and traveling in hallowed water for long distance sailors. We are crossing and re-crossing the wake of Columbus' first voyage and exploration of the Bahamas and passing just 50 miles west of his landfall.

During my night watch on Saturday, April 25, I listen on the VHF radio and hear chatter from other yachts talking to two boats that identify themselves as the *Niña* and *Santa María*. As we approach these northbound vessels, I contact them on the radio, talk to the captain of *Santa María* and find the boats are reproductions used in the filming of the movie "1492," with Sigourney Weaver. While talking with the captain, I can hear in the background what sounds like a Gardner (British) diesel, a highly regarded engine. Boaters know the sound of a Gardner like teenage boys know that of a Ferrari. I tell the captain, "I knew Gardner has been making engines a long time but I didn't realize they supplied them for *Santa María*." He laughs and says he wishes it were a Gardner. It is instead a French engine built under license from Gardner and has given him immeasurable trouble.

Also during that night we are beating into the wind on a collision course with a trawler that has her nets in the water. She has the right of way. Until she gets close, her running lights – and thus her course – are obliterated by floodlights trained on her trawling booms and nets. The lazy watch keeper/Captain on *Lusty Wind II* is hoping something will happen to make a course change unnecessary. The appropriate change will put us in the irons. The concerned crew of the trawler begins sweeping us with her spotlight; we finally furl the genoa and motor into the wind out of harm's way.

Approaching the Windward Pass we begin more intense navigation by checking the G.P.S. every 15 minutes with radar confirmation. We want to be sure we are at least 20 miles off the coast of Cuba well outside the 12 mile territorial limit. It is misty and we can not see well; but on radar, we can detect a boat trailing six or seven hundred feet behind on our starboard – Cuban – side. We suspect this is a Cuban gun boat making sure we do not wander into their territory. The Windward Pass which can be very treacherous is as smooth as silk. When dawn comes, we can see the eastern end of Cuba and the western end of Haiti (both, of course, on radar all night) and the water is smooth enough to be able to see our reflection. We are in the lee of Hispaniola and sheltered from the trade winds and are getting radio reports that a gale is expected in 24 hours and that the Windward Pass will become very difficult. We dodge that "bullet."

The expected 15 knot tradewinds out of the east in the Caribbean Sea give us a pleasant beam reach on our southbound course all the way to Panama. A beam reach (wind just aft of the beam) is the smoothest of the points of sail. Boat motion and sail handling are at the minimum. If the wind drops, a sailor can motor-sail; and on a beam reach, the wind and engine both contribute to boat speed. Downwind motor-sailing just further reduces apparent wind and beating into the wind the extra speed generated by the engine brings the apparent wind angle closer to the bow.

Occasionally at sea, sailors view a green flash just as the sun disappears below the horizon. Most crew members, until they see one, think the green flash is akin to the elusive snipe. They do occur. The probable cause is refraction of the sun's light as it decreases in density while dropping below the horizon and a green flash only lasts for a fraction of a second. I look on every sunset at sea and see one, not my first, on April 29th.

Three times over the next few days *USS Antrim*, a guided missile frigate, stops us after aircraft buzzed us as we sail south and a bit west toward Panama. In all three instances, they ask many questions on the VHF radio including our port of departure, our intended destination, and the names, nationality, and occupations of all crew members. In each case we must have satisfied our interrogators, for they do not board or search us. We are probably under less suspicion as we are traveling south instead of north. Carrying drugs – that which they are looking for – south would be like carrying coals to Newcastle. The three separate watches of *USS Antrim* that quiz us are very formal, polite, interested in our voyage, and ask if they could be of any assistance. In one instance, at our request, they switch us to their meteorologist for a forecast. It is good to know she is nearby as we are only 200 miles north of the coast of Columbia – waters frequented by ruthless drug traffickers.

We aren't on a shakedown cruise, but we are still discovering where some of our planning has gone awry. In specifying our AM radio system, we have gone out of our way to assure long-range reception. Long range AM is used for weather reports, news, and entertainment. FM is not used much in blue-water as its range is too short. While equipping the boat, we bought a high quality Kenwood automobile radio and installed a long antenna. Unbeknownst to us, AM stations broadcast in increments of 10kHz for Canada, United States, the Bahamas, and Mexico but most of the rest of the world broadcasts in increments of 9kHz. "No problem." To modify the digital radio to tune to 9kHz multiples we just have to wait for a full moon, stand on our left leg, push button 4 seven times and button 7 four times. We do this over and over to no avail. Later, reading the small print in the manual, we find radios made for the US market can not make this change. Therefore, for the remainder of the trip we can only receive ten per cent of available AM stations.

As we approach Panama, we encounter a navigational hazard more commonly found on the Ohio River: large trees with leaves at one end and a root system on the other. These trees are floating in the ocean in surprising numbers.

Because the Isthmus of Panamá twists northeast, boats approaching Colón are traveling southwest along the east coast of Panama. In fact, there are areas on the west coast of Panama where one can watch the sunrise over the Pacific. I am on watch this morning and thinking that someone could come on deck and think our landfall is south and that we are making up the difference by traveling north. Just then crew member Ted Blackwood comes on deck, looks around, thinks it through and asks if our landfall is south of Colón.

A sailor has to be perceptive to be the Captain!

4

CHAPTER FOUR

White Paper

May 2, 1992 – May 11, 1992

Panama Canal

We enter Limon Bay with great excitement, find The Flats – the prescribed yacht anchorage at the Caribbean end of the Panama Canal – and drop the hook. For several hours, we settle in and try to raise Panama Immigration and Customs on our VHF radio. We believe the difficulty contacting the authorities is that on weekends, in Latin countries, officials are difficult to find or possibly our radio is again not working. We take the dinghy up the old French canal to the Panama Canal Yacht Club to see if we can contact Immigration and Customs from there. On our arrival, the yacht club staff tells us not to venture out as there is a political insurrection going on and it is dangerous. We walk to the chain link fence in front of the yacht club where we can see a boulevard separating the towns of Cristóbal and Colón from the port area. Along our side of this boulevard, we see soldiers with rifles and bayonets. Several overturned trucks and a bus are on fire. We can see civilians on the other side of the boulevard and can occasionally hear gun shots from the city. The Club staff also tells us that Immigration and Customs will probably not show up as long as this insurrection persists.

A bright spot – we met an attractive young English girl, Sally, who is living in a pup tent on the grounds of the yacht club. She is waiting for an English boat built in Finland (a Swan), with a name, *Tenereze*, from a French wine region. Sally is to crew from Panama to French Polynesia and is on leave from her regular job as cook on a Virgin Islands charter boat. Before going back to the boat, we make dinner arrangements at the yacht club and, of course, invite lonely Sally to join us. During dinner and beer, my crew members begin making advances toward Sally which might be expected from sailors who have been at sea a long time, but we are only six days out of George Town. Sally leads us to believe that she has a contagious skin disease; and for a time, that solves the problem. After a few more beers, the crew wants to invite Sally to move aboard *Lusty Wind II* where, they reason, she will be safer than in her pup tent. After a few beers, the contagious skin disease apparently isn't looking so bad. I decide, and I think Sally's mother will agree, she is safer in the pup tent in the middle of an insurrection. Also Pat's requests at my departure are "be careful" and "no girls on the boat."

By Monday morning, the gunshots have subsided and both the bus and trucks are no longer ablaze but the soldiers remain in place. We persuade a taxi driver to help us find Immigration and Customs and to take us to the Canal Administration Office. The office is on our side of the boulevard and separated from the insurgency by the line of soldiers. The driver takes us to a small office where an Immigration officer, for $20 US, agrees to stamp our passports and crew list, clearing us into Panama. After this, our cab driver takes us to another small office where he thinks we might find a Customs official. We find a uniformed man who, for $20 US, agrees to clear us through Customs. He gives us no clearance papers but announces in the only English he knows, "No problem."

We then locate the Canal Administration Office where we attempt to schedule our canal transit. The authorities look at the stamps on our passports and crew list, note our lack of customs clearance papers, and state we can not transit until we have formally cleared. They do, however, agree to complete all the necessary canal forms and take our money, documenting us in large leather ledger books on expensive-looking paper with very fine blue and red lines – all looking like a 1930's bank mortgage journal. The officer estimates costs will be $170 and collects this amount in travelers' checks. When I return home from Australia, I find, among five months of mail, a refund check from the canal authority for $53.80; our transit fee is thus $116.20 – quite inexpensive considering it saved us an 8,000 nautical mile voyage including a winter passage around Cape Horn. Tentatively they schedule our transit for Thursday. Yachts are allowed to transit on Tuesdays and Thursdays.

Upon our return to the yacht club, we find Sally to be very happy because *Tenereze* and her crew have finally arrived, although a week late. Enthusiastic to start on her journey, Sally has already folded and stowed her pup tent aboard *Tenereze*.

We spend Tuesday changing the engine oil and watching for Gary Foy from Louisville, Kentucky, who is to be with us through the canal and to the Galápagos. Later in the day at the yacht club, we find a pile of video cameras and luggage with Gary standing in the middle. He has been checking with Immigration and Customs, but they have no record of our arrival (somehow he got through to them but they never answered when we called).

The insurrection heats up again; and through the chain link fence, we can see soldiers shooting real bullets in the direction of real people. At times our eyes smart from drifting clouds of tear gas. A newspaper account of the insurrection discusses four days of shooting and burning but has no mention of anyone's being hurt.

Late Tuesday an Admeasure Officer from the canal authority comes to the boat in a launch and measures the length (125 feet) and diameter (7/8 of an inch) of the four required dock lines. They also start our engine, look at our fenders, measure the entire boat, and approve her for transit. For their final transit fee calculations, they consider the boat's length as 56.2 feet, adding two feet eight inches for our anchors and davits.

Wednesday another group from the canal measures our dock lines, looks at our fenders, and again approves us. The insurrection has abated and we nervously take a walk through Cristóbal and Colón. Gary and I take a dinghy ride past the yacht club to the end of the old French Canal. There we find a collection of rusted abandoned French equipment which has been there since 1890. Skies are grey; and except for the verdant jungle growth, the scene looks like a black and white photo of an abandoned turn-of-the-century Kentucky strip mine.

The canal authorities require a captain and four line handlers aboard small yachts; we have only three crew members. A waitress at the yacht club suggests for a fee of $30 plus $5 bus fare back we might hire her son, Alfredo. She promises he has experience. We agree and ask if he can be aboard in the morning in the event permission is given for us to transit.

* * *

We are now about to navigate a strategic and historic strait of commerce. The Spanish conquistadors named this land Panama after they asked the native Indians where to find gold and the savvy Indians pointed and said *panamá* – the conquistadors didn't realize this meant "far away." The strategic importance of The Panama Canal is that the alternate route takes a voyager so far away.

If we accept the theory that at least some South American natives came from Asia via North America, Panama's importance began as a land bridge, or at least a shoreline to canoe past, for the first settlers of South America and possibly much of the South Pacific. Panama's importance in recorded history began with the mule trails used by the Spanish to move Inca gold from the Pacific to galleons for transport to Spain. As development in the United States moved west in the early nineteenth century, Panama became an important link in travel between the United States East Coast and California. Two steamers and the old Spanish trails are used. This route avoided an arduous overland trip across North America or a voyage around Cape Horn. Some sections of these ancient mule trails can still be found in the jungle a few miles from the canal. U.S. investors completed a railroad across the Isthmus in 1855. It prospered until completion of the North American transcontinental railroad in 1869.

By 1878, the French Compagnie Universelle du Canal Interocéanique formed by Ferdinand de Lesseps bought the nearly defunct Panama railroad to use in the construction of their proposed canal. De Lesseps was the celebrated builder of the Suez Canal and planned to build another sea-level canal across the isthmus. He estimated completion in six years; but after a decade, he completed less than half the project and spent the equivalent of 325 million dollars. French engineers could not stop mud and rock slides from filling newly dug cuts, nor could they control malaria, the "black vomit" that killed 20,000 workers. De Lesseps (by then 85 and senile), his son, and other associates were convicted in French courts for the financial collapse of their company which had nearly destroyed the French economy.

In 1904, President Theodore Roosevelt bought the canal assets from the French company, bankrolled a successful revolution in Panama that was then part of Columbia (so he wouldn't have to deal with the latter) and built the canal. The canal opened in 1914 at a cost of 375 million dollars. Equivalent cost today would be 10 billion dollars. The United States engineers were, of course, able to control malaria and wound up with a valuable asset. Mud and rock slides continue to be a problem.

Eight principal parts make up the Panama Canal, a 51-mile-long engineering marvel:

- The first part is a seven mile sea level canal that runs from the Atlantic Ocean and Limon Bay to the Gatun Locks bypassing part of the canal dug by the French.
- The Gatun Locks with six chambers, in parallel sets of three, raises ships 85 feet to Lake Gatun.
- Lake Gatun which provides a 24-mile channel from Gatun Locks to the Gaillard Cut as well as providing the massive amount of water necessary to operate the locks. This artificial lake is formed by Gatun Dam just west of the Gatun Locks.

- The Gaillard Cut, a 500-foot-wide channel, transports ships eight miles over the Continental Divide. Here the original maximum elevation was 312 feet and the cut was to 85 feet plus the 40 foot canal depth or a total cut of 267 feet. The French intended to cut 350 feet for a sea-level canal. This cut, where the French foundered, was successfully completed by the Americans.
- The Pedro Miguel Locks with two parallel chambers drops ships 31 feet to Miraflores Lake.
- Miraflores Lake provides a one-mile-long channel to Miraflores Locks.
- The Miraflores Locks with four chambers in parallel sets of two drops ships 54 feet to the Pacific level. The last lock here is the tallest since it must allow for the big 16 foot Pacific tides.
- A sea-level dredged channel from Miraflores Locks to the Pacific complete the canal. This channel also bypasses part of the original French dig.

Each of twelve lock chambers is 1,000 feet long and 110 feet wide. Each transit uses 52 million gallons of water – an amount that will fill 2,000 average sized home swimming pools. Daily usage will fill 80,000 pools. As Lake Gatun supplies all this water and is at the highest canal water level, all the water moves without pumps.

When the canal was new, 800 to 1,000 ships transited per year, but today 14,000 transit – nearly 40 per day. Ships are also many times larger now. The average merchant vessel pays a transit fee of $33,200.

* * *

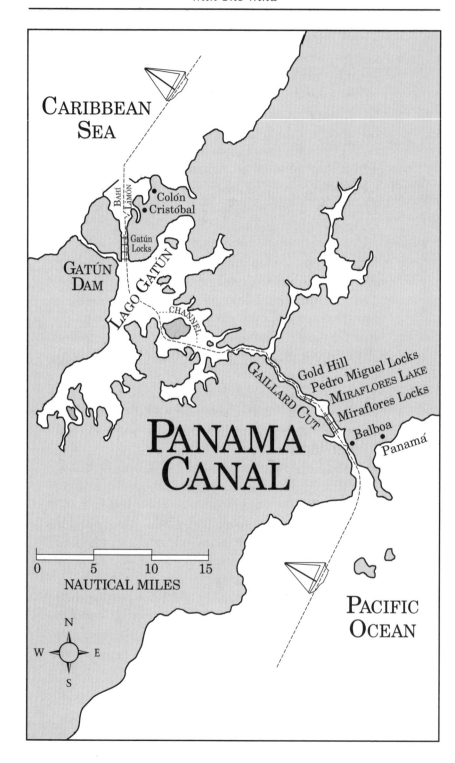

Thursday morning at 7:45 a canal pilot, Campos, comes aboard and asks if we are ready to transit. We tell him we have not yet cleared customs and he merely says, "No problem." At 7:55 Alfredo, our line handler, a fine young man, arrives; we pull up anchor and begin our transit at 8:00.

A German yacht of about our size, *LaRoca*, is also to transit this day. Campos informs us we will raft up to *LaRoca*'s port and transit the locks together using two lines on our port and two of *LaRoca*'s lines on her starboard to center us both in the lock. We raft before entering the locks, carefully putting fenders between our vessels and being sure our masts are not aligned so violent movement will not damage the rigging of either boat.

Campos tells us rainfall has been light and the water supply in Lago Gatún is low. To conserve the water, *Lusty Wind II* and *LaRoca* will transit with a large ship; "this is dangerous and normally not done." He also says light rain happens every several years. Can it be El Niño caused the rain to be light; and if the rain is light, what washed all those trees out into the Caribbean?

As we enter the Gatún Locks, we pass the statue of Ferdinand de Lesseps. It rains harder than I've ever seen it rain. I know now where all the canal water comes from but I have difficulty understanding any present shortage. With *LaRoca* we motor into the east, or left-hand chamber behind *Petersfield*, a 615 foot long freighter with a beam of 95 feet. Cables connect to the canal locomotives to keep *Petersfield* in the center of the chamber; and as the water fills the chamber, both sailboats and the ship rise. We take in our port lines and *LaRoca* takes in her starboard lines to keep us near the center. Alfredo is on the stern line, Ken and Ted are on the bow line, and Gary Foy is photographing the whole operation from under his umbrella. As the water begins to pour into the chamber, the turbulence puts a great strain on our lines and line handlers. Crew members, Ken and Ted, have been pulling the bow line in by hand and have one wrap around the windless capstan; normally, one wrap is sufficient for control. We reach the top, the water is still, and we are standing by to see what will happen next. Unbeknownst to us, the gates separating us from the next lock are opening; *Petersfield* is, of course, in our line of vision. In an instant, *Petersfield* engages her engines and suddenly tosses us about like a cork in the wash of her massive propellers. I glance at the knot meter; we are still tied to the chamber sides but the gauge is showing 12 knots indicating *Petersfield* is passing this speed of prop wash past us. The wash violently pushes both sailboats toward the west wall – on *LaRoca*'s side. Very quickly our 7/8 inch port bow line stretches down to the size of a little finger and Ken and Ted are no longer able to hold on. When our line slips, the prop wash hurls both boats against the rough concrete west wall doing surprisingly little damage to *LaRoca*, which took the hit and no damage to *Lusty Wind II*. The damage to *LaRoca* amounts to a bent bow roller, bent bow pulpit, and some scrapes on her hull. Hearing of our plight from her stern watch, *Petersfield* quickly reduces screw and everything quiets down. As our masts are not aligned neither yacht suffers rigging damage.

Every picture I've seen of the Panama Canal shows the locomotives. I have always supposed the purpose of these locomotives is to pull ships through the canal. It becomes clear that the real purpose is to hold large vessels in the center of the lock and the vessels propel themselves.

In the next two chambers of the Gatún Locks, *Petersfield* engages her engines slowly and there is no difficulty. *LaRoca*'s crew has, of course, now deployed more fenders to her starboard.

In the west locks, which are also being used for south-bound traffic, USS *Henry Clay*, a nuclear ballistic missile submarine, is locking through under tow – two Kentucky boats transiting at the same time.

It is still raining as hard as I've ever experienced and we are now in the fresh water of Lago Gatún, 85 feet above sea level. That is the highest *Lusty Wind II* has ever been. As fresh water is not so buoyant as salt water, *Lusty Wind II* settles down into the water 1-1/2 inches lower than she would be in salt water. We are thus at our highest and lowest point at the same time.

Campos is very eager for us to complete this transit in one day, presumably so he can go home; so we motor across Lago Gatún at full steam. Most yachts and pilots take two days. The channel is around the east side of Isla Barro Colorado but *LaRoca* and *Lusty Wind II* both receive directions from the pilots to take a short cut around the west side of the island. It is a very interesting trip with thick jungle on either side complete with monkeys and tropical birds. Half way across the lake the rain stops.

After crossing the lake we enter Gaillard Cut. The original name of this eight mile stretch, Culebra Cut, comes from the Spanish word for snake, a word that accurately describes its shape. Alongside the Gaillard Cut, is a monument to the tens of thousands of workmen who lost their lives there. Dominating the south end of this cut is Gold Hill, where many of the massive landslides have occurred. Gold Hill was named by the French who, as construction dragged and costs accelerated, claimed there was enough gold in the hill to cover the entire cost of the canal. This was a bit of salesmanship on the part of desperate engineers and contributed to their fraud convictions.

After the Gaillard Cut, we reach a wide place just before Pedro Miguel Locks. Campos said we will wait here for the *Universal Trader* with which we will lock through the Pedro Miguel Locks and the Miraflores Locks. Campos confers with Señor Guard, the pilot aboard *LaRoca*, and decides rather than bobbing around we will tie up at a maintenance dock on the east side of the canal. Campos directs me to sail toward these docks. Suddenly we go aground on something hard. On his portable VHF radio, Campos asks Guard and *LaRoca* to come by and pull us off. *LaRoca* approaches our stern at about three knots. We expect her to stop, take a line, and pull us off in reverse; instead she passes our portside, asks for a bow line to tie to her stern and attempts to pull us off while still under way. When the line tightens, *LaRoca*'s stern swings to starboard and the protruding stock of our Danforth anchor rips a three foot gash in her new inflatable dinghy that is hanging in davits at her stern. In the process, the wash of *LaRoca* and/or the jerk on the line breaks us free. It's amazing that the two pilots arrange this maneuver as the canal computer printout that shows the dimensions of both boats lists our draft as six feet five inches and *LaRoca*'s as seven feet six inches; a boat that draws seven feet six inches shouldn't try to pass close to a boat that draws six feet five inches and is aground. Also a boat isn't normally pulled off a grounding in the direction she is going.

Now after two accidents, I am in shock and Harry Birkholz, the captain and owner of *LaRoca*, is both in shock and understandably upset. He is, however, a reasonable man and agrees that, rather than shouting at each other, we should wait until the next morning at the Balboa Yacht Club to discuss the two events.

North and South America, Japan, and Korea are in Buoyage Area B of the world and the color scheme of markers is "red right return." That means when sailors are returning from the sea the red buoys are on the right and the green or black buoys are on the left. In the rest of the world, Buoyage Area A, it is the opposite – green right return. When a boat is passing through the Panama Canal, obviously the first half of the trip is returning from the sea and the second half of the trip is returning to the sea; the buoys on the starboard hand should thus change from red to green at the halfway mark. To ease the confusion, the change occurs not halfway but at the Pedro Miguel Locks; the locks closest to the Continental Divide.

The *Universal Trader* is due and Campos tells us to precede her into the lock chamber, presumably to avoid the prop wash problem. Our pilots instruct us to raft together again which is difficult when the two captains are avoiding eye contact. Very soon the *Universal Trader*, with a length of 675 feet and a beam of 100 feet comes in behind us. I think for sure she was going to push us right through the gates to drop us all into the next lock. With a width of 100 feet she has just five feet of leeway on each side. All, however, works well and soon we are through the single Pedro Miguel west chamber, the two Miraflores west chambers, back in salt water, passing the huge French cemetery, and approaching the yacht club.

Finally, after the worst boating day of my career, we moor off the Balboa Yacht Club a respectable distance from *LaRoca*. We are tired and upset, and it is a little late. Compos departs quickly without any mention of the customary $20 tip. We go into the yacht club dining room for dinner and some over-indulgence in wine and beer.

*   *   *

On the Caribbean end of the canal, tidal range is 1.5 feet making docking and anchoring easy. On the Pacific end the tidal range is 16 feet; the fuel and dinghy dock at Balboa must float requiring a long ramp to the shore. The tidal pull of the moon and sun is the same on both sides, but the shape of the shore and rate of rise of the sea floor affects the way the tide slouches up against the continent.

* * *

Early the next morning I notice Harry alone on the deck of *LaRoca* and take that opportunity to dinghy over to come to some agreement. Harry, graciously, welcomes me aboard. He has contacted a lawyer in Panamá City during the previous evening to discuss the two incidents. I'm confident the lawyer informs him that the accident at Gatun Locks was either the fault of the Canal pilots or the crew of *Petersfield*, depending on who has ordered the excessive power. Ships are responsible for damage caused by their wake, or prop wash. The pilot on *Petersfield* should have been aware of all other vessels in the lock chamber. We are glad the damage to *LaRoca* is as minimal as it is. The second accident, before going through the Miraflores Locks, is probably also not our fault considering we are not moving and *LaRoca* was. A Ft. Lauderdale port pilot once told me that if I ever became involved in an accident to be perfectly still at the time. *LaRoca* was aware we are "not in command" as we are aground. Also *LaRoca*'s crew requested and accepted the line our crew had thrown to them.

Neither accident is Harry's fault – certainly not the first; and during both, our canal pilots are in command.

Harry and his pregnant wife, Maria, who is now on deck, are, however, distraught with the damage done to their new dinghy. I tell them I understand the extenuating circumstances of his coming to our aid when the damage to his dinghy occurred. I made a proposition. Either we submit a claim to my insurance company for a new dinghy or I will pay the cost of repair but not replacement. He quickly agrees to the second proposition and

Ken Wandstrat helps him transport the dinghy to a repair station. The cost is $275. Unfortunately, Harry now has an unsightly looking and a questionably seaworthy dinghy. The cost of our canal transit is now up to $466.20 – still a bargain.

In Cristóbal and Colón, I am obviously unable to get to a hospital to have my leg checked since I do not want to pass through the midst of an insurrection. We are now in Balboa and Panamá City with no insurrection; so by taxi we find a hospital. I take one look at this hospital with its bullet pocked stucco walls and crowds of people waiting and decide to take a pass. In truth, I know my leg is twisting and see no way to leave *Lusty Wind II* in this hostile environment, not to mention incurring further delays in my carefully planned schedule.

Ted Blackwood must leave us in Panama to go back to Florida and one day at the yacht club bar we find Dick Dicken of Ft. Thomas who is to be our fourth crew member to the Galápagos. I am very happy to see Dick but even happier about his bringing all my new credit cards. Dick will be my first crew member with any offshore experience; he served aboard *USS McKean*, a destroyer, during the Korean War and retired a captain. His being a retired naval officer will allow him to take us to the PX in Panama for provisions he informs us. Saving money and finding US goods sounds great but the lady at the door of the PX is unimpressed with Captain Dicken's credentials and refuses our entry. So by taxi we do the provisioning we need to do at a local grocery.

Panama is to have one more crack at us. Returning that night after dinner and a glass or so of *vino blanco*, we climb aboard the boat and secure the dinghy. Normally the last thing I do before going below and to sleep is to check the security of the dinghy. Unfortunately, I have had just a shade too much wine and go to sleep before checking the line. The next morning, I get up, walk around the deck and find people on other boats yelling to us that our dinghy is gone. The crews of neighboring boats are now pointing out to sea where I can see in the distance a small fishing boat with our orange dinghy in tow. If the fishermen haven't noticed we are the only boat at anchor without a dinghy, the crews of other boats are all now pointing to us for them. We are appreciative and a $100 reward overwhelms these two good fishermen. Fortunately for us, salvage rights don't apply in harbors as they do on the high seas.

Our final job in Balboa is to obtain a *zarpa*, or exit permit. The United States does not give exit permits; however, most other countries of the world do. A sailor cannot gain entry to the next port until he can show a satisfactory exit permit from his last port or show some evidence that the last departure was from the United States. They take this seriously. We apply for a zarpa at the immigration office in Balboa and find we have not really entered the country and can thus not leave. Their solution is for us to transit back through the canal, gain entry, and return again through the canal to Balboa which is like hearing I need root canal work two more times. Fortunately for all, Dick Dicken has another chance to prove his worth. His seat mate on his flight from Dallas to Panama has been the wife of the Ambassador to Panama. One call to her, a second to the Ambassador, and a third from him to the Panamanian Authorities smoothes over the whole deal and Dick returns triumphantly with our *zarpa*. The government official does have the presence of mind to extract $40, double the customary tip.

5

CHAPTER FIVE

"And a Star to Steer Her By"

May 11, 1992 – June 8, 1992

Balboa, Panama – Nuku Hiva, Marqueses

We negotiate a spot at the Balboa Yacht Club floating fuel dock just ahead of *LaRoca*, fill our tanks, and with *zarpa* in hand depart for the Galápagos. By now we and the crew of *LaRoca* are smiling and waving, but not yet rafting up.

The Pacific Ocean, which will be our home from May until September, covers one-third of the entire earth – an area 11% greater than all the land. When Balboa climbed over the mountains of the Isthmus of Panamá, he saw an ocean of placid water and named it *Pacífico* or peaceful. True enough, the Gulf of Panamá, which he was viewing, is usually quite peaceful, but the Pacific certainly has all the tempest one can imagine with its hurricanes, typhoons, cyclones, and gales. Even though Balboa escaped punishment for this mistake, he was later publicly strangled in Panamá City for numerous other offenses.

Our planned trip to French Polynesia will cover 3,800 nautical miles from Balboa to the Marquesas with one stop in the Galápagos for rest, fuel, provisions, and crew change. This distance is equal to sailing from New York to San Francisco then back to St. Louis. The best time for this passage is April through June and the worst, because of possible hurricanes and occasional El Niño effect, is October through March. May should be perfect.

We spend our first night and morning avoiding fishing fleets and merchant ships bound to and from the Panama Canal. In the morning we are busy on the single sideband radio talking to our friends on *Tenereze*. They left Balboa early the morning after we had departed and are now about 100 miles behind us. We have agreed to contact each other every morning at 8 a.m. on 6,230 kHz. We also call home via Whiskey Oscar Mike in Ft. Lauderdale, and talk to son John who is packing for our rendezvous in the Galápagos. Twenty-four hours later we again speak to *Tenereze* now 90 miles behind us.

Near this position in 1973, Maurice and Marilyn Bailey lost *Auralyn* to a whale attack and were adrift in their life raft for a record 117 days before rescue.

We cross the equator as we approach the Galápagos while all on board, except Ken Wandstrat who is asleep, watch the GPS observing the N after the indicated latitude change to S. It is a time honored seafaring tradition that experienced crew members haze sailors crossing the equator for the first time to gain the favor of Neptune, the Roman God of the sea. Crews do not dare haze captains and as both Gary Foy and Dick Dicken have previously crossed the equator, the three of us storm into Ken's cabin to give him a brief hard time. Upon awakening, Ken looks a bit concerned, probably for our sanity, but is quickly grinning and joins in our celebration.

* * *

The Galápagos Archipelago consists of thirteen large islands and six smaller islands all of volcanic origin. Since there is not much rain, vegetation is sparse. These volcanic islands are relatively new; so not much soil has developed. In the ITCZ there is little wind, but there are swift cold currents caused by centrifugal force of the counter clockwise currents of the trade system of the southern ocean.

In the 18th century, pirates used the Galápagos as a base for raids. In the 19th century, whalers and sealers came in search of food and water and were responsible for the near extinction or total extinction of many species of animals including some seals and tortoises. Whalers and others would take the giant tortoises alive to preserve their meat for later use; they captured well over 100,000. Today most visitors are scientists, divers, tourists, and circumnavigators.

The most famous visitor to the Galápagos is Charles Darwin. Darwin obtained a non-paying position as naturalist with a British expedition aboard *HMS Beagle* for an 1831-1836 around-the-world voyage. Numerous English and French scientists including Darwin's grandfather, Erasmus Darwin, had been discussing evolution much to the consternation of the Church of England. Ironically Darwin's charge as a naturalist was to find evidence to refute these theories of evolution.

In the Galápagos, Darwin noticed that many species including the finches had obvious common traits but were adapted to each particular island. Each of the thirteen types of finches identified had a beak particularly suited to the ecology of the island on which it lived and to the food supply on which it depended. With strong currents and little wind between islands, there was very little intermingling of sub-species of the different islands and the Galápagos were thus an excellent laboratory to observe this morphology.

* * *

By dawn we can see the knobby gently sloping outline of volcanic Isla Santa Cruz, Isla Santa Fe and the remaining volcanic cones known as Islas Plaza. By 10 a.m., we anchor in Academy Bay just off Puerto Ayora, Santa Cruz. By dinghy, Gary and I go ashore and find a floating dinghy dock lashed to steps cut into the lava. The steps lead to the streets of the town. Twice a day the tide floods these steps making them moss-covered and slippery. There is no handrail and it is difficult to maneuver up and down with or without crutches. A Chinese gentleman who owns a restaurant near the top of the steps comes to our aid. He orders his restaurant staff to keep an eye out for me and help as I come and go. I get to the Port Authority Office, clear Equadorian Immigration and Customs, get permission to stay for several days, and order fuel from the Ecuadorian Navy.

Sons, John and Andy, have spent the previous two nights at the Hotel Galápagos and have now gone for breakfast. They discover *Lusty Wind II* at anchor. It is great to see family after our previous ordeals but a bit shocking to catch their expression when they see my leg which is by now substantially twisted.

About 5 p.m., *Tenereze* with Sally and our other friends arrives. After clearing Immigration and Customs, they join us for dinner.

The crew of *Tenereze* goes on and on about their great speed with a few subtle remarks about having left a day later than we had and arriving on the same day. By my calculations, the 883-nautical-mile trip has taken us 140 hours for an average speed of 6.31 knots and took

Tenereze 132 hours for an average speed of 6.69 knots. Not much difference considering they have five feet of waterline on us. Displacement hull boats such as *Lusty Wind II* and *Tenereze* reach their maximum speed when the length of the wave made by the vessel moving through the water exceeds waterline length and begins to cause suction; thus longer boats with longer waterlines can go faster. Mathematically, we did just about the same as *Tenereze*. We are glad to see each other anyway.

I have a corny habit of confronting cab drivers, waitresses, bartenders, etc., after a demonstration of my inability to speak Spanish with the only phrase I've mastered *"¿Cuantos anos tienne usted?"* (How old are you?) They usually throw back a couple of words followed by *"¿Y usted?"* (And you?) and I quickly respond *"Veinte y uno"* (21) to the great amusement of everybody, except family and crew who have heard all this before. Ken Wandstrat has been to the Darwin Institute on Santa Cruz, observing the pens of frequently fornicating tortoises, and tells me it was something I shouldn't miss. One afternoon I am in town alone with some extra time and hitch a ride in the back of a pickup truck to the Institute. After visiting the museum, I hobble up the dusty trail, passing a concession stand and bar along the way, to the breeding pens where, with great fascination, I watch the five-hundred pound tortoises. Afterwards, hot and dry, I stop at the bar for a rest and a cold drink. The bartender is an Ecuadorian girl with a degree in biology. After establishing that I don't care what kind of beer I get, I just want the coldest, in Spanish I ask her age. She screeches and says, "I know your son!" It is obvious Wandstrat has picked up and is using my very best line.

The giant tortoise of the Galápagos is a wonderful animal. The name Galápagos originates from the Spanish word *galápago* meaning tortoise. Looking at their expressive faces, it's easy to understand how they were the inspiration for the appearance of E.T.

May 19, I take Gary and Dick into town as they need to take a 7:30 a.m. bus and ferry to the airport on Isla Baltra to catch their flight to Guayaquil, Miami, then Louisville and Cincinnati respectively. About 10 a.m., after the crew is up and has breakfast, we go into town for supplies. There we find Gary and Dick sheepishly grinning and sitting alone on a bus with a flat tire. We will find out months later they somehow made all their flights.

John and I change the oil in the engine and generator, then John, Andy, and Ken dinghy the used oil ashore to try to find a proper and ecologically safe point of disposal. The manager of the only service station on the island tells them to pour the oil on the street to help keep the dust down. With pangs of remorse, they do so.

One of the most fascinating things for me, in reading about sailing around the world, is the description of the Barrel Post Box on Isla Santa María. Whalers on their way out to the Pacific from California and Central America would deposit mail in this barrel and returning whalers would pick-up the mail and post it when they reached home port. It was known that Santa María had the most dependable water supply and thus it was the usual stopping place for whalers. The barrel, at B. de Correo, on Isla Santa María, rebuilt several times, is still there serving yachtsmen and tourists. We have a one-week cruising permit for the Galápagos Islands and intend to include a visit to B. de Correo prior to our voyage to the Marquesas. The two big delays in our departure from Ft. Lauderdale have, however, disrupted our schedule and we have to forgo this opportunity. With papers in hand, I spend some time every day while in Puerto Ayora asking the Port Authorities to grant us permission to stop at B. de Correo on our way to the

Marquesas. They are beginning to show some weakening; they tell me of a requirement that after visiting B. de Correo we would have to sail back to Porta Ayora to clear out before departing. This involves a round trip of 70 nautical miles, a delay of three days; and as we have a schedule to maintain and are late leaving the Galápagos anyway, I reluctantly have to take a pass.

May 20, late in the afternoon, our fuel finally arrives by Navy barge. The two sailors who bring the fuel don't accept money as a tip; instead they insist on T-shirts. At 6:30 p.m., Andy, Ken and I go ashore to obtain our *zarpa*, or exit permit, and decide to eat aboard, get some sleep, and leave at dawn. Before returning to the boat, Andy and Ken pick up our laundry at the hotel plus a carry-out pizza for dinner. On their way back to the dinghy, they stop at a bar and find the two sailors proudly wearing their new "I Love Northern Kentucky" T-shirts.

By dinnertime on the first day out, we are motoring in a calm of the ITC and passing Volcano Cerro Azul and Volcano Sto. Tomás on the south end of Isla Isabela – a dramatic last sight of land before our 3,100 nautical mile, 18-day passage. On our second day out of port, we unpack and distribute the laundry. Among our effects we find several dish towels we don't recognize and two pairs of women's panties of a most alluring size. With enthusiasm not usually applied to chores, my crew ties the panties together and hoists them to the top of the starboard burgee halyard.

Two days out of the Galápagos, in 1971, the Robertson family lost *Lucette* to a whale attack and managed to navigate thirty-eight days before being rescued near the Central American coast. This position is known for its isolation from shipping lanes; it is 300 nautical miles north of the Panama to Tahiti route and 400 south of the Panama to New Zealand route.

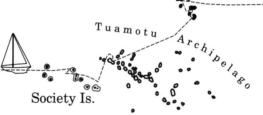

- *Tropic of Cancer* - - - -

Hawaii

NORTH
PACIFIC OCEAN

- *Equator* - - - - - -

Marquesas Is.

T u a m o t u

AMERICAN
SAMOA

A r c h i p e l a g o

Society Is.

FRENCH POLYNESIA

- -

Pitcairn Is.

EASTERN SOUTH
PACIFIC OCEAN

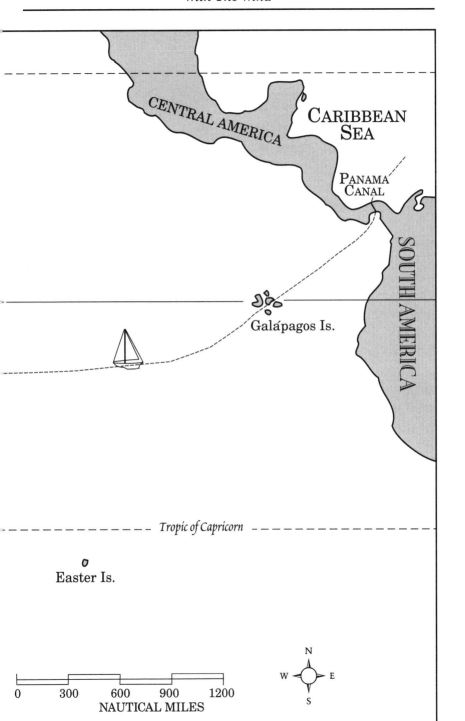

CENTRAL AMERICA

CARIBBEAN
SEA

PANAMA
CANAL

SOUTH AMERICA

Galápagos Is.

Tropic of Capricorn

Easter Is.

0   300   600   900   1200
NAUTICAL MILES

N
W ⬥ E
S

On Monday the twenty-fifth, Ken catches a small fish he identifies as a dolphin. It doesn't look like one or, as we learn later, taste like one. John is the cook for the day and adds Ken's catch to some frozen fish. While John is serving us, he doesn't notice we all push our oily tasting fish aside. After eating his, he discovers the bowl of discarded fillets and immediately uses Ipecac Syrup so the *poisson* won't poison him. For the remainder of this passage, John has a peanut butter and jelly sandwich when fish is served.

On long passages in the tropics, we know from experience that store-bought bread lasts no longer than six days. Thereafter, we must bake, usually, two loaves per day. The homemade bread is a treat for both taste and the wonderful aroma during and after baking. With our electric range, baking bread requires running the generator; we run the refrigerator, charge the batteries, and make water at the same time.

On Tuesday, the twenty-sixth, we do 193 nautical miles – *Lusty Wind II*'s second best day. Our best was between the Azores and Gibraltar in 1987 with 202 nautical miles. Both of these distances are through water which is measured by the paddle wheel of the knot meter. To determine speed over the bottom, adjustments for currents must be made or distance must be accurately measured by the GPS. On this record day for this passage, we lose four nautical miles over the bottom because of foul current – our total distance over the bottom is 189 nautical miles. The trade system is supposed to provide a favorable current.

We are on a broad reach with cool wind and big rolling seas out of the southeast. Now we can appreciate the value of aft reserve buoyancy. Today, Saturday the thirtieth, the wind gets up to an apparent 25 knots and we are becoming over-powered. As it is night, we furl the sails and turn on the cast iron spinnaker – our trusty diesel engine. By morning, reduced winds and daylight allow us to continue sailing.

As we approach the top of the tradewind circle, the winds gradually shift from out of the southeast to out of the east. We are running as the winds are nearly on our stern. We have a big unintentional jibe that snaps two stainless steel bolts on the traveler and sends the pulley that attaches it to the main sheet into the deep. We furl the sail, secure the boom, and replace the bolts and the pulley. *Lusty Wind II* is again under sail; however, with a more cautious skipper.

We now have some difficulty with the genoa furling system; so we reduce backstay pressure which seems to help. The bearing at the top of the furling assembly has disintegrated and a little later the entire furling rod, which is also the headstay comes apart. The halyard keeps the rod from falling on deck. It is going to take us the better part of an hour to drop the whole assembly gradually. In the process, because of its length, we put several bends in the furling rod and render it beyond use.

Without a headstay we run a line from the masthead to a snatch block at the bow then to the windless to give support to the mast. We reduce the main to about the size of the staysail, and motor-sail the remaining two and a half days to the Marquesas. We use a Hyde furling system with the furling rod becoming the stay and the weak points being the bearings at the top and bottom. Our rigger in Ft. Lauderdale recommended replacement of this system with one that wraps around a wire stay eliminating this weak point. I must have been feeling a little tight that day. I decided to proceed with what we had. Now, of course, I regret this frugality.

By now we should be well into the system and gaining the benefit of one to one-and-a-half knots of current. By all of my calculations, we are in a foul current of one-half knot. Assuming my calculations are correct, are we in a counter current? If so, will a move to a more southerly course gain more speed than it will lose in distance?

Our watch system on *Lusty Wind II* is four-hour, single-man watches 24-hours a day. Whoever both fixes dinner and washes the dishes gets credit for one watch. With four on board and counting cooking dinner as one watch of two hours, everyone has an average 6.5 hours per day. If one person becomes sick or disabled, the work day becomes 8.7 hours – still very easy duty. If two are out of commission, the work day becomes 13 hours. With the autopilot steering the boat and the GPS navigating, the job usually just requires monitoring the whole situation to make sure weather and wind are not changing, a collision is not imminent and the navigation and auto-pilot systems are working properly. He must also write down our position every two hours. Watch is the key-word. Reading or listening to a "Walkman" are not permitted. Watch keepers may sit or stand but may not lie down.

Night watches are one of the great delights of blue-water ocean voyages. When we are at sea and away from man-made airborne particles, the sky is clear and the view is a delight. Multiply the stars visible from our metropolitan areas by 10,000 and one has an idea of what I mean by this. Many of our crew members find out for the first time that the Milky Way is not a candy bar. Phosphorescence on the bow wake is another spectacle that makes four hours go by quickly. When Andy is asked what a night watch is like. He replies, "You know how just before you go to sleep you think about things? Well, it's like that except it lasts four hours."

The earth is divided into 360° and time periods are based on a 24-hour day. Thus time zones around the world change every 15°. Porta Ayora is at longitude 90° 18' and Nuku Hiva is 140° 06', a difference of 49° 48'. We, therefore pass through four time zones on this passage.

Because we are traveling westbound, we gain four hours. Whoever is on watch when the time zone changes gets a five hour watch instead of four.

Before leaving the Galápagos, we made arrangements with *Quest* which is to be about three days behind us, and *Tenereze*, about five days behind us to communicate every morning at 8 a.m. on 8,400kHz. As we are about 500 and 800 miles apart respectively, we are often in different time zones. In addition, we often forgot to call. The conversations are thus infrequent and not much help. We should be better organized. Every couple of days we call home via Kilo Mike India at Point Reyes, California (Whiskey Oscar Mike is now out of range). One call is intercepted, and completed by Victor India Sierra in Sydney, Australia, who share channels 1203 and 1602 with Kilo Mike India. Reporting our position is the principal purpose of the calls; however, a second purpose is reassuring Pat who is now about to fly to the Marquesas with daughter Katie and young son Sam to meet us.

* * *

Most of a pleasure-boat voyage around the world, like our passage from the Galápagos to the Marquesas, is traveling east to west. It is easy for circumnavigating sailors, even without electronic navigation, to accurately find their port of destination – knowing latitude. Pin pointing when they will arrive – knowing longitude – is not so easy. Of course, if a Mayday is being sent both latitude and longitude are important in speeding rescue.

Navigation has changed in many small and a few big jumps over time. Arab seamen devised methods of navigating in the Indian Ocean, hundreds of years before Columbus. They were able to determine their latitude with an instrument known as a *kamal* and best described as a 3x5 card with a string through a hole in the middle and with a number of knots in the string, each representing a specific latitude. If the navigator knew that the second knot on the string represented the latitude of Bombay, he could check his location by holding this knot between his teeth, and holding the card out at the length of the string. When the height of the card equaled the height of the North Star above the horizon, the vessel was on the latitude of Bombay. Destinations of higher latitude (closer to the North Pole) were represented by knots closer to the card. The navigator steered to come to the correct latitude in the number of days the voyage usually took. Sometimes depending on speed, the coast would appear early and the vessel needed to travel south. Sometimes they reached the latitude before the coast appeared and the navigator merely altered his course to due east. These sailors could also follow the sun during the day and a constellation, such as Orion, at night just as we do today. Sometimes, of course, they couldn't see any of these signposts because of cloud cover. Essentially this is the method Magellan used. Instead of a card and string, however, Magellan had aboard a quadrant – a large wooden protractor, with a plumb bob that measured the height or angle of the North Star over the horizon. A sight along one side was lined up with the North Star and the line of the plumb bob indicated the angle of elevation from which latitude was easily calculated. There is evidence of Phoenician use of the North Star in their navigation as early as 1,000 BC.

Navigators of those times were unable to determine longitude except by dead reckoning based on estimated speed and currents. Magellan knew the latitude of the Philippines and was able to navigate across the Pacific with some assurance. Astronomers of the day knew the method to compute longitude, but their computations required accurate time pieces which were not available until 1735.

Years later Mormon pioneers, including my forefathers, navigated the North American plains using the North Star. Every night as the campfires died, wagon masters would point the tongues of their wagons to the North Star so that in the morning they would know west even on an overcast day.

Latitude also can be determined easily by today's yachtsmen using a sextant when the North Star and the horizon are both in view. If a navigator is on the North Pole, the altitude of the North Star is 90°; if he is on the equator it is 0° (although in this case it is too low in the sky to be visible). Thus if it is at 39-1/4 degrees, he is at 39° 15'N latitude. Of course, south of the equator the North Star disappears and, unfortunately, there is no South Star. A dummy "South Star" can be imagined by lining up several stars including two of the Southern Cross; accuracy, of course, diminishes.

For centuries navigators had done extensive dead reckoning. They knew their direction from compasses and their speed through the water by throwing chips of wood overboard and marking the time it took the ship to pass the chip. With celestial observations, the navigator checked his latitude. Once accurate timepieces were available, he checked his longitude. His position, however, was primarily determined by dead reckoning.

Early Polynesians used the same arcs of the sun and the stars over each island group to navigate. They angled their catamarans north or south until they were in the proper relationship to the seasonal east-to-west track of the sun and the stars; then followed them to their destination. With the consistent trades causing consistent waves Polynesian navigators could maintain a constant angle to the waves when overcast skies obliterated their view of the sky. This is like our autopilot which steers the last compass heading if the GPS looses its signal. The Arabs, Europeans, Polynesians, and Mormon pioneers all used the same geometry to navigate – the same as used by navigators today.

Every night after we reached the latitude of the Marquesas, we had the Southern Cross to our port and the Big Dipper to our starboard. This gave watch keepers assurance that our GPS and autopilot were keeping us on course. Orion's course across the sky in late May and early June is just north of the Marquesas and a welcome signpost every night.

Most blue-water sailors are proficient with the "Noon Shot." To determine latitude, the navigator uses a sextant to measure the height, or angle, of the sun at its zenith, or highest angle of the day. Navigation Almanacs tell the zenith height of the sun at the equator for every day of the year allowing the navigator to compute his latitude.

To determine longitude, the navigator needs to know how far he is from the Prime Meridian in time which can be converted to longitude. The difference in time from the zenith at the Prime Meridian and the local zenith multiplied by 15° for each hour is the longitude.

It is easy to measure the zenith altitude of the

sun for latitude calculation. As it goes over the top of its arch, it is essentially at the same altitude for several minutes. It "hangs there" in the language of navigators. To determine the exact time of its zenith is more difficult. Navigators measure the altitude of the sun thirty minutes before the expected zenith, for example, and then watch with their sextants for the sun to return to the same altitude after the zenith, noting the time and computing the actual zenith to be half way between the two measurements.

The noon latitude calculation is related to the north-to-south movement of the tracks of the sun across the earth. The track moves at about one-half of a nautical mile per hour. A noon latitude determination is thus easy to measure and usually accurate. The noon longitude calculation is related to the east-to-west movement of the sun. The sun appears to be moving 900 nautical miles per hour. With the great speed and because two measurements are necessary, it is quite easy to be in error by a substantial amount. It is easy to see why this calculation depended on the development of accurate time pieces. A one-minute time difference could cause a 15-nautical-mile error. If the navigator's timepiece lost one minute per day his longitude calculation would be off by 150 nautical miles over a 10 day voyage.

There are numerous adjustments all necessary for accurate celestial fixes. These adjustments are ignored here for clarity.

Even though we now have GPS, navigation perfectionists still claim it is important to maintain a dead reckoning position. Very few yachtsmen practice dead reckoning; aboard *Lusty Wind II*, we do not. I have become convinced that the GPS system is either accurate or not working. It is obvious when it is not working because either the displays do not light or they tell the navigator the instrument does not have sufficient information to give a position. When at sea, every two hours we log the position displayed by the GPS. In the event it does fail, we would only have to use our memory back a maximum of two hours and begin our dead reckoning and rusty celestial navigation at that point. The beginning point of this dead reckoning would be much more accurate than a dead reckoning position kept over several days or weeks. Asking a crew member if he held the prescribed course during his watch is like asking a child whether he'll take care of a puppy if you get him one.

GPS works by measuring the distance to satellites that are in a known position and altitude over the earth. Distance is computed by the on-board receiver by measuring the splay, or increasing width of an electronic beam from the satellite. The satellite also transmits its altitude and position over the earth. The GPS receiver can thus calculate the vessel's position as somewhere on the circumference of a circle. The center of which is the position of the satellite over the earth and the radius is calculated from the distance to the satellite. The GPS calculates circles from three satellites and the spot where all three cross is the ship's position.

Early Arab navigators using the North Star knew the height by using their *kamal*, knew that the star's geographic position over the earth was the North Pole and assumed an altitude of infinity. They then knew their latitude which was, of course, the circumference of a circle with the North

Pole as the center; the same definition of a line of latitude. The geometry is therefore the same as has been used for 2,000-plus years. The difference is we use an electronic instrument to measure and calculate our position from satellites full of more electronic equipment and we no longer need a clear sky.

Joshua Slocum on his single-handed trip a century before us sailed approximately 5,700 nautical miles from Islas Juan Fernández to Samoa in 72 days or an average of 79 nautical miles per day (*Spray* had a length of only 36'9"). On this voyage, Slocum sailed within sight of Nuku Hiva in the Marquesas. He decided not to stop, but to proceed to Samoa. Slocum said things were going well and there was no need to stop, but the Marquesas' reputation for cannibals probably influenced him as well. We must remember that Slocum was single-handed, had no engine, electronic navigation, refrigerator, radio, CD player for entertainment, or watermaker. A Portuguese sailor at Isla Juan Fernández had traded some old potatoes that Slocum had for fresh ones. After going to sea, Slocum found these new potatoes were insect ridden and he had to throw them all overboard reducing his normal diet of potatoes, salt cod, and biscuits to salt cod and biscuits. A big deal is made by Slocum's biographers of this remarkable man's navigation using a wind up alarm clock with a broken face. Actually, as we know, this only affected his longitude calculation.

On his first voyage aboard *Yankee*, Irving Johnson, without an accurate timepiece, " . . . found Bermuda by the old method of coming in on latitude. After trying it a few times, one can easily see it would be quite possible to sail around the world without a chronometer, the only drawback being occasional time wasted in getting to latitude and staying on it under sail."

* * *

June 8, it's just before dawn and we can see Ua Huka on the radar. We pick up Polynesians on the VHF radio. Daylight is just starting to seep into the last edges of night when we see it – the eastern end of Nuku Hiva. The scent of land is intense after an eighteen-day absence. A school of twenty dolphins greet us by jumping and squealing at our bow. While watching this wonderful display, I take down and throw overboard the panties that have been serving as our "burgee" for the crossing. I know that "in the middle of France the ladies wear no pants," but I'm afraid we might offend the French Immigration and Custom officials in this remote outpost. I replace the panties with the Yellow Q Flag and the French Tricolor; the panties haven't attracted anyone anyway.

This leg is normally the longest one for westbound circumnavigators. Our total distance through the water from Porta Ayora to Nuku Hiva is 3,130 nautical miles. According to the GPS, our distance over the bottom is 3,060 nautical miles. Our time is 18 days 2-1/2 hours plus four hours gained, or 18 days 6-1/2 hours. Factoring in the extra four hours, our average speed over the bottom has been 6.98 knots, or 167.5 nautical miles a day, and our average speed through the water has been 7.14 knots, or 171.3 nautical miles per day. Normally the current adds 1 to 1-1/2 knots for 75% of the distance, an average of one knot. Our foul current of about 0.16 knots, we will learn later, has been due to a strong El Niño that has been in place from November 1991 through March 1992, and the revived trade winds of May and June have not yet massaged the temporary eastbound current to its normal westward flow.

We have used 256 gallons of fuel, or a little less than 70% of the 373 we had aboard when we left the Galápagos. We have used approximately one-quarter of the fuel in the last two and a half days after the genoa furling failed. If we hadn't had our large fuel supply we might have lost two or three days and missed Pat, Katie, and Sam's arrival. With the watermaker working, we have all four water tanks still full.

6

CHAPTER SIX

Who the hell is Jeannie Baré?

June 8, 1992 – July 23, 1992

Nuku Hiva – Bora Bora, Society Islands

We are approaching Nuku Hiva in the Marquesas passing Baie de Contrôlleur known when Herman Melville first visited the island as Typee. After eighteen days at sea, a stop is tempting but Taiohae, five nautical miles farther west, is the official port of entry. We enter the harbor sailing between Ile Sentinelle de L'Est and Ile Sentinelle de L'Ouest, two pieces of the volcano crater that are now Baie Taiohae. We are now in the Buoyage A region of the world and the red buoys will be on our port-left-side. *Lusty Wind II* at last is anchored in Polynesia – the most dreamed of destination of blue-water sailors. A stern anchor to hold her bow into the surf helps reduce the motion of the boat as the gentle wind would have held her beam to.

Polynesia is from the Greek *poly* "many" and nesos "islands," a name given by early French sailors. The Polynesians call their world *Moana-nui-o-kiva*, "The great ocean of the blue skies." Polynesia covers a huge triangle with Hawaii at the north tip, New Zealand at the West, Easter Island at the east, and Tahiti almost at the center. These islands are grouped together by the apparent common racial heritage of the original inhabitants. Original is the key word – in the two most populated areas, New Zealand and Hawaii, Polynesians are now a minority. We shall sail in this triangle for nine weeks; not nearly long enough.

In Taiohae, we find almost everything including the *gendarmerie* and stores closed because of a holiday. There are no Immigrations or Customs officials in the Marquesas and entry is handled by the *gendarmerie*, which requires us to post a bond with a bank in the Marquesas of enough money to buy airline tickets for all on board back to home territory, or in our case – Hawaii. We all have tickets home from Papeete, to be cashed in later, which satisfies this requirement. Later in the day the *gendarmerie* opens and we are issued a temporary cruising permit giving us official status until our arrival in Papeete. This *pratique* is followed by a series of telephone calls to California to order a new genoa furling system.

We look around the village a bit but rest most of the day. On the way to dinner at Snack Pakiu, I am suffering my only serious insulin reaction of the trip. Apparently the activities of today have greatly exceeded what I have experienced at sea the previous eighteen and the insulin shot I'd just taken is too large a dose. John waits with me while Ken and Andy run back to the dinghy and then to the boat for my Glucagon, an emergency sugar injection. Just after they leave, I discover some candy – Lifesavers – in my pocket and am soon much better.

There are two other occupied tables in the restaurant making it almost full. At one of the tables, is a young French doctor who runs the island clinic. This good man

With the wind in the Abacos.

Photo by Bruce Mirrielees

...ovisions stowed on the lower
...nk of the port stateroom.

Panama Canal.

Teiki, Katie,
Sam, and Pat on the
road to Baie Atihue

Photo by Andy Ellison

Sam in the
Mearae at
Baie Atihue, Nuku
Hiva, Marquesas.

Sam and friends
on Fatu Hiva,
Marquesas.

am changing engine oil
the South Pacific.

to by Ward LeHardy

Lusty Wind II anchored in
Baie de Verges, Fatu Hiva, Marquesas.

Photo by Andy Ellison

Katie and friends in
Fatu Hiva, Marquesas.

Andy,
Katie, Nick, Pat,
Sam, and John
moored at Papeet[e]
Photo by Carol Morgan

*Lusty Wind II,
Tenereze* and
LaRoca
moored at Papeet[e]

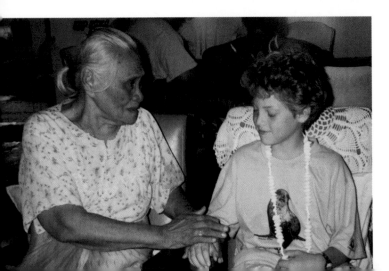

Tuana Utahia
and Sam
in Papeete.

The Captain,
Celina Hurahiatia
and Katie-
Three Party
Animals
in Papeete.
Photo by Andy Ellison

John and
Carol Morgan
on Moorea.

The Captain and
the Admiral on
Bora Bora.

Photo by Katie Ellison

John, Andy, and Sam near Moorea.

Lusty Wind II anchored near Moorea.

Photo by Andy Ellison

John writing home to Sam

Andy with Mahi-Mahi actually
caught by the Captain

Insulin and
diabetic supplies
in the Aft Head.

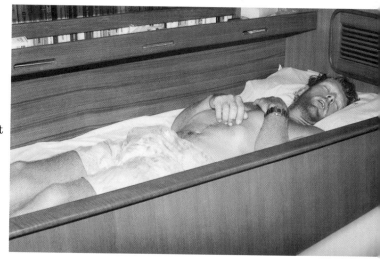

Erik Ramon
sleeping in pilot
berth along Great
Barrier Reef,
Australia.

Dave Townsend
and Andy taking
noonshot in the
Indian Ocean.

Bob Payne enjoying
a flying fish breakfast.

The spinnaker blow
in the Indian Ocea

Photo by Bob Payne

Lusty Wind II anchored at Adan, Yemen.

comes over and talks with me at some length to make sure I am all right. He invites me to come to the clinic for a checkup, but I decline. I am afraid he will call Dr. Bever and the two will have me with my leg shipped back home. Part of this doctor's concern is the combination of my being diabetic and having a twisted swollen leg.

Early the next morning Andy takes a ferry to the northwest corner of the island to meet Pat, Katie, and Sam. I ask Andy to see if our new furling system is at the airport. (As a boy I would mail a box top with 25¢ and wait the next day for the mailman.) We are all waiting when the ferry returns at about 11 a.m. but there is no Pat, Katie, Andy, Sam, or furling system. We get word from Rose Corser at the Keikahahui Inn that Pierre Teikitohe has met and made a deal with Andy to drive them all back from the airport, a drive she accurately promises will be spectacular. They should arrive at the inn about three. Pat and Katie are going to stay at the inn for several days, giving them a chance to acclimate and give us a chance to get the boat cleaned after a fifty-seven day voyage with men only. Pat lets me call myself Captain as long as I understand she is the "Admiral." All captains clean up before a visit from the Admiral. At three o'clock, we beach the dinghy on the black volcanic sand at Paha Tea and hike up the steep rock road to the Keikahahui Inn. Just as we reach the top of the hill, the truck carrying the rest of our family arrives for a reunion which is marred only by Pat's horror at the jaunty angle of my left foot.

Because of the serious illness of Frank Corser, Rose's husband, and the difficulty they have had in keeping responsible help in this remote part of the world, the services of the hotel are at a minimum and they are unable to accommodate us for dinner. Frank and Rose are ever vigilant – I seldom hobble down the road when Frank doesn't give me a lift in his pickup truck.

Ken makes reservations for us again at Snack Pakiu; and as it is necessary for him to specify our meal ahead, he decides we will all enjoy a native dish – chopped goat. The chopped goat turns out to be exactly as described – a goat chopped and made into a thick stew. It isn't really bad tasting but it is difficult to eat because it is full of little pieces of chopped bone and other unidentifiable chopped parts. None of us except Ken eats. And he's eating under duress; since it was his choice, he has to put up a good front.

* * *

Most historians think the Marquesas were settled over 2,000 years ago by Polynesians traveling east in dugout canoes from Samoa and Tonga. Thor Heyerdahl's theory is that South American Indians settled the islands by sailing west on balsa log rafts. Heyerdahl holds that early sailors could reach these areas only by sailing westbound in the system, as we had done. He supports his belief by the fact that many artifacts in Polynesia are common to those found in South America. The Quechua of Peru, the indigenous population, and many native Polynesians have a similar appearance.

Proponents of the eastbound theory assume many early travelers left where they lived because someone was making life difficult for them. It has been suggested they might have escaped to Polynesia late in an El Niño season, with a reversed system, hoping that by the time their enemies got organized the El Niño will be over and they could not be followed for several years. These historians have also found artifacts supporting their theory. Is it possible that both are correct?

The first Europeans in the Marquesas were led by the Spaniard, Alvaro de Mendana, in 1595. He and his men massacred more than two hundred of the Marquesans in the process of their explorations. Mendana named the islands after Marquis de Mendoza, his patron and the Viceroy of Peru. The Polynesians call these islands *Fenua*, the land of men.

The next Europeans were Captain James Cook and crew. Cook rediscovered the Marquesas on his second voyage around the world in 1772-1775. He attempted to keep the Marquesans from stealing all the iron off his ships and once ordered a volley fired over a particularly adventuresome group. Unfortunately, one man was killed. This was not Cook's style. He was quite cognizant of his intrusion on another culture and intended no harm to these people or their way of life. Cook later went ashore to find what kindness he could do for the son of the man killed but the boy had fled terrified into the hills.

After Cook documented the location of the Marquesas for the world (having an accurate timepiece, he knew both latitude and longitude), less sensitive whalers and slavers came leaving behind venereal disease, tuberculosis, and influenza. Beginning in 1798, missionaries came to compete for the souls of the Marquesans. The French Catholic missionaries eventually drove most other missionaries from the scene. Later when the first Mormon missionaries arrived, the Catholic priests told the native merchants they will be excommunicated if they sold anything to the Mormons – a strong theological argument effectively forcing the Mormons out of this Catholic domain.

In the middle of the 19th century, Herman Melville jumped ship and wrote the classic *Typee*, an account of run-a-ways climbing the hills from Taiohae Bay and down into Typee Bay to avoid capture. Typee Bay was known to be populated by cannibals; so his was a desperate escape.

When Thor Heyerdahl first visited Fatu Hiva in 1936, he wrote of encounters, although not invasive, with cannibals. Our visit 56 years later did not put enough space between us and the cannibals to satisfy Pat or Sam. I will admit I felt chills when at dusk I heard Marquesans practicing on their drums.

The population at discovery was 80,000. It fell to 1,200 just before World War II, and today is about 8,000 and increasing.

* * *

Pat, Katie, Andy, Sam, John, Ken and I engage Teiki, at Rose Corser's suggestion, for an all day excursion across the island. After an early breakfast, we climb aboard his Toyota four-wheel drive truck. The first leg of this trip is up and over the hill to Typee Valley. It is certainly easy to envision the difficulty of Melville and his fellow runaway, Toby. It must have been an arduous climb through this rocky, thick jungle up and down steep grades to hoped-for safety.

After visiting beautiful Typee Valley and walking through the ancient *mearae*, or temple, we again board Teiki's Toyota and climb over the mountain to Baie Atiheu. Baie Atiheu and the adjoining and easily accessible Baie Anatio are probably the home of the Happars, also cannibals and arch enemies of Melville's Typeeans.

The scenery on these truck trips over this relatively new and spectacular volcanic island must be one of the most beautiful and breath-taking rides in the world. We stop first at the *mearae* just before Baie Atihue. This *mearae* is cared for just enough to make it accessible without destroying its ancient allure. We have lunch in Hatiheu, the village on Baie Atiheu. Our reservations are at the restaurant, Hinakounu. Service is home-style with large platters of every kind of food imaginable. Barbecued lobster is the main course and we all have our fill leaving only one lobster on the tray. I am ready to grab it when the waiter takes the tray to everybody's amusement. A few seconds later, he is back again with the tray heaping with more lobster about half of which we are able to eat. This is the only time I've seen leftover lobster.

All the sailing guides of the South Pacific advise those who may need fuel in the Marquesas to write ahead – by as much as six months – to reserve an appropriate number of 55 gallon drums. We have done this; but now that we have arrived, we find a large sailboat from Antigua has arrived ahead of us and purchased our fuel; thus none is available from the "only" supplier. On checking around, Ken finds a native who has a number of barrels of diesel in his back yard and is happy to sell us the contents of three. There is no delivery system; so John, Andy, and Ken carry the fuel in the dinghy, in 15 gallon Jerry cans, from the dock to the boat.

It's a fine morning and we decide to sail for Baie Taioa on the southwest corner of Nuku Hiva – about one hour from Taiohae. About halfway, we encounter a strong squall accompanied by severe seas. My plan is to continue on to Baie Taioa for shelter. John looks into the bay surrounded by high and steep cliffs (1600 feet) and talks me into returning to Taiohae. He is afraid we may encounter severe down drafts in the bay. (John and I, on

Lusty Wind II under bare poles, had our spreaders nearly dipped into the sea by a down draft off Gibraltar in 1987, and John wants no more of that.)

During all of this, we begin to smell diesel fuel in the cabin and see traces of fuel on the water when the bilge pump cycles on. Back in Taiohe, John and Andy find the problem – a leaking banjo fitting on the engine's return fuel yoke. I temporarily fix it with a collar of stick epoxy.

The next day is clear; so we motor back to Baie Taioa and anchor in L'Anse Hakate, the east side of this beautiful heart-shaped bay. John, Katie, Andy, Sam, and Ken hike to the "cascade," a spectacular 2,000 foot waterfall and lake. While swimming in the lake, Sam loses one shoe which means he must be carried much of the three miles back to the dinghy over the steep rocky trail. His return to terrified parents, stranded on the boat in this bay that by then has "cannibal" written all over it, is well after dark.

Tenereze arrives in port late one night after a sixteen-and-a-half-day passage from the Galápagos, beating our time by a day and a half. Again remember that she's longer.

The best time to cruise French Polynesia is May to November when the Southeast trade winds are perfect and the hurricane season of December to March is over. June and July are perfect.

It is an over-night sail from Nuku Hiva to Hiva Oa, our second stop. About six in the morning, we anchor in the open just off the village. Later in the morning, by dinghy, we explore the yacht anchorage and find it crowded. Our friends on *Quest* are getting ready to leave and they suggest we take their position in the anchorage, which we do at about 1 p.m.

While resting aboard, another sailboat comes into the harbor. The master is asking on the VHF radio in a gruff voice if there is a *Lusty Wind* in port. We answer, not knowing what we have done or where we have done it. The call is from General Ward LeHardy (US Army, retired), aboard *Cormorant*. He is demanding the return of his wife, Judy's, underwear, not to mention several dishtowels. Apparently when items were missing from her laundry, the Hotel Galápagos told her they must have gone with *Lusty Wind*. We return the dish-towels and I offer to replace Judy's missing garments but Ward, now grinning from ear to ear, doesn't think it is proper for civilians to be buying this sort of personal item for the wife of a General. We sail with Ward and Judy all the way to Tahiti and have since kept in touch with them by mail and telephone.

The access to town from the boat at Hiva Oa is more difficult than at Nuku Hiva, particularly if one is on crutches. Without a protective reef, both anchorages get a heavy swell, but Hiva Oa is worse. Sam was going ashore one day on his own and got caught in a sudden swell. The dinghy was tossed upside-down onto the rocks. Somehow, Sam escaped injury and got the dinghy back into the water – all again to the horror of his parents who were watching helpless from the boat. Several yachties in the harbor were quickly off to Sam's aid, one picking me up on his way.

After several days wandering around Atuona and visiting the graves of Paul Gauguin and French crooner Jacques Brel (Brel is not alive, well, or in Paris), we motor against the wind to Baie de Vierges (virgins) on Fatu Hiva, the southern-most island of the Marquesan group.

Baie de Vierges is often called, and I will without hesitation add my vote, the most beautiful anchorage in the world. Fatu Hiva gets more rain than any other Marquesan island and the rough volcanic shore has richer and more varied greens than one can imagine. The heavy mysterious mist in the hills adds to the picture.

Several lava formations around this bay look like statues guarding the entrance and one is in the likeness of George Washington – at least it is to Americans. Many think the name of the bay comes from early French sailors thinking another formation here looks like the Virgin Mary. I vote with those who think the name was an unkind joke attesting to the Europeans' misunderstanding of a difference in sexual mores between the indigenous culture and their own. This sounds more like sailors.

* * *

In 1936 when Thor Heyerdahl brought his bride, Liv, to Omoa on southern Fatu Hiva, the settlement consisted of 197 Catholics and four Protestants. Thor and Liv being Protestant settled in with the smaller group. The Catholics, upset by this change in the balance, according to Thor, began to hassle them. Frank Corser had another theory. Frank suspected the natives were upset because Thor was looting the burial grounds of their ancestors.

* * *

John and Sam go ashore to the village of Hana Vave to find the Chief and report our arrival. Reporting to the Chief is a custom on islands without a *gendarmerie*. The Chief is at a special Fathers' Day service at the church but welcomes us to Fatu Hiva at its completion. John, Katie, Andy, and Ken hike to the "cascade," another beautiful waterfall up in the mountains. Sam is running out of shoes; so he and I visit the village full of many happy children. Some of these youngsters get a little too enthusiastic trying to help us; and as I am trying to hoist myself from the water into the dinghy, they start the engine, which, unfortunately, I have left in gear. The revolving propeller could have done more damage to my dangling legs and feet, but it turns out all right. We give these children Pringles, which they love. Later their parents come in dugout canoes to try the Pringles. This may sound like a meeting of "the noble savage and technology"; but, back in their *fare*, or house, these people wash their dishes with Fairy Soap and diaper their babies in Pampers, both of which are also made by Procter and Gamble headquartered in Cincinnati.

This afternoon, Katie and Andy take me along to visit a *fare* to buy home-made *tappas* they had seen earlier. The *tappas* are wall hangings produced from the bark of Mulberry or Breadfruit trees and dyed in wonderful native designs. The woman who makes *tappas* is in her *fare* with her mother, daughter, and granddaughter. Katie and Andy need to go on up the trail to deliver some promised chewing-gum and candy to children they have met there earlier. Since the trail is steep, I stay with the *tappas* lady and her family. Katie and Andy are gone for over an hour and these women do not quite know what to do with me. They offer me some type of sweet-drink with cake and they, particularly the grandmother, do not understand my refusal. I am finally able to make them understand with the word *diabetico*. "*Ooooooooh diabetico*," they repeat. They then bring forth some other form of goody they indicate will be all right for me. I'm sure it isn't, but I take it anyway. A lesson – it is important for traveling diabetics to know how to communicate the words diabetic and sugar or candy.

Cormorant joins us in Baie de Vierges and we share some cheese and wine with Ward, Judy, and Ward's brother-in-law who is along with them. Early the next morning, *Cormorant* leaves for the Tuamotus and we depart much later in the morning. We motor-sail with the main and staysail but treat our rig, which still has a temporary forestay, with caution. During the night, we pass and have radio contact with *Cormorant*. She is also slowed as Ward has found a crack at the weld on the boom gooseneck and is not using his main. We consider a panty-raid but think that might be pushing our new friendship with Judy and the General.

We and *Cormorant* are now crossing Magellan's wake. After celebrating his navigation through the strait and entry into the Pacific Ocean, Magellan started on a north course seeking a meeting of the coast of Asia with the West Coast of South America at about latitude 35°S. This coast was assumed by map makers of the day. Upon passing 35°S and reaching latitude 32°S, Magellan saw no sign of this imagined coast and steered northwest. Being able to determine latitude, he sailed northwest until reaching the known latitude of the Philippines, then sailed due east. After just missing Islas Juan Fernádaz and Easter Island, Magellan discovered a low lying atoll at about 15°S. The island is very likely Pukapuka in the Tuamotus. Magellan then without sighting other islands of the Tuamotus slowly crossed the doldrums of the ITCZ at the equator and saw only one other island before reaching Guam and the Philippines.

Magellan just missed many of the most wonderful places in the world and he and the rest of the crew suffered inordinately from lack of food and water while passing close to prolific providers of both. This happened because the calculations of the circumference of the earth were 3,000 nautical miles short and Magellan "came in on latitude" too early. One wonders what voyagers may be going by our galaxy and not noticing. They may be in dire need or their immune systems may be masking devastating disease.

* * *

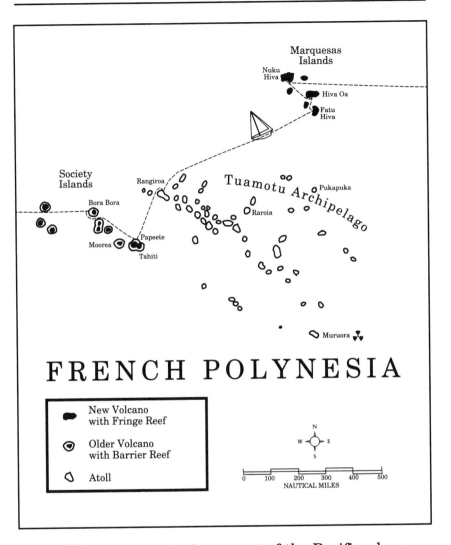

Marquesas
Islands

Nuku
Hiva

Hiva Oa

Fatu
Hiva

Society
Islands

Rangiroa

Tuamotu Archipelago

Pukapuka

Bora Bora

Raroia

Moorea

Papeete

Tahiti

Muruora

FRENCH POLYNESIA

New Volcano
with Fringe Reef

Older Volcano
with Barrier Reef

Atoll

N
W — E
S

| 0 | 100 | 200 | 300 | 400 | 500 |
NAUTICAL MILES

We are now entering a part of the Pacific where
coral reefs affect a big part of daily life. Reefs are
built over many years by small sea anemones.
These creatures have the ability to secrete lime
which becomes their external shell and the main
building block of reefs. These reef builders require
water at a temperature of 77° to 84° Fahrenheit
with a level of salinity that is normally found in

oceans. These temperatures are generally found between the Tropic of Cancer and the Tropic of Capricorn. The band narrows on the west shores of continents as the currents of the "system" bring cold water and widens along eastern shores where the currents bring warm water. Where salinity is reduced by fresh water, there is limited or no coral. A major example is a large area around the mouth of the Amazon. Coral growth requires photosynthesis from the sun and, thus, is best in clear water and in depths of usually not more than ninety feet. Pollution threatens the reefs of the world both in the form of chemical poisons and debris that reduce the needed photosynthesis. These pollutants are spread over the entire world by the currents of the system. Geological records show that natural phenomena, such as volcanic eruptions, also affect coral growth by putting ash in the air and water again diminishing photosynthesis.

Before Charles Darwin crossed the Pacific, he formulated his first theory: this one on the growth of coral islands. His findings while crossing the Pacific and Indian Oceans supported his theory. Darwin published *The Structure and Distribution of Coral Reefs* in 1842, which explained how reefs begin growing in the shallow water, up to ninety-feet or so, around islands where water temperature and salinity are suitable. With the melting of the polar caps, the water-level of the oceans has risen about four-hundred feet in the last twenty-thousand years. As the sea-water rises or the islands sink or both, coral reefs grow by building upon the old reef. The old coral, as it gets into lower colder water without sufficient sunshine, dies and becomes the foundation for the new living coral.

There are three types of coral islands in the South Pacific. The first type is the new island with very minimal fringe reef. An example of this is the Marquesas. The lack of reefs is the reason the anchorages are rolly and the natives tend to gather fruits and vegetables rather than depend on fish. The lack of lagoons and barrier reefs make harvesting of the sea much more difficult.

The second type of island is the more mature volcanic mountain where the reef has begun on the shore. As the sea-levels rise or the islands sink and the coral grows upward, it becomes a barrier reef and the distance between the reef and the sinking mountain, or the lagoon, expands. This lagoon is then filled by the sea to a shallow depth with sand. An example of this type of island is the Society Islands such as Tahiti, Moorea, or Bora Bora. Here the mountains still precipitate rain and enough time has elapsed for soil to develop; thus the natives may gather or farm. The Barrier Reef makes fish abundant and fishing easy; so fish provide a big part of the diet. Because of the easy living conditions, the population of these islands is the largest. It is easy to find the passes through the reef in relatively still water where the absence of surf reveals their locations. These passes are opposite valleys where the fresh rain water runoff has reduced the salinity and the coral has been unable to grow.

The third type of island is the coral atoll where the rising water has completely submerged the volcanic mountain and the ring of coral has continued to grow as the water rises. The principal examples of this type of islands are the Tuamotus which must have been, aeons ago, an unbelievable collection of volcanic islands. On the coral reef in

CORAL ISLAND FORMATION

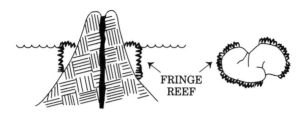

New volcano with fringe reef
(Marquesas)

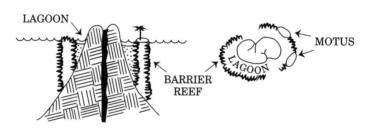

Older volcano with barrier reef
(Tahiti, Moorea, Bora Bora)

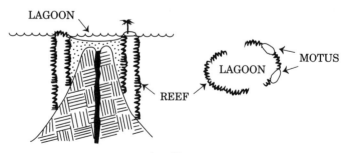

Atoll
(Tuamotus, Bikini)

some spots, sand driven by the water has lodged and *motus*, or small islands, have developed. There is little agriculture on these islands since they are not high enough to precipitate water and the soil is sparse. The principal diet of the natives of these islands is coconut meat and fish which, of course, are extremely abundant and easy to harvest. The passes must be either observed by the lack of crashing surf or from charts since the rivers of the mountain valleys that prohibited the coral growth have been below the sea for a long, long time.

*   *   *

Our sail from Fatu Hiva to Rangiroa in the Tuamotus is 715 nautical miles and has taken 95 hours for a speed of 7.5 knots. By now the current is going our way. We motor sail in light air using the main and staysail as we, of course, still do not have a headstay. We are now 3,600 nautical miles from Kilo Mike India at Point Reyes, California, but still can easily make radio telephone calls. One call is to check on the furling system.

The pass into the Rangiroa Lagoon is on the northeast side of the atoll and thus should be negotiated in the morning with the sun behind the helmsman and Polaroid glasses on so reefs in the water are visible. But it is afternoon, the sun is in our eyes, and I am a bit nervous because this is our first Pacific reef passage. However, the pass looks pretty clear-cut; and after four days at sea, we are all ready for a quiet night. As we approach the pass, it becomes apparent there is a strong tidal current coming out of the lagoon through the pass. The current, as it fans out, pushes us a bit to the west. Unbeknownst to us we are now steaming toward some reefs we, of course, cannot see with the sun in our eyes. A skiff with two fisherman, working a bit from us, sees our predicament, and rushes

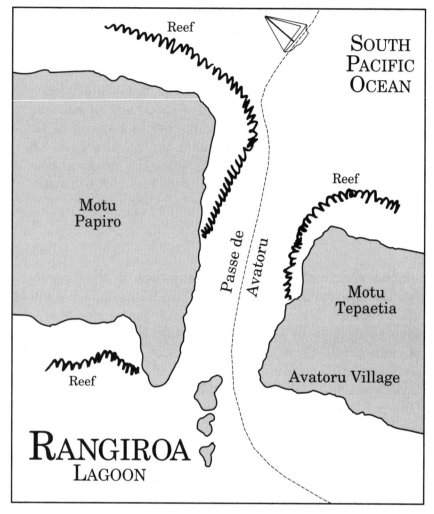

to us pointing and yelling for us to alter our course to the south. Once in the pass, the current is quite strong and with full power we are just able to make three knots over the bottom. It takes a great deal of concentration to hold the boat straight as a little bit of a turn might well spin the boat 180° and require us to go back to the ocean for the night.

Once we are in the lagoon, all is peace and quiet as well as breath-takingly beautiful. Lesson to be learned –

a navigator must know the tides and transit passes at or near slack tide, particularly in narrow unmarked passes at large lagoons. Everyone doing this should follow the old advice – plan the arrival or wait to enter when the sun is over the helmsman's shoulder. And have Polaroids handy.

We motor in the lagoon east about four nautical miles to anchor off Hotel Kai Ora. We dinghy over to Tiputa to call home, to call California to check on the furling gear, to report to the *gendarmerie*, and to buy *baguettes*. At the post office where the telephone is, we meet the Post Mistress who is Mormon and find that the President of the Mormon Temple in Papeete has my aunt and uncle as house-guests waiting our arrival. The President is anxious not because of the house-guests, but because of their concerns about our lateness. He has asked all Mormons in the Tuamotus to be on the lookout for *Lusty Wind II*. Before handling our calls, the Post Mistress calls Tahiti to report our whereabouts and anticipated arrival date in Papeete.

Since leaving the Marquesas, Sam and I have developed sores on our arms and legs. One sore on my ankle is swollen to about the size of a golf-ball. (Liv, Thor Heyerdahl's wife, had suffered from the same "teacup sized" sores at Fatu Hiva in 1936.) We pull up anchor and motor the four miles back to Avatoru where John, Andy, and Ken carry fuel from a gas station to the boat and Pat takes Sam to the clinic. After landing the dinghy, Pat asks a native who is clearing some brush along the road where the clinic is. He seems to be asking what is the trouble. Pat shows him Sam's leg, and he responds, "*Ooooooooh mosquito*," and drives them in his truck to the clinic. The young French medic sprays to kill the mosquitoes (so small we hadn't noticed), cleans and dresses about 40 bites then gives Sam some antibiotics – all at no cost. Our return to the anchorage is well after dark and, on our approach, we pass close to but safely away from an anchored boat. The next morning several ask if I saw the boat I nearly hit – I still occasionally wake up wondering if there was another I didn't see.

John, Katie, and Andy join a dive group to "shoot the pass." When the current in the pass is strong, divers starting upstream rush through the reef-strewn pass to a waiting boat. They are accompanied by sharks who seem to have invented this sport. Sam and I, called the boil twins by Katie, stay out of the water.

Joining us at this anchorage are *Cormorant*, *Pegasus*, and *Quest*. We all celebrate Judy's birthday aboard *Cormorant*.

* * *

Tuamotus comes from the original Paumotu; *pau* means "low" and *motu* means "small island." Beginning with the first discovery by the Spanish in 1606 through recent times, they have been known in English as "The Dangerous Islands." This name and reputation is the result of many reefs, some of which are below the surface, coupled with strong, and in some years reversing, currents that have caused the demise of many ships. During the early days of World War II, these islands were charted since there was a possibility that the war with the Japanese will come this far. Now, of course, we have accurate navigation systems and radar which coupled with good charts substantially reduce the danger of traveling among these atolls.

* * *

While on Rangiroa, Sam and I read *The Hurricane* by Charles Nordoff and James Norman Hall. Fortunately,

Sam doesn't watch old "B" movies; so the plot is new. *The Hurricane* is a story of Terangi, a native of an island in the Tuamotus who was wrongly jailed in Tahiti and escaped many times. On his last escape, he finds his way on a log back to his home atoll in time to be a hero when a major hurricane arrives. The extreme low pressure raises the water level over the highest land on the atoll, and drowns most of the inhabitants. This novel exposes one of the two blemishes in the seemingly peaceful and easy life of the natives of the Tuamotus. The other major flaw is nuclear testing by the French on Mururoa in the southern Tuamotus.

Now much the wiser, we wait until late in the afternoon and slack tide to exit the same pass we had entered earlier. This time we have the sun over our shoulders and Polaroids in place. After an uneventful navigation of the pass, we sail around the northwest corner of Rangiroa and turn south-west for our overnight sail to Papeete. Our afternoon departure times our arrival at Papeete for morning.

Tahiti means "high and holy place" and Papeete, the city, means "water basket." The shore line and the barrier reef form the basket.

* * *

Long before Europeans came to Tahiti there was a prophecy that "strangers will one day arrive in a vessel without an outrigger and bring change enough for the sacred birds of sea and land to mourn." This prophecy was fulfilled in 1767 with the arrival of *Dolphin* and Captain Samuel Wallace. Wallace claimed the island group for England by "Right of Conquest" and planted the British flag. The welcome from the Tahitian women overwhelmed Wallace's sailors; and by all accounts, the crew planted a few flags of their own. The Tahitians wanted things from the ships and the women were useful. Iron was new and astounding to these people and nails would buy drinking water, fire-wood, fruit, chickens, pigs, and women. Sailors having nails in 1767 was not unlike infantrymen having silk stockings in Paris in 1944. The sailors were understandably pulling nails out of the ship for this trade to the point that the structural integrity of the ship was becoming questionable and guards had to be posted twenty-four hours a day to keep things, shall we say, nailed down. Many of the sailors were required to sleep on the deck all the way back to England for lack of nails with which to hang their hammocks. No doubt.

Before Wallace had returned to England with news of his discovery, the French explorer, Louis Antoine de Bougainville, sighted this new land. He anchored at Papeete in April 1768 and immediately claimed all the surrounding islands for France. Bougainville experienced the same structural problems with his ship and also posted guards.

The Tahitians surmised that the Europeans had come to Tahiti for women since there was none on their boats and, it followed logically, none on the islands from which they came. One day a Tahitian man noticed a servant of one of the officers and called out that this person was a woman dressed as a man. He was right! This young woman had come all the way from France to Tahiti undetected, we are told, by her master or the crew. She was Jeannie Baré. Jeannie was an orphan trying to improve her situation by going to sea. Now revealed to the crew, Jeannie went ashore and was first raped by members of the fired-up French crew and then by the Tahitian men who were looking for a new experience. Jeannie, thenceforth, stayed aboard and protected herself with loaded pistols. The ability of Jeannie to disguise her sex on the long voyage from France to Tahiti does not speak well of her or the French crew. She completed the voyage back to France and was thus the first woman of whom we know to sail around the world.

Early in the eighteenth century, Edmond Haley of comet fame presented a method of determining the distance from the earth to the sun during the transit of Venus. This would occur, by his calculations, in 1761 and 1769. Haley's method required observing the time lapse of the paths of Venus across the sun taken from two different places in the world. Accuracy depended on extending the points of observation to the longest possible north-south distance which made an observation somewhere like Tahiti critical. The distance from the earth to the sun was important to these scientists of the "Day of Enlightenment" as it would give dimensions to the known universe and enable a better understanding of the move-ment of the planets. This knowledge would also expand the ability to navigate ships.

The Royal Geographic Society obtained the use of *Endeavor*, a ship of the British Navy. It was commanded by a young officer, James Cook who was to deliver a group of astronomers to Tahiti for these important observations. Cook's resulting voyage of exploration contributed much other valuable information on their world. The scientific work of Joseph Banks aboard *Endeavor* was so remarkable that scientists were thereafter assigned to voyages of exploration by most nations. The most notable was, of course, Charles Darwin.

The missionaries came to stay in 1797 and the

French came with three warships in 1843 to take formal possession of the island group.

* * *

Tahiti is, of course, the symbol of the South Pacific and its most famous island. Its bounty of food, scenery, easy living conditions, and the friendly populace earned it its reputation. The climate is best described by my Uncle John who says that in summer a person sleeps very comfortably with only one sheet over him and in the winter perfect comfort requires two sheets.

We arrive in Papeete about three o'clock in the afternoon and find all the good berths along the sea-wall in the inner harbor occupied. Outside the inner harbor, there is a beach, of sorts, with trees close to the water. With much excitement, we drop our hook; and while letting out chain, back in between two other boats. We then dispatch John and Katie in the dinghy to pull long lines to tie our stern to the trees. We are just getting settled when we see a familiar couple walking down the beach looking for somebody. It was John and Carol Morgan – a wonderful reunion except my father's youngest sister is close to tears when she sees my leg.

John Morgan, my uncle from Layton, Utah, had been a missionary in Tahiti and the Tuamotus from 1947 to 1950. John and my Aunt Carol were called to work for a couple of years in the Papeete mission office in 1988 after his retirement. They quickly accepted our invitation to join us in French Polynesia and are now staying in the Mormon compound in Papeete waiting our arrival.

Uncle John had been in Papeete when Thor Heyerdahl's raft with five other Scandinavians washed over a reef near Raroia in the Tuamotus. The raft and crew were brought to Papeete for a grand welcome including a gift of *The Book of Mormon* from John.

POLYNÉSIE FRANÇAISE   RÉPUBLIQUE FRANÇAISE

Liberté . Égalité . Fraternité

CIRCONSCRIPTION TERRITORIALE
DE LA POLICE DE L'AIR
ET DES FRONTIÈRES   PORT DE PAPEETE, LE   01 JUILLET 1992

POSTE de PAPEETE

DÉCLARATION D'ENTRÉE D'UN NAVIRE DE PLAISANCE
(Arriving Declaration of a pleasure vessel)

NOM DU NAVIRE ! Name of the vessel	LUSTY WIND	PAVILLON ! Flag AMERICAIN
DATE D'ENTRÉE EN POLYNESIE FRANÇAISE! Arriving date in French Polynesia	08.06.92	PAR ! First port GALAPAGOS

ITINÉRAIRE !   USA PANAMA GALAPAGOS   NUKU HIVA HIVA OA RANGIROA PAPEETE
Itinerary

DATE PREVUE DE SORTIE DE POLYNESIE FRANÇAISE !   15 JUILLET 92
Sailing date from French Polynesia

LISTE DES PERSONNES À BORD
Persons on board

NOM ET PRENOMS Name and Given Name	DATE ET LIEU DE NAISSANCE Date and Place of Birth	NATIONALITE Nationality	QUALITE Quality
- ELLISON Nicolas	09.02.39 à SINSINATY	AMERICAINE	CAPITAINE
- ELLISON Andrew	23.02.73 à FORT THOMAS	"	EQUAPAGE
- ELLISON John	17.10.68 à KENTUCKY	"	"
- WANDSTRAT Kenneth	05.10.67 à OHIO	"	"
- ELLISON Samuel	03.08.80 à OHIO	"	"
- ELLISON Priscilla	04.06.40 à KENTUCKY	"	COQUERIE
- ELLISON Katharine	23.01.72 à OHIO	"	"

MENTION / Les trois derniers passagers sont arrivés par voie aérienne à FAAA
le 08.06.92 et ont embarqué à bord du voilier à   NUKU HIVA.

POLICE NATIONALE
PORT DE TAHITI PAPEETE
- 1 JUIL. 1992

RESERVE AU SERVICE   SIGNATURE DU CAPITAINE !
(Captain's Signature)

Entry Paper—Papeete June 8, 1992.

Heyerdahl's trip had been to prove the possibility that South American Indians sailing on balsa rafts to populate Polynesia, also a belief of the Mormons.

With son John, I hobble around to the Immigration and Customs Office where we fill out forms and crew-lists for over an hour. They need special document stamps for the passport and boat clearance, which are available only at the Post Office. The Post Office is, by now, closed. The officials tell us to enjoy ourselves for the evening and come back in the morning. Dinner our first night is along the commercial quay. Natives with trucks provide local delicacies. This is tailgating Tahiti style.

On the insistence of one wife, one aunt, and one uncle, I agree to go to the Clinic Paofai to have my leg examined. We are first directed to the emergency clinic where the doctor sends me to X-ray and on my return has an orthopedic surgeon waiting to see me. The surgeon first asks if I am diabetic then examines my X-ray, looks at my leg, does a Doppler circulation test, and tells me I need surgery. I ask him when, thinking he means right now, and he says, "No rush but when you get home, they will recommend surgery." The doctor's measurements indicate my leg is bent inward 57° just above my ankle. My cost for all this is a little less than $40 US. I call a concerned Dr. Bever in Ft. Thomas saying the bad news is my leg is bent 57° but there is good news – I just won the Bastille Day Coconut Palm Climbing contest. The actual good news is they aren't going to send me home.

The next morning Sam is on deck and notices we are dragging anchor, have angled sideways, and are moving very slowly toward the beach. I wake John, Katie, Andy, and Ken. The six of us untie the shorelines, pull the anchor up, reanchor the boat with more scope and tie her stern to the trees again.

During the day, Ken Wandstrat leaves us to camp on Tahiti for a week and then to return home; we re-count our nails before we let Ken go. We also complete our paperwork with Customs and Immigration. John and Carol then move aboard and in the evening we are all invited to the home of Chantel and Lyses Terooatea for dinner.

Dinner is served on a covered terrace between their home and the swimming pool and includes every conceivable type of Polynesian food. Sam has his bathing suit and goes swimming with their son, Tani, two boys about the same age. We leave with breadfruit, bananas, and grapefruit from their yard and several leftover casseroles from their table.

We have promised the harbor officials we will depart early the next morning as the Bastille Day celebrations are beginning and the *pirogue* (outrigger) races will need our stretch of the beach that day. We motor, with very little wind, over to Baie Oponohu on Moorea where we meet *Cormorant* again. Ward and Judy, who also have had to move because of the *piroque* races, come aboard to celebrate the Fourth of July and finish all the leftover food we have from the Terooatea dinner.

The next morning I wake with a fever of 102.5°. Apparently I have Dengue Fever – probably picked up from one of numerous mosquito bites. Dengue fever had plagued early explorers to the area and had caused the death of many. I begin to take 750 milligrams of Ciprofloxacin twice a day plus more frequent blood sugar tests and insulin to control my blood sugar now high because of the infection. In 24 hours I am much better.

Uncle John and Aunt Carol help Sam prepare for an Arbor Day project that will be waiting for him at the beginning of the upcoming school year. They jointly develop a list of all the benefits to the Polynesians of the coconut palm. From this list it is easy to understand the reverence these people have for their tree *Tumu Haari*.

The complete tree:

Beauty, shade, to hang hammocks, and birds nest in dead trees.

The tree top:

Palm heart found at the tree top is quite delicious.

The trunk:

Wood for *fares*, furniture, boats, bridges, cooking fires, and logs make great outdoor seating.

The leaves:

Roofs, house siding, mats, hats, brooms, baskets, torches, fish and lobster traps, fences, and Palm Cabbage. Palm Cabbage the center of the leaf, is a food eaten like celery.

Leaves also are used for cooking, much as we use aluminum foil.

Husks of the Nut:

Brake fluid, rope fiber, dishes, bowls, cups, scoops, brassieres for dancers, masks, and souvenirs.

Milk:

Skin tonic, drinking, sauce for food, and an ingredient in fancy cocktails. Milk is the consistency of bread as the coconut takes root. In this form it was used as sacramental bread by Uncle John when he was a missionary.

At Man-O-War a drink called swigel is made with coconut milk, condensed milk, and water.

Meat:

Cooking, baking, manufactured as margarine, and as a condiment. Children eat old, dry meat as a candy. Coconut chips are thin cut meat deep fried.

Blossoms:

A sweet drink called *tuba* is made from the sap of the tree's blossoms.

Copra:

For many years copra, the dried kernel of the coconut from which coconut oil is expressed, was the main cash crop of most of the tropical world. It is used in the manufacturing of perfume, soap, suntan oil, and plasticizer for safety glass.

Copra Meal:

Livestock feed and fertilizer.

When we return to Papeete, the port authorities, in consideration of my leg, give us one of only four berths in the entire harbor on a finger pier. This makes going ashore much easier. As an added bonus, we are sharing the finger pier with *LaRoca*. Marie is now very near to having a baby and the port authorities feel they too should have this convenience. Several other boats near us are *Tenereze*, *Cormorant*, and *Quest* plus new friends on *Quest II*. Talking to fellow yachties, we notice American circumnavigators talk of where they are going and Australians talk more of what they will do when they get home.

One day a small sloop comes into the harbor with a mast broken about four feet from her deck. The skipper is Lowell North of sail-making fame. Every day North and I meet at the Post Office. He is calling California expediting his new mast and I am still calling for my roller furling.

The finger pier is especially helpful because our new roller furling finally arrives. Assembly and installation are much easier working from a level surface. In the process of this work, I run an ice pick through a finger and out the other side. Pat, Carol, Katie and Sam should not hear the remarks that follow, but I'm afraid they do.

We have several other memorable meals in Papeete. The first is at the home of Yolande and Erroll Bennett. This wonderful couple have two sons Naea and Rio and five daughters. The girls ranging in age from 18 to 3 are Noelani, Erroline, Gilles, Vaite, and Ester. Whether one starts with the youngest or oldest, these girls get more beautiful as he goes along. Son John in love with Sara at home plays it pretty cool, but Andy's eyes glaze over and he is in semi-shock the whole evening. After dinner, the women dance for us, starting with the youngsters. After the girls finish dancing, their mothers dance; and after their mothers, their grandmothers. Three-year-old Ester never stops.

After the dancing, the girls want to sing for us. Vaite goes to a group of shelves on the wall and opens a cabinet with a PC and a printer. After several commands, the printer produces song sheets – one for everybody. I hope our technology doesn't bring more change "for the sacred birds of the sea and land to mourn."

The Bennetts ask the Ellisons and Morgans to sing some American songs. We are all caught up in the moment and think we can. Our hosts politely relieve us and continue their singing.

One of the Bennetts' sons, Naea, is a noted soccer player. Erroll Bennett, is local celebrity being the unquestioned best soccer player in Tahiti and probably the best in the South Pacific. As a young man, Erroll was often unable to play because most games were on the Sabbath and Mormon teaching required him to reserve that day for spiritual matters. As a result, all sports schedules for Tahitian soccer were changed – including the Tahitian Cup and the Pacific Games. We leave this remarkable family late in the evening again with bunches of bananas, baskets of breadfruit, and platters of other wonderful foods. We don't know what they all are, just that they are delicious.

Another memorable meal is at the home of Celina Hurahutia. Our host and her sister, Rosalie, have for several days been cooking various foods wrapped in palm leaves. A specialty is *ioata* – raw fish, soaked in lemon juice and served with coconut milk. Celina and Rosalie, as young women had lived on Tabuai in the Tuamotus and had known Missionary John Morgan.

On a motor trip around the island, we stop to see Tuana Utahia who had been a young girl on Raroia, in the Tuamotus, where she also was a friend of Missionary Morgan. Utahia is overwhelmed by our visit and it is a warm, emotional time. She takes a particular and tearful liking to Sam, which embarrasses him to no end. Utahia gives us wonderful gifts including a homemade rug we treasure and homemade shell leis for everybody.

Strangely, we don't meet any males Uncle John had known.

It takes two days to do another major provisioning, obtain fuel, and clear out of Papeete. We sail overnight to breath-taking Bora Bora and are soon joined by *Tenereze*. Bora Bora was the inspiration for Bali Hai in James A. Mitchener's novel, *South Pacific* and later Rogers and Hammerstein's musical of the same name. For several days we swim, change oil and filters of the engine and generator, and adjust to shipboard life without Carol and John.

Today Pat, John, Katie, Andy, and Sam rent bikes and start on a counter clockwise (we are, after all, south of the equator and certainly on a high) all-day ride around the island. With my bent leg, this is not for me. After they leave, I get lonesome and rent a motor scooter to catch up. We have lunch at Bloody Mary's and later in the afternoon, meet Sally and the crew of *Tenereze*, who are biking clockwise. We rest and have a beer with them.

Another day John, Katie, Andy, and Sam join a snorkel group for a shark trip. The dive master ties a line in a large circle and has the participants hold on outside the circumference. He then throws "chum" to attract sharks to the inner circle. The sharks swim between the individuals to their great surprise. The dive master throws a piece of meat near Sam and a shark darts over too quickly, eats it, and elevates Sam's heart rate.

While buying beer for our passage to Samoa, I complain about the cost of about $4 per can. The shopkeeper tells me a big part of the reason for the cost is a $2.40 deposit. We properly disposed of about $300 since entering French Polynesia.

7

CHAPTER SEVEN

"...where it won't bother anybody."

July 23, 1992 – September 12, 1993

Bora Bora – Manly, Australia

We reluctantly depart French Polynesia for a pleasant seven-day sail to Pago Pago (pronounced Pango Pango), Samoa. It is great to have a full complement of sails again; however, *Lusty Wind II* is not performing so well as she had before losing the headstay five weeks ago. The new headstay we installed is two inches too long and can't be tightened for good sail shape. We start in light winds with the spinnaker pulling us. After dinner the halyard parts and the sail goes into the water. We motor for the night and put the genoa back up early the next morning.

We begin using canned food purchased in Tahiti and find our otherwise fine U.S. can opener will not open French cans. The lip design is just enough different. The lesson is – when a traveler buys canned goods in a foreign country he or she should buy a can opener as well.

Our original planned course from Bora Bora was to Tonga, Fiji, Vanuatu, New Guinea, Thursday Island,

Darwin, then to the Maldives to wait out the cyclone season before crossing the Arabian Sea. My need to fly home for leg surgery necessitates a break in the trip earlier than the Maldives and Australia is the best choice. Reports of unusually bad weather near Tonga extending towards Fiji suggest a better course to Fiji is through Samoa keeping north of the trouble. We also know provisioning is less expensive in Samoa.

We trawl for fish most of the time at sea. One rule – before dark we pull the line in and do not fish during the night. The reason is, which all crew members understand, if a fish would strike during the night, I have little doubt the lone watch keeper would leave the cockpit to start to bring it in. There is always the chance in his rush he will lose his footing and go overboard. If no one is with him, we would not know he is gone and could very well sail for the remainder of his watch before discovering his absence. If the next watch keeper doesn't wake up, we could go for another four hours. Also we usually have at least four crew members but only one fishing pole.

It is early morning, with someone else in the cockpit, and I, the watch keeper/Captain put the fishing line into the water, let it out until the lure is about at the end of the wake, then go back to my watch. At about three in the afternoon with Andy on watch, we have a big strike. I am below, asleep, but the noise of the strike and Andy's scramble for the rod wakes me. It takes a bit to wake up, dress, and get on deck with my crooked leg, and by the time I get there, Andy almost has the nearly five foot, 40 pound *Mahi Mahi* landed. It is a bittersweet catch. We have what we know will be several magnificent meals coming aboard, but his mate is thrashing nervously in the water knowing the fate of her fish. We put fillets for several meals into the freezer, have a wonderful dinner, and grilled dolphin sandwiches for lunch the next day.

Now for the big question – who caught the fish? I claim I put out the lure and thus I caught the fish. I have no issue with Andy getting credit for landing the fish; but as surely as if I had shot someone with a gun, I caught the fish with the rod, reel, line, and lure. If a gunshot victim dies while being transferred from the scene of the crime to the emergency room, the EMS hasn't done the killing. John, Katie, Andy, and Sam all feel Andy caught the fish since he has brought it aboard. Fortunately Admirals don't become involved in such issues and thus the Captain has the final word; this final authority, however, only lasts until we are back ashore.

I have a tendency to be a bit uptight on blue-water passages. These blue-water passages are, however, a great responsibility for the master of the ship; so a joyful facade is not always possible. Son John, one day, has his fill of my bull – and sits me down for a talk. The gist is if I don't lighten up he will fly home from Samoa. I understand and try to lighten up. One fortunate thing – neither John nor Andy (the two who received the brunt of my nervousness) ever find my gallon of frozen strawberries.

Before dawn, July 30th, we see the lights of Pago Pago. Our first impression is a magnificent old volcanic cone, now a beautiful harbor. Our second impression is the rusty tuna fishing fleet which was blown ashore by Hurricane Val in 1991. We anchor with other yachts in the harbor and begin to get settled before clearing Immigrations and Customs. While enjoying the scenery and the activities of the harbor during breakfast on deck, the wind shifts and we are suddenly downwind of a fish processing plant. For an hour or so before the wind shifts again it is enough to gag a maggot. We later learn this plant is managed by Pet Heinz, headquartered just four miles from our home in Kentucky.

* * *

At least 2,000 years ago the Polynesians populated the Samoan Islands and the first European discoverers were the Dutch in 1722. Imperial Germany claimed the islands in the late 1800's and the United States Navy built a coaling station at Pago Pago around the turn of the century. A treaty in 1899 divided the islands between the United States and Germany with the United States taking possession of the eastern islands including Pago Pago. The US Navy presence lasted until 1951. American Samoa is now left with our administration, welfare, and catfood factory. The residents of American Samoa are American citizens and can freely come and go to the United States. Many have including "The Throwing Samoan," Jack Thompson, a former quarterback for the Cincinnati Bengals. When natives we met found out we are from Greater Cincinnati, they wanted to talk about Jack Thompson, their personal friend.

* * *

The process of dealing with *pratique* in American Samoa is not technically difficult or restrictive, but there are three sets of officials to deal with. The first is Customs which handles this efficiently and politely on the fender of a Chevrolet at dockside. The second is Immigration which is in the port district, up several flights of stairs, in offices over a rusting warehouse. We are first directed to the wrong set of stairs climbing at least two-and-a-half stories to find out we have to climb back down and back up another comparable set. This may not sound like a big problem; but with crutches and a leg bent 57°, it is a major effort. No surprise – the Port Authority is back up the steps we first climbed in error.

The next morning at the dinghy dock, we meet a pretty, perky, tall "California girl" who takes an immediate interest in my leg – not the good one. She is a physical therapist from San Diego and is in Pago Pago to meet her boyfriend who is sailing around the world alone. Her interest in my leg is, unfortunately, professional and she came to the boat to prescribe for me a number of exercises to maintain the mobility of my ankle. Doctors at home assure me that if I had not followed her advice, I would not be walking nearly so well as I do now.

American Samoa, of course, does not have duty on American goods and the United States Government subsidizes the shipping of these goods; thus, the grocery stores are well stocked with familiar American products at prices comparable to those at home. It seems inappropriate to subsidize plentiful paradise with peanut butter and canned baked beans. We all work most of the day to restock the boat with enough to last until our arrival in Australia. It is great to find beautiful red apples from the State of Washington for 50 cents each. These are also available in Papeete but were about $3 each.

Pat and Katie are fascinated by the Samoan men who wear skirts. John, Andy, Sam, and I are unwilling to "go native" and adopt this style.

On Saturday evening after a pizza dinner ashore, we depart for a 13-hour overnight sail to Apia in Western Samoa. We anchor in the Apia Harbor about 9 a.m. Sunday, and find, by radio, that Customs and Immigration are closed. They ask us to stay aboard until Monday morning. We take the day to relax aboard *Lusty Wind II* and to do some cleaning.

* * *

During World War I, New Zealand troops captured Western Samoa from Germany and operated the islands as a territory under charter from the League of Nations. Western Samoa gained independence in 1962 and Malietoa Tanumafili II, a member of one of the Samoan Royal Families, now rules and is Head of State for life. Essentially, he is a constitutional monarch. In Samoa, however, he is carefully referred to as Prime Minister.

* * *

Monday morning many warm and happy people direct Sam and me to the government offices which are in an old Victorian house near the center of Apia. Everybody there is happy to see us and wants to be helpful but cannot understand where we want to go. We finally find a distinguished gentleman in a business suit who asks in perfect English what we are looking for. He introduces himself as the Secretary of State and the Western Samoan delegate to the United Nations. He takes us to his office where he tells us Immigration can be handled. His entire staff of two are elsewhere; so he agrees to clear us himself – a bit like meeting Henry Kissinger on Ellis Island. Our guide books indicate we need special permission to see two places. That is reason enough for us to want to visit. We ask the Secretary how we can get permission to visit the Scottish novelist Robert Louis Stevenson's old home and the Island of Savai'i where the government is attempting to keep foreign visitors to a minimum. He tells us we must petition the Prime Minister. I ask, "How," and he says, "Follow me."

Sam and I walk to the next office where the Secretary knocks on the door. When a grunt of approval comes, we enter and find the King sitting at his desk. After introductions and shaking hands, our request is explained. The King gestures his approval, we thank him; then we go back to the Secretary's office to receive proclamations attested to by the Secretary of State that we may visit these places.

Later in the day we take a taxi up to Robert Louis Stevenson's old home. Stevenson lived in Samoa from 1888 until 1894 and is buried up the hill from his home. Stevenson is highly regarded by Samoans and is called *Tusitala*, or teller of tales. We discover why it is necessary to receive special permission from the King to visit. The King lives in this home and we can see "Mrs. King" waving to us from inside the house.

Sam still is working on his Arbor Day project and is looking for information about more trees. Not to take anything away from the coconut palm, but our taxi driver's favorite is the Teak. There is a large Teak tree, at least three feet in diameter, knocked down by Hurricane Val and blocking the driveway into the Royal home. Our taxi stops before the tree and we follow a path around and walk the rest of the distance. I assume the King does the same as his limousine is under a carport and looks like it hasn't been moved in a long time. Our driver explains to Sam all the uses of the Teak tree which includes the special lumber which is long-lasting and nearly rot-free. He further explains two uses for the leaves. They can be used as a kind of sandpaper because of their rough surface; or they can be crushed and be made into a red dye.

Stevenson's wife's diary includes notes of a visit in 1896 from Joshua Slocum. Slocum anchored *Spray* very near where we are and received an invitation to dinner from Mrs. Stevenson. I'm sure this is a welcome respite for Slocum after his 72-day voyage eating salt cod and biscuits.

That night we make reservations for dinner at Aggie Grey's Hotel owned and operated until her death in 1991 by Aggie Grey and now by her two sons. Aggie was a young entrepreneur at the beginning of World War II. When our military began occupation of these islands, she was the supplier of anything needed. The G.I.'s wanted cheeseburgers; so she set up a shop and made cheeseburgers. They wanted beer – she had beer. Aggie is the character inspiration, not appearance inspiration, for James Michener's and Rogers and Hammerstein's character, Bloody Mary. One of my childhood favorites and part of my long inspiration for this trip is Bloody Mary singing:

"You got-ta have a dream,–
If you don't have a dream–
How you gon-na have a dream come true?"

Dinner is complete with a *fiafia* (fun) show including Samoans with spears and dancing girls with coconut husk bras. One of Aggie's sons notices my bent leg and instructs all drivers of their fleet of tour buses to look for me and offer a ride.

With the eleven hour time difference between Samoa and Kentucky, I have not been able to make a long overdue call to the office. I awake early (knowing the telephone office opens at eight) and take the dinghy to the dinghy dock. Then I hitch a tour bus ride to the Post Office and the only available telephone. After being given a turn number, I wait an hour for a chance to talk to my office answering machine.

About noon on August 5, we depart Apia and sail around the northwest corner of Upolu Island, through the Apolima Strait to an opening in the reef and small anchorage at Palauli Bay on the island of Savai'i. The silhouette of Savai'i is the same knobby gently sloping hill as Isla Santa Cruz in the Galápagos. The geological origin of these two islands must be similar.

The wind is building a bit and our anchorage in this lagoon surrounded by reef becomes worrisome to us. While we take a swim, the boat begins to drag anchor. We reanchor. While Pat and Katie are preparing dinner, we drag anchor a second time. The wind is building and the Captain decides to forgo our permission from the King and depart before dark for Fiji. Two reasons – the anchorage is obviously dangerous with bad weather building; and if bad weather comes and we cannot leave through the reef pass, we will be in danger of Pat, Katie, and Sam's missing their flight from Fiji back to Kentucky and Colorado to meet their school schedules. By 7:30 it is dusk. We clear the reef and are soon back at sea in building winds on our southwest passage to Fiji.

The winds, still building, are coming out of the Southeast and we are on an aggressive beam reach. In heavy seas this can be a dangerous point of sail because the combined action of the winds and waves can trip a boat and roll her. I have been previously warned that I should not be on a beam reach in seas exceeding 15 feet. The seas are getting near that height.

By the morning, it looks as if we are in for a gale. Jimmy Cornell in *World Cruising Routes* warns that on a westbound passage to Fiji during July and August when the trades are their strongest, one may encounter gales. He is correct. By midday, we are experiencing a full-blown gale with sustained winds of 40 knots gusting to 45, a bit of a lusty wind, to say the least. Seas are building to 30 feet. The crests are, however, mostly far apart and *Lusty Wind II* is handling the conditions very well. John, my conscience, is warning me we should change course and get off our beam reach. I change course about 15° which reduces the danger somewhat. We are under sail with the staysail partially furled and a matching amount of our loose-furled main and with the boom lashed in the gallows for safety. My principal concern is chaffing of the outhaul line for the main; however, it would have been too dangerous to leave the cockpit to freshen nip. I do not feel conditions warrant getting our storm sail out. As all sailors know, often by the time a decision is made to reduce sail, it is too late. During these weather conditions, John, Katie, Andy, and I handle watches. We are taking two hour watches fastened into the cockpit with a safety harness and tether.

I now realize that I should have gotten the sea anchor and its rode out of the lazarette. If conditions continue to deteriorate, the sea anchor we need will be beyond safely getting. Our sea anchor is a large parachute made of heavy canvas webbing and used to hold the bow of the vessel into the seas and wind. In this manner the vessel may ride out the storm with less possibility of pitch-polling. Pitch-polling is a vessel riding down the face of a wave and the bow driven into the water. The wave pushes the stern over the bow. That's right – the boat is upside-down. Cruising sailors normally have no practice with sea anchors. They don't work at all until winds reach 35 knots or so; and in those conditions, few of us are looking for additional learning experiences. By the time wind reaches 45 to 50 knots, it is too late to practice.

In a storm, sailing diabetics have an additional concern to keep a sharp weather-eye on. Good diabetic control requires taking insulin shots before eating. The insulin works as a catalyst on the food. As long as they eat, it will process their food and not reduce the sugar level of the diabetic's blood which in turn can cause a dangerous insulin reaction. An insulin reaction can lead to loss of consciousness. If a diabetic becomes sea-sick and unable to hold down food after he has taken the insulin, a reaction is a probability. Understanding the problems and an appropriate reduction of insulin reduces the risk. It is important to keep a handy supply of Glycagon (a glucose injection) on board plus crew members who know its location and how to use it.

During the night, Pat opens the companionway and puts her head up, which of course, immediately causes a wave to break over the boat. After drying off, and with the automatic bilge pump running, she asks if we know where we are – which we do – and if everything is all right – which it is. Pat says to Katie, "I'm 52 years old and supposed to be on a cruise ship worrying about what I'm going to wear to dinner."

People often ask me what it is like standing watch under these conditions. My response is, "Like having a seat on the outside of a barrel going over Niagara Falls for four hours."

In the morning, still in a gale, I attempt to call home through Zulu Lima Bravo in Wellington, New Zealand, and Victor India Sierra in Sydney, Australia. I can hear both stations but cannot elicit any response nor can I gain response from Kilo Uniform Quebec in Pago Pago, Terrathree Delta Papa in Suva, or November Romeo Victor in Guam. We can hear all the stations but none responds to our call. With our 25-watt VHF with a range of 30 miles not broadcasting, we are down to our five-watt hand-held VHF with a range of about five miles. We are probably alone within this range.

We are not in a desperate strait as we have two EPIRBs (Emergency Position Indication Beacon Radios) which will, I'm confident, solicit help if we need it. When activated, the EPIRB sends a message to satellites which can determine the vessel's position and relay the distress signal and position to a shore station. The radio also sends a coded signal that identifies the vessel in distress. The authorities may then call any of the three numbers the owner has filed to help ensure they are not answering a false alarm before launching a rescue effort.

After draining the batteries with our attempts to broadcast with the single sideband, we start the generator to recharge. The generator starts and runs fine but is soon overheating and shuts itself off. Conditions are not conducive to climb down into the bilge to find out what is wrong. We start the main engine to charge the batteries. This wakes and upsets Pat. She has thought the engine has been on all along and has not realized we are under sail. She has good reason to be concerned. The forestay, with its Norsemen fitting, has just been put together by me and is now being tested in severe conditions.

When my friend and then medical student, Dr. Jeff McMath, taught me to do sutures; he also told me all bleeding will eventually stop. The same can be said of severe weather – eventually it will get better. By midday we are beginning to see an improvement in conditions. We gleefully report to those below when sustained winds drop to 30 knots. We are ecstatic when they drop to 25 knots and we know all is well.

A serious storm like the one we have just experienced gives one a great deal of confidence in his boat. These conditions reaffirm my belief that the most important piece of safety equipment is the design and construction of the hull.

At home watching television, I often will be reminded of this gale. Television weathermen describing strong storms will say, "...then the storm will go out to sea where it won't bother anybody." I know someone is out there hanging on by his fingernails and plagued by *kaput* radios and generators.

August 8. Saturday. Wind is sustained at 15 knots gusting to 20 and seas seven to eight feet. By noon, everyone is starting to eat again. We come through Lakemba Passage into the Kero Sea. Katie makes salmon patties for our first dinner of the passage. By midnight, we cross 180° longitude, the wind is down to ten knots, and seas to four or five feet. We have crossed the Date Line just after leaving Saval'l; however, we are too busy with a building storm to notice. The Date Line is an agreed-to deviation from 180° longitude to keep Tonga and Chatham Island on the same day as New Zealand.

Master

Time/Date	From/To	DMG	Source	Log	DistEng	EngHour	GenHour	Crew	Notes
Mon Aug 3	APIA Lat 13:47.885 Lon 171:45.77w		GPS	23870	2396	2046	861	M Ellison P Ellison J Ellison A Ellison S Ellison	Reach consul for breakfast. Sam and Vice cleared pratique and met Prime Minister. Had dinner at Aggie Grey's Hotel. Katie tried to steal ashtray and got caught.
	APIA Lat 13:47.885 Lon 171:45.77w			23870	2046			0	
Tues Aug 4	APIA Lat 13:47.885 Lon 171:43.77w		GPS	23870	2348	2396	861	Same	John, Katie, Andy & Sam went on snake tour. We had tea with Aussie Grey's son. Had dinner again at hotel. Successfully stole ashtray.
	APIA Lat 13:47.885 Lon 171:45.77w			23870	2348	2396		0	
Wed Aug 5	APIA Lat 13:47.885 Lon 171:45.77w		GPS	2386	2361		861	Same	Up early to call office - got Alisuoraus machine. Departed Upasau for Savaii. Drop anchor at Vunon Savaii Yacht Lodge for safety & sea.
	Lat 14:09.815 Lon 172:53.6w			81	13	2348		0	
Thr Aug 6	Lat 14:09.815 Lon 172:53.6w		GPS	24109	2385		861	Same	By 2 PM wind was 27 and seas 10-12. So to rebuild. By 5 PM we were in gale. No dinner. Crossed International Date line but to busy to notice.
	Lat 15:38.085 Lon 175:08.26w			158	24	2361		0	
Fri Aug 7	Lat 15:38.085 Lon 175:08.26w		GPS	24354	2397	2385	861	Same	By 6 AM wind to 35 kts with gusts to 45. Seas 14'. All crew green. No dinner. By midnight wind down to 25 kts. and seas 8'.
	Lat 17:02.265 Lon 177:20.16w			45	12			0	
Sat Aug 8	Lat 17:02.265 Lon 177:20.16w		GPS	24447	2403	2397	861	Same	By 6 AM wind down to 18 kts and seas 8'. 1 to 8 feet. Moon came through. Lake cuba pass into Kebo Too. West before midnight. Crossed 180° long and skipped one day.
	Lat 18:06.905 Lon 179:57.38w			123	6			0	
Sun Aug 9	Lat ... Lon ...		Day	WOOT					
	Lat ... Lon ...			24515	1935	12234			

CROSSING 180° Longitude

LUSTY WIND II LOG From Aug 3 to Aug 9, 1992

Log Page

When Magellan's ship returned to Western Civilization after the first circumnavigation, the carefully kept log was found to be a day short. They thought it was Wednesday but it was Thursday. This was serious as they had thus been eating meat (when they had it) on Friday and had celebrated Easter on Monday. The bureaucrats of the day went over and over the log to determine what had gone wrong. The men who went the whole way were quizzed to see if the missing day could be found. Finally, after going to higher authorities, astronomers were summoned and determined one loses a day when circumnavigating westbound.

Westbound sailors gain an hour 24 times on their circumnavigation and then lose one day. Eastbound sailors lose an hour 24 times and gain one day. If one recalls, Phileas Fogg, the hero of *Around the World in Eighty Days*, thought he was a day late to win his wager. But he found, to his surprise, that he had returned to England in 81 days, 24 of which had 23 hours. Because his trip was east bound trip, he had gained a day and won.

Sunday, August 9, is noted in our log as, "Day lost due to crossing of 180° longitude." Saturday, August 8, is followed by Monday, August 10.

By Monday morning, wind and seas are down substantially and forward motion requires motor-sailing. We arrive in Suva Harbor on the island of Vita Levu about one in the afternoon. This harrowing passage has taken about 90 hours and covered 623 nautical miles, at an average of almost seven knots. The entrance through the reef to Suva Harbor is easy. There are buoys and lights but the best markings are island freighters wrecked on the reef at either side of the entrance. On instructions received on our portable VHF radio, we dock between two freighters at the commercial dock and John and I proceed on a three-hour process of *pratique* including carrying our guns three miles and up a steep hill to the police station for safe-keeping while we are in Fiji.

* * *

Fiji (properly pronounced Fidgee) is part of Melanesia, a name from Greek that means "black islands." Until recently, belief was that these islands were settled 3,600 years ago. But recent theories differ. Prior to the sea's rising over the last 20 thousand years because of the melting of the polar ice caps, a tremendous area around Fiji was once above the surface of the sea. Evidence of settlements as much as 20 thousand years ago are probably now obscured by the sea. On entering the Kero Sea, seamen can see evidence of this huge land area since the reef is many miles from shore. Cannibalism was a perfectly normal part of earlier Fijian life. Victors of war ate their enemy and in this way showed them the ultimate disgrace. The first European discovery, in 1643, was by Abel Tasman, the Dutch navigator sailing for the Dutch East Indian Company. Fiji became a colony of Britain in 1874 and Fijians fought bravely for the Commonwealth in both World War I and World War II. Fiji gained its independence in 1970.

* * *

After dealing with all necessary officials, we return to the boat and motor deeper into the bay to anchor off the Royal Suva Yacht Club where all courtesies are extended. We go ashore to gain a courtesy membership in the yacht club and to attempt to find a technician to repair our single sideband radio. We are exhausted; and after dinner at the club, we return to the boat to sleep.

The next morning, we explore Suva which has a few new buildings and many old. Suva gives the impression of an old colonial port and a modern commercial center. A number of street vendors push their wares. One enterprising vendor approaches Sam with a carved wood knife saying he would like to give it to him. He presses Sam for his name and before we know it "Sam" is carved on the handle of the knife. The vendor then demands payment. Sam must have a little Armenian blood, for he quickly sees through this scheme and refuses the vigorous pressing of the salesman. The vendor's line is, "What will I do with a knife with Sam carved on it?" We later see a US Marine on shore leave proudly carrying his new wooden knife with his name carved on a handle which is a somewhat smaller diameter.

The ancient ceremony of *kava* drinking, important in Fijian life, is not performed indiscriminately and to this day retains great significance. Social *kava* drinking goes on all the time. The social drinking is much like morning coffee with the "good old boys" of a small southern town except that it has mild narcotic properties. For over an hour I have been sitting in our rental car in front of a tire repair shop resting my leg. The shop has a large bowl of *kava* on a table and all the good old boys of the neighborhood are stopping by to take a cup full and talk. I really expect an invitation to a cup since Fijians are outgoing but I have a definite feeling this is a special thing and not for an outsider. The *kava* is made from the root of the pepper plant. In early days, virgins of a village prepared the *kava* by chewing the pieces of root into a pulpy mass before adding water. Today it is pounded into a powder and water added. *Kava* is not very appetizing for us Westerners as it is the color of antifreeze. The cups are half a coconut husk.

The next morning at the Royal Suva Yacht Club, I meet the radio technician and his apprentice from the Suva Furuno dealer and transport them in our dinghy to the boat. This technician speaks perfect English in a voice like the actor James Earl Jones and has a huge

Melanesian head of curly black hair. His appearance personifies "Cannibal Islands," the name given by early European explorers of these islands. Only a bone in his nose would complete the picture.

When we board *Lusty Wind II*, I explain to this man what I think is wrong with the radio. I am sure it has a bad circuit in the transmitter. He tells me and instructs his apprentice that we will start with the antenna and work toward the transmitter. He first inspects the wire connected to the insulated backstay which acts as one of our antennas. He approves this connection by taking it apart, cleaning, and rebuilding it and says that it certainly is not the problem.

He then instructs the apprentice to climb into the lazarette to inspect the connections there. The apprentice in a few minutes climbs out with a Radio Shack relay that selects, by a switch at the Navigation desk, which of the two antennas will be operative. Somewhere before the gale, the RF power of my 300-watt transmitter overwhelmed this relay and melted it down. We are, therefore, not connected to an antenna. The technician says I need a much heavier relay but none is available in Fiji. He said he will connect the antenna directly eliminating the need for the relay. With an RF indicator which indicates the transmission power of the radio, he tests a wide range of frequencies with each antenna. It is apparent at high frequencies, used for long range, that the whip antenna is better. The backstay is better at low frequencies used for short range communication. I ask them to connect the whip antenna since our main communication will be through Sydney, Australia, or San Francisco to call home. The technician says no. San Francisco or Sydney will not come to our aid in an emergency and I will need to talk with someone close. Therefore, he will only connect the backstay. This man,

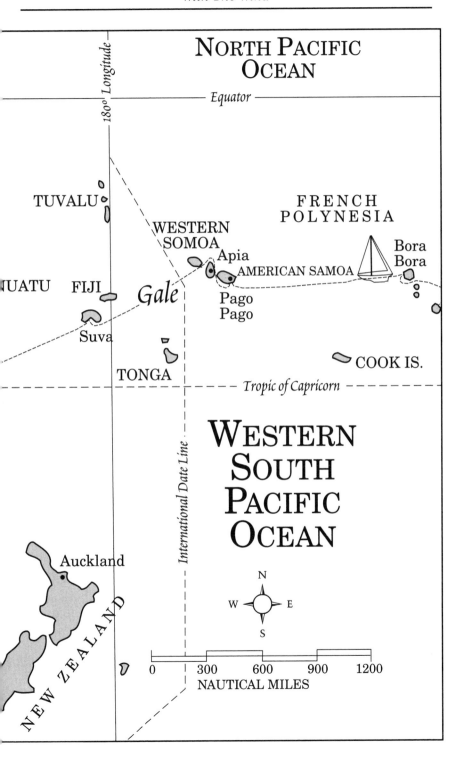

whose ability I now highly respect, is absolutely correct. Radiotelephone operators are trained to relay a distress message but it is better to talk to a ship just over the horizon. The single sideband ends up working perfectly for the remainder of the trip.

The Furuno technician recommends a diesel mechanic to help me with the overheating problem of the generator engine. This mechanic and his apprentice quickly find the problem – seaweed in an elbow immediately before the strainer for the generator's sea water cooling system. He points out that this is not a good design. The strainer needs to be directly attached, without elbows, to the seacock. He points out that the design of the US-made strainer requires a remote location or an elbow when used with a seacock that is below the curve of the hull. This mechanic finds a ground wire on the generator that has burnt insulation indicating an overload. He removes the old wire and replaces it with a heavier one. Katie says the old wire looks like Eeyore's tail.

We later find a Profurl dealer who sends a very qualified English rigger who with me as a helper is able to shorten our forestay and double check my installation of the forestay and Profurl furling system.

Sadly the day has come for Pat, Katie, and Sam to fly home. Their departure is 2 p.m. from the Nadi Airport on the opposite side of Viti Levu. There is only one main road on Viti Levu and it goes in a circle. The only mistake one can make is to go counterclockwise instead of clockwise, and the time difference between the two directions is negligible. The road has no markings or directions on it; so Pat is absolutely convinced I am lost and they will miss their flight. She has not forgotten the gale of the week before and does not want to chance having to sail on to Australia. Pat keeps insisting that I ask for directions; but between the language barrier and the fact there is only one road, I won't do it. I make a side remark to Andy, "This shortcut doesn't look like it's working out," which nearly ruins the whole day. It is a quiet ride back for the three of us after watching their departure for home.

On arrival back at the Royal Suva Yacht Club, we dinghy to the boat to find Dick Pearson, my friend from Madison, Wisconsin, aboard and waiting for us. He flew in to Nandi this morning, missed us at the airport, took the bus to the Suva and was transported by the yacht club launch to *Lusty Wind II*. As our communications with the outside world have been less than perfect, I am a bit apprehensive about Dick's time of arrival. Dick adds much experience to a sailboat crew. He has sailed with me before, is a mechanical engineer, and understands more than we will ever need to know about diesel engines and electricity. Dick was Chief Engineer aboard *USS Holmes County*, an LST. He now designs heating and air-conditioning systems for cruise ships. Dick's cruising skills stop there – he is trading a watch with John and Andy for a cooking turn since his skills do not include cooking.

Wednesday, August 19. We motor to the commercial wharf to clear Immigrations, Customs, Harbor Patrol, and to recover our guns from the police. After clearing the harbor and setting sail, John fortunately spots a reef and corrects my course – it is afternoon and the sun is again in my eyes.

We sail on the broad reach almost all the way to New Caledonia. With the forestay now the correct length, sail shape is easy to control.

Approaching New Caledonia, I realize we will come to the pass through the reef before dawn. I debate slowing the boat down to time our arrival to be about 9 a.m. when the sun will be over our port shoulder and the reef easy to see. But I decide to keep going because all is going well and to reduce sail would require waking someone up. We can always lay ahull when we arrive.

By 5:15 a.m. I can pick up the range lights provided by the French authorities and one is directly over the other indicating we have a perfect approach after 800 miles. Our true heading is 247° which when checked against the chart is a further indication we are exactly on the recommended course.

By 5:30, I see the flashing navigation lights off Cap des Cannibales marking the two sides of the channel. As indicated on our chart, a merchant ship that sits wrecked on the Komekame Reef further marks our course. Thus with a little trepidation, we enter Canal de La Havannah on the east-end of New Caledonia just at sunrise. We turn to sail downwind into the Canal Woodin past the beautiful Baie du Prony into a large reef strewn lagoon and towards the harbor of Nouméa.

We quickly find the new floating marina built by the French government and are waved into a convenient slip. We complete *pratique* in 15 to 20 minutes and are quickly off to Nouméa to look around, to buy a few supplies, and to rent a car.

* * *

New Caledonia, just as Fiji, with its wide lagoon could have been first settled as many as 20,000 years ago. Evidence has been found of cultures as much as 4,000 years old. European discovery was in the late 16th Century by Spanish expeditions looking for Terra Australis, land to the South. Captain Cook spotted New Caledonia in 1774 on his second scientific expedition and named it, because of its resemblance to the Highlands of Scotland. Caledonia is the name given Scotland by the Romans. In 1791, the French took over, uncharacteristically accepted the name, and have been there since.

New Caledonia is a very wealthy community because of the high pay of the workers in the bauxite mines and subsidies for the infrastructure from France and the mining company.

During World War II, the French people in New Caledonia and the local population overwhelmingly supported the free French forces as opposed to the Vichy regime. The colony took it upon itself to give the United States and her allies permission to set up military bases and nearly 400,000 American and New Zealand personnel arrived. From there, the allies launched attacks against the Japanese in the battle of the Coral Sea and the invasion of the Solomon Islands and the Philippines.

*   *   *

The highlights of our stay are a drive to Yaté on the east end of the island, wonderful French cuisine, and stores that would rival many of Paris.

On Thursday, August 27, I send John and Andy to clear with Customs, Immigration, and the Harbor master. After they return, we depart. We need to sail around several reefs in the lagoon to Passe de Dumbéa on our course for Australia. On the chart this looks clear-cut and I am not being particularly careful. We learn quickly that all the exposed reefs look alike and I am disoriented. We are now 9,700 nautical miles into our trip and for the first time, I am not at all sure of our position although we can still see Nouméa. On the assumption that the best thing to do before a reef encounter is to stop, the crew holds the boat as close as they can to still and I go below with the

GPS, the radar, and the chart to determine our exact location. I do so and we are quickly on our way.

Our original course was to have been across the Coral Sea to Thursday Island and we have aboard excellent charts of that area. Our course now is south of the territory of cyclones in Australia, which is generally considered to be Brisbane, or south. Discussions with various Australians we'd met indicated the most pleasant place to moor a yacht and to stay is Mooloolaba 50 miles north of Brisbane. But Mooloolaba is not a point of entry. We need to enter either at Bundaberg or Brisbane. We cannot find Australian charts in French Polynesia and Samoa. We find charts of Brisbane in Fiji but no charts of Bundaberg. Our course is thus determined – Brisbane to clear Customs.

Unfortunately there is a large low pressure centered over New Zealand; and since we are in the southern hemisphere, the low is generating a fairly strong clockwise system. It seems all the winds and the seas are coming right out of Brisbane. We make just shy of five knots and at that speed we are using two and a half gallons an hour indicating a range of about 700 miles with a distance to cover of just over a 1,000. We alter our course 35° north and find ourselves beating directly for shoals and reefs in the middle of the southern part of the Coral Sea. Also we are heading straight for Townsville, Australia – well into hurricane territory.

The tropical storm season will not start for nearly four months but we need a place to leave the boat for a period beyond that. Before reaching the area of shoals and reefs, we turn our course again toward Brisbane and motor using our now limited supply of fuel. For two days we motor sloppily into the wind and seas before the low pressure moves, the winds become favorable, and we are finally under sail.

It is 8 a.m. – the beginning of my watch. The sea and

wind are perfect. Dick breaks the spell by waking and quickly stopping up the head. Dick, John, and Andy remove the hose between the head and the seacock. Dick's story is that it is clogged with a long term build up of "stuff." We know better. Repair jobs don't go fast at sea and at the end of my watch, extended to eight hours, the three finish their job. For obvious reasons, I volunteer to prepare dinner.

Our first exposure to Australia is in the Coral Sea where we hear on our VHF radio a ship of the Australian Navy asking questions of the sail boat at our location. We cannot see them but they apparently see us. They ask the name of the vessel, our port of departure, and our intended port of entry – all very officially. They then ask our nationality and port of registry. We answer on our portable VHF United States and Ft. Thomas, Kentucky. There is a pause followed by an enthusiastic Australian seaman saying, "Well, g'day mate." From that point our relations with Australians are full of nothing but good will and fellowship.

As wonderful as the Australians are, they have brought bureaucracy to a science that puts the rest of the world to shame. After calling on the radio and getting directions to the Customs dock, we arrive, call on the designated phone, and very quickly two staff cars arrive with eight uniformed inspectors. Each one has two or three long forms to complete, each form with its own crew list. The boat is thoroughly inspected and any meat, fish, fruit or vegetables are confiscated. We knew ahead of time this would happen and have secretly stowed an entire case of canned Dixie Chili which includes meat. We depend on it. After stooping to this deceit, we find only canned food from French speaking areas is confiscated; canned goods containing meat from the United States are allowed. The inspector explains, "We can't have any of that 'frog' meat in this country. You know, mate?"

We are given some papers and told to report the next day to the Immigrations and Customs office in Brisbane for our final clearance. We ask where we might anchor for the night and are directed Doboy Creek – almost directly across the Brisbane River. We motor up this creek and find the method of mooring to be a row of pilings along each side of the creek, 50 feet apart with boats tied fore and aft. We find a vacant space between two. We are the largest boat in the creek and tie our bow to one piling and our stern quarter to another. Since we exceed 50 feet in length we are at an odd angle, looking a little like that bird pointing the wrong direction on a *New Yorker* cover.

Pearson's wife, Noel (you can guess her birthday), is to meet us at a hotel in Brisbane and we are a little overdue. We call a cab, wait, and eventually have a reunion with Noel, who, instead of worrying about us, has been busy sightseeing, petting wallabies, and making plans for excursions with Dick.

We arrive at the Customs office in downtown Brisbane. In time we are greeted by Roy Pugh, director of the office and the whole bureaucratic plot begins to unfold.

We tell Mr. Pugh we intend to sail from Brisbane to Mooloolaba and to leave the boat until my return in five and a half months. He explains that we cannot leave Brisbane Harbor without filing a sailing plan to continue. To stop outside Brisbane for more than a fortnight is not permitted. Mr. Pugh tells us they have tried repeatedly to get Mooloolaba to become part of the official Brisbane port which would then permit us to stay but to no avail. I then explain that I want to leave John and Andy on the boat for several months to redo all the brightwork (varnish) and to see some of Australia.

Live-aboards are not permitted in the port of Brisbane. This probably explains why Mooloolaba has opted to remain part of the Port of Bundaberg which does permit live-aboards. We learn later that if we had entered at Bundaberg, we could have then gone to Mooloolaba and stayed as long as our visas are valid.

John, Andy, and I take a 20-minute cab ride to Manly and the Royal Brisbane Yacht Club. The gatekeeper is a distinguished looking gentleman in pressed khaki Bermuda shorts, white shirt, and a monocle. He directs us to the dockmaster who is very pleasant and wants to be helpful. The dockmaster asks us if we are members of a yacht club. As we aren't, he is very sorry and but he cannot accommodate us. He directs us to the nearby East Coast Marina. We like the informal look of the East Coast Marina and go to the office to inquire about space. The receptionist explains, we cannot have live-aboards; so if we keep the boat at the East Coast Marina, the boys will have to get lodging ashore. We are soon introduced to Peter Hanson, the extremely accommodating manager of this marina. He offers us a ride to Doboy Creek and tells us by the time we reach the marina the offices will be closed. But he shows us our space and tells us to make ourselves at home for the night.

6 p.m. We are getting cleaned up and organized but happily we are interrupted over and over by yachties in the marina who come by to meet us and offer any help we may need. We talk to one gentleman about finding accommodations ashore. He says, "You can bloody well stay on the boat – the office has to say you can't. Only the port inspector would care; and if that bloody bastard comes around, the boys might have to move ashore."

One man returns after a half hour and says he has been home and his wife has asked him to bring us to their home for dinner. Gary and Elizabeth Gray become our good friends and it is comforting to know that someone is nearby if the boys have any emergencies or have to move ashore. After my departure, Gary and Elizabeth loan the boys a television, have them over for meals, and take them on tours of the countryside. Norm Uhr aboard *Shoestring*, the sailboat to our starboard, volunteers to watch *Lusty Wind II* and run the engine and generator weekly after John and Andy fly home.

After I leave, John and Andy will stay on to varnish the brightwork and some touring of Australia. They plan to visit second cousins in Sydney. I am flying home for scheduled leg surgery.

8

CHAPTER EIGHT

"We Don't Get Many Boats From Kentucky Here"

February 15, 1993 – April 16, 1993

Manly – Darwin, Australia

While the boat is in Manly, Brisbane's suburb John and Andy stay two months to redo all the exterior brightwork (varnished Teak), supervise the servicing of the engine and generator, and have all sails taken to a sail shop to be laid out, inspected, cleaned, and repaired.

I return to Brisbane after four flights from Cincinnati. Jobs are to install another new VHF microphone, have the boat hauled and the bottom painted, install new Australian-made strainers (not requiring an elbow), have all electronics serviced, and replace the return fuel yoke of the engine.

After a couple days in Manly, I come down with the worst case of flu I've ever had. I am surprised since at home I had taken my flu shots but I suspect this is a strain that shot did not protect me against. The massive infection brings high fever and affects my diabetic control. Infection reduces the effectiveness of insulin and high blood sugar reduces the body's natural process of fighting infections, altogether a dangerous situation. I am taking blood sugar tests and insulin shots every two hours, day and night, plus 750 mg. of Ciprofloxin twice a day. For about a week, very few of my chores are accomplished.

Sailing plans from Brisbane include being in Darwin for a planned April 5-9 visit from Pat and Sam plus Dr. John Bever, his wife Sue and son David. I also have to meet son Andy's expected May 17 arrival in the Seychelles on the other side of the Indian Ocean. Andy's arrival, we trust, will allow us to be in Turkey and Greece to meet Pat, Katie, and Sam. Unfortunately, this schedule requires starting north before the end of hurricane season which is the end of March. The quick way to travel the roughly 1,000 nautical miles to the Torres Strait is through the Coral Sea outside and east of The Great Barrier Reef, a voyage of about seven days. This isn't an acceptable route to me as if a cyclone occurs all the passes through the reef to sheltered water and shore become difficult. The best alternate route seems to be up the Great Barrier Reef passage with plenty of places to hide in the event of trouble. The best hiding place is tied into a mangrove. "Have plenty of bug spray, mate." The downside to this decision is that our schedule will require nighttime sailing; and through these sometimes narrow reef passages, this is not to be taken lightly.

Certainly any reef passage ranks high as a navigational challenge. The 30 minutes it takes to negotiate the North Man-O-War Pass in the Bahamas or Passé D'Avatoru at Rangiroa in the Tuamotus are as intense as any 30 minute stretch along the Great Barrier Reef. But the Great Barrier Reef seems to go on forever. Of its 1,000 nautical miles of reef piloting, most is the equivalent of sailing Hawks' Passage of the Florida Keys – if it went from Key West to New York City. The Great Barrier Reef passage increases in difficulty as a vessel proceeds north. For daytime sailing and cruising, these 1,000 nautical miles are one of the great delights of the yachting world. Sailing at night, delight is not exactly the operative word.

My crew consists only of Ted Blackwood, I am short-handed and desperately need some local knowledge. The Grays ask me to consider their son, Murray, who is available but has no local knowledge of the Great Barrier Reef passage. However, Murray would be good crew.

Peter Hanson, the manager of the marina, suggests I speak with his father Ron who has reef experience. I meet with Ron and immediately form a friendship. Ron is full of questions about the details of this venture. I tell him I will buy him a ticket back home and his question is, "What about the *tucker?*" I think he has a dog he wants to bring along and am not too excited about that but I'm inclined to agree to anything. After a few minutes of confusion, I find out tucker is one of those words that makes Australian a language foreign to us; it means food. Ron also wants to know if beer is allowed and adds, "In moderation of course." That concerns me because the most serious grammatical rule in Australian is that the words drinking and moderation may not be used in the same sentence. After signing on, Ron is at the boat early every morning and it is a delight to see the big smile and positive gait of this gentleman coming down the dock.

One morning I see Ron coming and from 300 feet I can tell something is wrong. The tall, cocky gait is slumped and slow. Close up Ron's grief is obvious. I help him aboard and it is a while sitting with my friend that I learn that the night before, his young son and Peter's brother, Philip, had died suddenly. Ron's grief seems compounded by the idea that he is letting me and the ship down by not being able to go. I'm not sure we ever convinced him to the contrary. Everyone in Manly and surrounding towns attend the services for this member of an obviously highly regarded family. Ron is around the marina the next day telling everyone, "Would you believe it – even that Yank was there."

Peter Hanson suggests I drive to Mooloolaba and helps me make appointments at the Mooloolaba Yacht Club to talk to several prospective crew members. The marina manager in Mooloolaba recommends Eric Ramon, a yachtsman turned rigger, living with his girlfriend Brenda, aboard *Orion*, in Mooloolaba. I meet with Eric and quickly recognize he is the man for the job. My assessment is an understatement.

Walking around the Mooloolaba Yacht Club, I find *Cormorant* but Ward and Judy LeHardy are on an automobile tour of Australia waiting out the same hurricane season we are preparing to sail into. After separating from us, Ward and Judy, had sailed to the Solomon Islands to commemorate the 50th anniversary of the death of Ward's father there during World War II. In sailing from the Solomon's to Bundaberg and then Mooloolaba, they sailed into a gale and lost their forestay. In bad weather and without the ability to sail, they were running out of fuel, *Comorant* was aided by another yacht with radio arrangements to transfer fuel from one boat to the other. Judy and the first mate of the other yacht did a reported marvelous job of maintaining course and speed while Ward and the other yachtsman transferred fuel. They came from the North; thus their natural port of entry was Bundaberg and their live-aboard stay in Mooloolaba is perfectly all right. While there Erik Ramon rebuilt their forestay.

Brisbane is an ideal place to provision for a long voyage. "Woollies" (Woolworths) is a high quality grocery store with many familiar US-made goods. Elizabeth Gray also takes me to "Cash and Carry" every bit as well supplied and economical as a Sam's Wholesale Club. Out in front of "Woollies" at the mall is Leonard's, a franchised chicken specialty shop that sells boneless, skinless chicken breasts, chicken salad, chicken stir-fry, etc. all of a higher quality than we are used to finding at home. I leave instructions and Leonard's pre-freezes everything to order. We will still be eating this frozen chicken when we arrive in Cyprus in July. A butcher shop close by in the mall provides steaks, beef stir-fry, and lamb stir-fry – again all packaged and frozen to order.

One trip to downtown Brisbane is to get our cruising permit and file our sailing plan. We ask for Roy Pugh and he tells us he will soon have a new job in charge of uniforms for Queensland – "I'll be in charge of socks and jocks." When we complete all *pratique*, the affable bureaucrat grins and remarks, "You know, we don't get many boats from Kentucky here."

Our departure from East Coast Marina and our friends there is delayed a few days by Cyclone Polly which is about 150 miles north of Brisbane and 100 miles north of Mooloolaba. Polly has gone out to sea "where she didn't bother anybody" and we sadly depart Manly and the East Coast Marina with Ted, Gary Gray, Murray Gray, and Helene Dyer (Pat, Helene is Murray's girlfriend). It takes us six hours to get to Mooloolaba where Eric has arranged a slip at the yacht club. Elizabeth is waiting for us with a picnic basket and takes Gary and Helene back to Brisbane. After a few days in Mooloolaba, we are off to the Tropic of Capricorn and the southern end of the Great Barrier Reef.

The counterclockwise rotation of the South Pacific system would indicate that the predominate current and wind would be out of the Northeast. Because of typical local high pressures in southeast Australia, the wind up along the Great Barrier Reef the greatest percent of the time is from the southeast caused by the counterclockwise rotation around these highs. This local weather pushes the system further east. The currents, however, outside the reef are typically southward against the wind causing choppy conditions and hard going.

After considering all, I decide to sail to the Torres Strait inside the reef. My self-imposed schedule forces us to run at night. This is regrettable because one cruising delight of the Great Barrier Reef is thousands of wonderful anchorages. The Great Barrier Reef, which we will transit in two and a half weeks, can provide a lifetime of cruising. Cook spent three and a half months doing this passage and was afraid during several incidents that it would be a lifetime. We must remember Cook had no charts, local knowledge, navigation aids, GPS, radar, guidebooks, or diesel engine. Eric would have been worth a king's ransom.

*   *   *

Cook's *Endeavor* drew 14 feet and *Lusty Wind II* six feet five inches. This is not much of an advantage to us because reefs grow up like a wall as the land sinks or the water rises; and in reef areas, a boat is either in deep water or deep trouble. Unknowingly, Cook was entering this huge lagoon which is certainly one of the world's most treacherous waterways. Noticing the narrowing width of navigable water and the ever constant wind from the southeast, Cook feared becoming embayed. Embayed is to a sailor a bit like a person painting himself into a corner except the corner is unnavigatable water and the paint is constant winds blowing him toward that shallow water. Just north of Cape Tribulation Cook was cautiously sailing *Endeavor* in the moonlight but still struck the coral of a reef he named Endeavor Reef. After 12 hours of throwing cannons over-board and pumping the bilge, the current of the receding tides canted *Endeavor* and she floated free. Cook, always the able seaman, had buoyed the cannons for later recovery. The ship was leaking badly; so Cook rushed toward a small river, now named Endeavor River, beached her, and began repairs on her bottom. Aborigines living in this area, now called Cooktown, attempted to rid themselves of these ghostly looking invaders by building upwind grass fires which kept Cook's crew busy protecting their camp and ship. But the crew finally completed the repairs and they were able at last to leave.

Shortly after leaving the Endeavor River, Cook came to Lizard Island rising above the coral, climbed to the top of the hill, and saw the surf hitting the reef exposing a gap now called Cook's Passage out into the Coral Sea. Cook quickly took this opportunity and was a day later in a calm in the Coral Sea with a strong tidal current pushing him back towards the reef and certain destruction. Just before being dashed against the coral the crew saw a second narrow channel that they named Providential Channel and were pushed by the current back into the lagoon which then widens toward the Torres Strait. Cook could be thankful that less salty tidal current prohibits reef growth.

* * *

Cook's passage was a frightening combination of seamanship and luck. I silently pray for both as we enter the waters of the reef.

To begin with, there is the problem of staying off the reef itself. Despite what its name implies, the Great

Barrier Reef is not one continuous reef, but thousands of smaller ones. They are all charted but most are unmarked. It is one thing to work past a reef in the daylight when the tell-tale water colors assure that all concerned are where they ought to be. It is quite another to negotiate the same passage in the dark when the only warning may be the sound of crunching fiberglass.

A four-knot current generated by tides of up to 18 feet can be intimidating enough in the daylight when visual references help determine the effect of current as it fans out from bays and rivers running with, against, or across a sailor's intended course. But at night, it is quite another story. Traveling north with good timing, tidal currents can be an aid, slack as one passes the bay, and with one again as the vessel proceeds north. With bad timing, the current can be against the sailor as he approaches the bay, set him out into the coral as he passes, and against him again as he continues north. Tide tables are thus vital for planning.

Under such conditions, it is easy for us to imagine some of the less savory creatures waiting to greet us should we happen to lose our boat on the coral and wind up in the water – man-eating sharks, salt water crocodiles so huge they should have running lights, and – the most feared of all by the locals – the box jelly fish whose sting is often fatal. Lucky for us, sharks, crocodiles, and box jelly fish remain products of our imagination. The real problem – the new problem created by running at night – is the fishing trawlers. Many commercial vessels including container ships, bulk carriers, and tankers travel the channel inside the reef. We watch out for them because their size and relative lack of maneuverability make them a hazard in such a narrow channel. Without exception, they are courteous and announce themselves on the VHF radio well ahead of blind turns and restrictive channels. However, the trawlers are a different story.

During the day, we see hundreds of trawlers anchored in the bays and inlets or out around the reefs as if they are nocturnal predators holed up in their lairs until after dark. At night, they come out in droves and travel in groups often in the narrow channels where good fishing helps them overcome any qualms they may have about the fact that trawling in channels is illegal. Their massive working lights obscure their running lights complicating our ability to deal with them. We first encountered this problem in the Bahamas. With the running lights obscured, we can only guess as to their direction of travel. They refuse to acknowledge our calls on the VHF. Some yachtsmen, I've been told, turn all their lights off so the trawlers get a radar image but can't see anything. This gets them on the VHF with satisfying speed.

Despite these problems, we have some things going for us. They include excellent Australian charts and navigation aids, the navigation gear aboard *Lusty Wind II*, and the local knowledge of Eric Ramon.

Especially useful among the navigational aids are RACON beacons to which the Great Barrier Reef piloting is my introduction. A RACON equipped navigation light sends to the vessel's radar a signal of a particular characteristic that flashes on the screen as a bar broken into segments representing a Morse code letter marked on the chart. For example, the chart may say RACON G and will flash on the radar screen as follows:

■ Morse G Identification
■ (flashes like the light - two long and a short)
▬

● Radar reflector (always on).

Additionally, if the light flashes once every ten seconds, so does the Morse symbol on the screen. The system allows a pilot to identify positively a mark at important points where visual characteristics may not be clear, all quite reassuring. I wonder what Cook would have thought of all of this.

A pilot must remember that along the reef he is navigating parallel to the coast and not returning from or going to sea. Lateral buoyage rules apply. As Australia is in Buoyage Region A, if a vessel is circling the main body of land clockwise, the red markers should be on the left and green on the right. We are traveling counter clockwise so we should keep red on the starboard hand.

Of the electronic gear I have aboard, it will come as no surprise to experienced reef pilots, that my depth sounder, so valuable in other piloting exercises, is of little use. Its limitation is that when piloting among coral, it cannot give advanced warning of the difference in depth because of the shear walls of the coral. The electronic gear that proved most useful were the GPS, radar, and autopilot. The combination of these three plus Eric makes a possible what, for me, would have otherwise been a fool-hearty passage.

It may seem like an over kill, but I feel the margin of error is so small (almost non-existent) that I take the additional step of comparing my positions with visual and radar plots made by Eric, who always seems to have the tide book in his hand. Eric has never navigated with GPS and is at first suspicious. After a few days, however, and comparing its accuracy with the accuracy of his bearing plots, he gives it his favorable approving pronouncement: "no drama."

Eric and I realize that our greatest risk for error is incorrectly plotting waypoints, incorrectly entering them into the GPS, or using a position when the GPS signal is weak and indicated position inaccurate. To guard against error, we mark each waypoint on the chart and then hand plot magnetic course and measured distance. We then enter waypoint into the GPS and compare the course and distance it computes with what we plotted first on the chart. On several occasions, this reveals our errors in plotting or entering waypoints. Several times the GPS signal is less than acceptable. We continue to plot the position but increase our emphasis on radar plots at night or visual and radar plots during the day.

Our GPS interfaces with the autopilot and can steer to the next waypoint compensating for drift caused by the tidal currents. We use this feature but continue to plot our GPS position often, in some places as often as every 15 minutes, and take visual or radar bearings. Not having to steer allows time for all this. The GPS and autopilot can determine the correct course to steer, and then steer it. In order to compensate for the set of strong currents, often the heading compensation, or crabbing, is 25° to 30°. Meanwhile Eric is making his visual or radar bearings and comparing them to the GPS positions. We, of course, have to remember not to filter out targets on the radar and to take bearings over our "bum" to be sure the electronics of the GPS and autopilot have tidal sets figured correctly. We also must remember that submerged reefs do not appear on radar.

At the Mooloolaba Yacht Club bar, we meet several Aussie sailors on a stop while delivering a racing sailboat from Sydney to Cairns. They are leaving several hours ahead of us in the morning. A day later, off Lady Elliot Island, we are motor-sailing in light air and passing our friends. They call and tell us we can't use our engine in a race. We tell them we're just running our generator. "Sure, mate, and we're pulling a bloody drogue!"

We enter the lagoon of the Great Barrier Reef and pass Ellison Reef. Our first stop is Hamilton Island in the Whitsundays. The Whitsundays are named by Cook to honor the day of his discovery. These islands are beautiful and outstanding cruising grounds. I wish we could spend several months here.

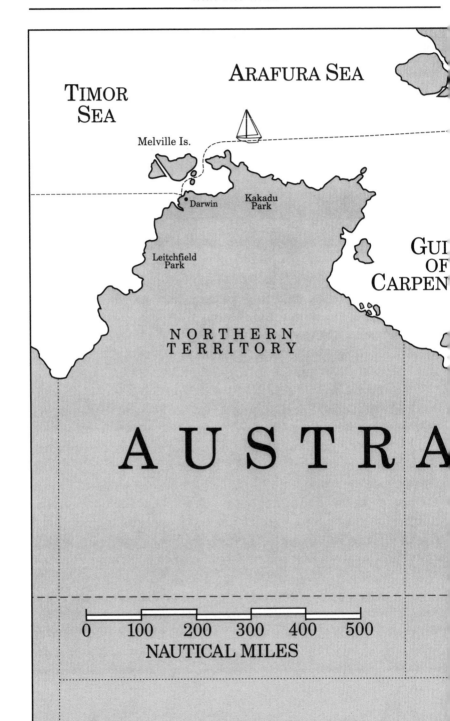

SIA

PAPUA NEW GUINEA

Great Barrier Reef

CORAL SEA

PROVIDENTIAL CHANNEL
Bligh Boat Entrance

Cape Melville
Cape Bedford
Cooktown •
Cape Tribulation

Cook Passage
Lizard Is.

Ellison Reef

Whitsunday Islands

IA

ENSLAND

N
W ✦ E
S

Tropic of Capricorn

Bundaburg •

Mooloolaba •

Brisbane •
Manly •

We stop for a couple days of rest and to wait out Cyclone Roger, which we know from radio and weatherfax reports is coming generally our way. We tie up at the Hamilton Island Marina, rigging a spider's web of bow lines, stern lines, breast lines, and spring lines to the floating docks. Nervously we watch Cyclone Roger creep within 80 miles of us. Even at that distance, the winds reach 40 knots and the storm surge puts the floating docks within a few feet of the tops of the pilings (we later hear the pilings had been designed and built higher but for "esthetics," the resort developer had the top six feet lopped off).

While at Hamilton Island, Eric is perpetual motion. He cleans anything he finds dirty and repairs anything broken. Eric re-rigs my whisker pole, making it much easier for me to handle. He is fascinated with some of my tools - particularly my handheld nicropress and hydraulic cable cutter. Murray meanwhile takes his guitar ashore and entertains a delighted crowd gathered around a gazebo.

Passing Cape Tribulation (named by Cook in retrospect) and pondering all of the obstacles we are encountering, it is easy to understand how some can't understand why sailing is so much fun.

At Cape Bedford where the channel narrows to 400 feet, I am on watch alone and on the radar I count seven trawlers abreast in the channel, again with running lights obliterated by the flood lights on their trawling gear. I am unable to get any response from these English-speaking fisherman on the VHF radio. There we are with this all-star line bearing down on us. I consider taking a detour through the coral on the side of the channel but it troubles me that it is midnight and the only advice I can recall about coral piloting is to keep the sun behind me and my Polaroids on. I wake Eric for his consultation. "Just pick a bloody spot, mate, and go on through," he says.

That's what we do and sure enough the trawlers give way just in time to prevent me from having a stroke. Their sudden willingness to yield is due to the fact that they are trawling in the channel illegally and have no interest in explaining at a court of inquiry why an accident had occurred.

Our next stop is Lizard Island. When we arrive very early in the morning, the wind is from the northeast making the usual anchorage on the northeast side of the island untenable. We enter the remote reef-strewn pass to the lagoon on the southwest side of the island and go ashore to explore and have a $7 beer at the resort. Before dinner, the wind shifts 180° and now our lagoon is unsafe. We weigh anchor, sail around the north side of the island, and anchor in Watson's Bay. We cook aboard because the least expensive entree at the resort is $75.

After departing early in the morning, Eric catches a two-and-a-half foot Spanish Mackerel which is unquestionably the best tasting fish I've ever eaten. Erik teaches us to lasso the tail of a fish and hang it head down off the stern to drain all the blood to the sea. This eliminates a mess on the deck.

Between Lizard Island and Cape York, we pass the Bligh Boat Entrance (channel) where in 1789 Captain Bligh and 18 of his crew on part of an epic 3,400 nautical mile small boat passage from Polynesia to Timor, after the famous mutiny, crossed the reef. We also pass Providential Channel where Cook's boat was saved.

In the afternoon near Cape Melville, we have coming towards us USS *Warden*, a guided missile cruiser, and USS *Reed*, a frigate. I ask on the VHF if USS *Warden* is going to interrogate us as USS *Antrim* had in the Caribbean. Aboard the cruiser, there is a pilot from Thursday Island. Later when I meet him, he tells me the "old man" said, to the amusement of the crew on the bridge, "not here." The radio operator replies formally, "negative to that." The lesson is if you're the captain of a deadly guided-missile cruiser, your crew will laugh at your jokes.

World War II has left some additional hazards in this area. Many passes along the reef are marked "Former Mined Area." Early in the war, intentional errors are put on charts in hopes of costing an unwary enemy a ship or two. We can only hope all have been corrected but some still have not. Hal and Margaret Roth on *Whisper* went on the reef one night near Bramble Cay northeast of Thursday Island. The light on the chart had been marked on the wrong end of the Cay.

Our approach to Thursday Island is through reefs and we unfortunately do not have a good chart of the area. It is, however, morning and we have the sun over our shoulder and our Polaroids on. By noon, we safely anchor just off Thursday Island. Eric and I, after two and a half weeks of intense piloting broken only by several days in the Whitsundays and one day on Lizard Island, somehow find the strength to join the rest of the crew for a visit of Thursday Island.

Thursday Island is the northern most settlement of Australia and a remote outpost. When we enter town, it appears most of the populace are in saloons disguised, at least in name, as hotels because of Australian liquor laws. Needing a beer, we select the Royal Hotel and enter the first room; it is a pool-hall with a wild looking cast of characters playing the game, watching it, or passed out. In the back room is an empty unattended bar where we take seats. We hear someone working in the storeroom behind the bar. In a few minutes, Clare appears. Clare is the precise tonic our tired eyes need. She is a young English girl working her way around the world from Southhampton eastbound to Southhampton. Fortunately it is easy to follow Pat's rules as we are going westbound. We do, however, stop back at the Royal Hotel several times to down a few tubes with this *friendly bird*.

On Tuesday morning, March 23, we weigh anchor and go to the fuel dock which because of the big tides is a long dock. We attempt a graceful landing with five knots of tidal current coming towards us. We get to the dock; but in the excitement and some unfortunate gear changes by the captain, Eric smashes one of his fingers between a piling and the bow pulpit of *Lusty Wind II*. This will turn out to be our only navigational injury of the entire circumnavigation. He cleans the wound with Peroxide and bandages it.

Now with charts and five knots of current behind us, we speed at 11 knots over the bottom through Normandy Sound into the Arafura Sea between the Gulf of Carpentaria and New Guinea. By 4 p.m., we are past all the markers and out into open water for the first time in three weeks. This navigator has some idea of how Cook must have felt at this same point.

We are rounding Coburg Peninsula into Van Diemen Gulf towards Clarence Strait, our last reef passage for a while. Eric and I are back to our navigational practices of the Great Barrier Reef passage. The importance of Eric's plotting and dead reckoning proves itself spectacularly this squally night when lightning strikes the water about 500 feet from the boat freezing the GPS screen. The screen is still lit but our position, course, speed, bearing, and the UTC times are not changing. We immediately begin more frequent radar bearings to determine position and course. We also reduce boat speed! I remember a remedy that worked for me before with electronic gear – I turn the GPS off and after a few seconds turn it back on. It proceeds through its initialization program then goes back to working as if nothing had happened except for a "black hole" in the course line on our plotter screen. With the GPS working again, we resume speed. For the remainder of our circumnavigation, this Furuno GPS works perfectly.

The north and northeast coast of Australia is as are Florida and the Bahamas, an area of high incidence of lightning. I feel our lightning protection system to be another key element to our successful passage and it unquestionably saved much electric gear tonight. A lightning strike can even remagnetize and change the direction a compass points. We are alone in a large body of water with a 71-foot aluminum pole and antennas sticking up into the air and the water is struck 500 feet away. Something kept it from hitting us.

The heart of our lightning system is a large ground plate near the base of the mast and wired to the mast and the chain plates plus a pom-pom-like device mounted at the masthead. The short sharp wires of the pom-poms are designed to bleed off the electric charge developed by the rigging moving through the air. The idea is to reduce the chance of becoming the counterpoint to the opposite charge developed as a thundercloud moves through the air. Experts estimate this system reduces the chance of a strike by 20-percent. Of course, predicting what lightning will or will not do is an inexact science at best, but I feel our system paid for itself tonight.

Thoughts of serious consequences bring us back to the Clarence Strait. It is just past midnight, squally, and we are preparing to pass through the Strait with the width between unyielding reefs of about a mile. The current is with us at about two and a half knots. The current is a help as it got all of this over with quicker. Notations on the chart like "reef uncovered at half tide" add to my anxiety, but soon we are in Beagle Gulf and in the clear.

At 5 a.m., we anchor off the Darwin Sailing Club at Fannie Bay and all is well, including; Eric's finger which seemed to be healing all right but for him not fast enough for the golf tournament he is flying home to.

This passage from Manly is 2,097 nautical miles and

took 24 days – much too fast. The Whitsundays alone deserve 24 days.

Being in Fannie Bay, we have thoughts of Clare again, but our immediate task is to figure out how to handle transportation to shore with a gradual sloping bottom and 20 foot tides. Where *Lusty Wind II* is anchored, the water depth is about seven feet at low tide. This puts us almost a mile from the beach. The real problem is that between high and low tides the shore line here moves nearly a half mile. If one beaches the dinghy at low tide, he needs either to carry it a half mile through the mud to the permanent beach or to provide adequate anchor line and prepare for a long swim on his return.

The tropical storm season is nearly over and we are the first yacht of the season to anchor off the Darwin Sailing Club. The yacht club extends all courtesies. Members who keep their boats in more protected areas during the "willy-willy" season have not yet returned their boats to Fannie Bay. It is important to be far enough from shore that the boat will not be careened at low tide and just as important not to anchor in an area where the bottom is fouled with the remains of the World War II submarine nets. I can imagine trying to recover an anchor out of a submarine net is quite a job and we don't have John Wayne to swim down and snip it free.

*   *   *

Darwin is named after Charles Darwin who was never there. It was first visited by *Beagle* on a trip after Darwin's epic voyage. In the early days of World War II, Darwin was a very sleepy outpost with a small British garrison. The tremendous demands of the early war years forced the British to vacate Darwin at a dark time when it appeared the Japanese were coming that way. The void was filled by U.S. Seabees and Marines who fully understood the strategic importance of Darwin. They built in record time the highway from Alice Springs to connect Darwin with the rest of Australia for the first time and to provide a reliable means to supply a defense. Australians, particularly in Darwin, remember to this day those events and have very high affection and appreciation for Americans. An American can't have a drink at a bar, particularly in Darwin, without someone buying another and again telling him this story.

Darwin was severely damaged by Cyclone Tracey in 1974 and, as a result, there is not much old architecture to see. Today Darwin is the political, commercial, medical, and transportation hub of the Northern Territory.

* * *

After one day of dealing with the tides of Fannie Bay, we make arrangements to dock *Lusty Wind II* for our stay in Darwin at the "Duck Pond." The Duck Pond is built to encourage a fishing industry in the Northwest Territory and fishing vessels have first priority to available space. Water is kept at the mid-tide level and as the tide rises or drops past this level, lock doors are opened and vessels may come or go for a period of about a half an hour. Prior arrangements must be made with Scottie, the operator of the lock. At the appointed time, we motor out around Emery Point into Port Darwin and into the Duck Pond. We are immediately befriended by Otto and Helen Eijkman, their daughter and son, Makicka and Lakeen, aboard *Wind'f Change*. Makicka is 14 going on 19 and Lakeen is 10. This courageous family had purchased *Wind'f Change* and are preparing for a sail to the Netherlands, Otto's homeland.

I will bring back a stack of photographs from this trip, but a scene not recorded on any film is one of my favorites. It is 10-year-old Lakeen rowing about the Duck Pond, dragging an anchor for treasure. He snagged a bicycle and spent several days trying to restore it, using the threads of a huge bolt to file off the barnacles. Suddenly, the bicycle was gone. Lakeen's explanation was direct – I chucked it in the bin.

After getting settled in the Duck Pond, we take Eric and Murray to the airport for their flight back to Brisbane and Mooloolaba. In a few days, Pat, Sam, John, Sue, and David Bever arrive. Our quick four-wheel-drive tour of the Northwest Territory includes a crocodile-feeding trip on the Adelaide River, fording streams, and viewing marvelous vistas and aboriginal petroglyphs in Kakadu National Park. The next day we go to Leitchfield Park for swimming and rock sliding in lakes and rapids and take a difficult off-the-road trip to the "Lost City."

John Bever takes me to the Darwin Hospital for X-rays and a Doppler circulation test. He and the hospital doctors agreed I am fine. This must be one of the most distant house-calls in history.

All too soon I take my family and friends to the airport for their trip half way around the world and home.

Ted and I spend the next few days loading *tucker* aboard and making advance arrangements to clear Australian Customs. My friend and journalist, Bob Payne, arrives at 3 a.m. on a flight from Bali. The next morning at mid-tide, we have Scottie "beam" us out of the Duck Pond and steam to Fisherman's Wharf where arrangements have been made for fuel and for the return of our guns which had been surrendered in Brisbane. When the customs officials bring the guns, they ask me to unzip my case to make sure all three are there. I apparently didn't rezip the case; and when I passed it down to Ted, the pistol falls out into 30 feet of water and mud. Our departure is delayed a bit while we hire a diver for recovery. The gun is by now in 40 feet of water as the tide is coming in.

9

CHAPTER NINE

The Flying Fish Run
April 16, 1993 – May 30, 1993
Darwin – Adan, Yemen

Most circumnavigating yachtsmen set sail from Darwin for Bali, Singapore, the Strait of Malacca, Sri Lanka, then across the Arabian Sea to the Red Sea and the Mediterranean. Reports of pirates in the Strait of Malacca and civil unrest in Sri Lanka put a damper on this route. More important, because of our timing, I want to take a wide berth of the May-November cyclone season in the Arabian Sea. We are departing Darwin just at the end of the willy-willy season on the northwest coast of Australia; however, with today's excellent weather forecasting and all the information available on the radio and weatherfax, I feel comfortable with our April 16th departure for Cocos Keeling Islands.

We anticipate little or no wind until we reach the Indian Ocean system. From there to the Seychelles, we should find some of the greatest sailing conditions in the world. The system in the Indian Ocean south of the equator is a counterclockwise rotation just as that normally experienced in the South Pacific. Most of our crossing will be at 10°, or 600 nautical miles south of the equator where we expect to find the most consistent trade winds and current.

Of all the great oceans, the Indian generally is the kindest to sailing ships. Its crossing has been long known among sailors as the Flying-fish Run:

"I'm a flying-fish sailor,
 Just in from Hong Kong:
 Oh-way-oh, blow the man down!"

In *The Voyage of American Promise*, Dodge Morgan writes of his fear of this ocean. Dodge crossed the Indian Ocean in the "Roaring Forties," between 40° and 42° south, about 2,500 nautical miles south of the equator where the system goes east – his way. Conditions, however, are often severe at this latitude. We, of course, are westbound 1,900 nautical miles north of his wake in beautiful sailing conditions and climate.

The ability to propel a boat into wind was probably first discovered in the Indian Ocean by Arabs, Persians, or Indians in their sea going dhows. Their big lateen sails were ideal both with and against the wind. A dhow with its lateen-rig could sail upwind to 50° off the bow. After 2,000 years of improvements, modern cruising yachts will sail upwind to about 40° and racing yachts to 32°.

It is believed Phoenicians first sailed around Africa to the Indian Ocean 2,600 years ago. Romans 2,000 years ago built ships in the Red Sea and traded in the Indian Ocean. Recorded direct sea trade with Europe was not until 1488 when Bartholomew Dias of Portugal and his unwilling crew were blown 230 miles east of Cape of Good Hope by a gale. After Columbus' famous discovery for Spain, King Manuel I of Portugal financed Vasco da

Gama to follow Dias' lead. Da Gama knew the system and the counter clockwise rotation south of the equator. He followed the South American coast – with the system – crossing the South Atlantic instead of hugging the African coast – against the system -- like his predecessors. After rounding the Cape of Good Hope, the system in the southern Indian Ocean was against him to the monsoons north of the equator which these seamen understood. Hippalus, a Greek pilot, wrote of these monsoons in A.D.80.

Da Gama's opening of new trade routes by-passed centuries of profit-taking by Arab merchants and pirates as well as the Italian merchants in the trading cities of Venice and Genoa. For a while, the wealth would flow to Lisbon.

Pirates have roamed the Indian Ocean since trading vessels first began to ply these waters. Marco Polo tells of a band of 30 or more ships whose crews would string them out at intervals of three to four miles forming a net 100 miles long that traders could only avoid with much luck. Later in the nineteenth century, fleets of bloodthirsty pirates would take a ship and slash the throats of all on board. The *Koran* taught these Muslims not to steal from the living, but said nothing of the dead. The southern coast of the Arabian Peninsula is called the Trucial Coast, a name that comes from the Arabic word for pirate.

The navies and coast guards of the world have reduced pirates to a minimum but there are still dangerous areas. We heard of one English woman circumnavigating solo who was robbed of everything she had of value by a group of fisherman off the coast of India. She made port where she received neither help nor sympathy from local officials. She bravely faced all her hardships; but when she found fellow yachties after sailing to the Red Sea, she cried for several days before continuing her odyssey.

In the Indian Ocean north of the equator, the Indian subcontinent breaks the sea and system in half and sailors don't find the system of wind and currents of other oceans. The heating and cooling of the huge Asian land mass causes monsoons. The word comes from Arabic mausim meaning season. There are two of these seasons: the Northeast Monsoon and the Southwest Monsoon.

The Northeast Monsoon occurs as the winds blow out of the Northeast when the sun is south of the equator from November through March. The wind is generally very steady at 10 to 15 knots with occasional gales. This monsoon does not produce much rain. Excepting occasional gales, sailing conditions in the Northeast Monsoon are as nearly perfect as possible; unless a sailor is traveling northeast.

The Southwest Monsoon is caused by the heating of the Asian land mass during the summer months. The wind is out of the Southwest and is strongest from June through September. As the wind comes over water and collects moisture, this monsoon has a tendency to produce a lot of rain. Hence the "monsoons" of India. In the Southwest Monsoon, the winds average 20 knots and frequently reach gale force.

For present day circumnavigators, who are usually sailing northwest, both of these monsoons allow pleasant sailing beam reaches – again, excepting frequent gales and cyclones in the Southwest Monsoon.

Our plan takes us north of the equator in May and requires constant monitoring of weather as gales in the Arabian Sea are from late May until the middle of June as well as from October until the middle of November. We are again at the fringe of danger.

The first few days of our passage out of Darwin are as expected and we motor-sail in very light air. We occasionally experience squalls which provide a short rest for the engine and fuel supply. Things have been going so well I let up a bit and don't review menu and cooking procedures with Ted who is to cook the evening meal. Ted decides to pan fry chicken in oil and very quickly the oil, chicken, and range are on fire. Bob, on watch, comes from the other direction with a box of baking soda with which I put out the fire. Fortunately the mess is easy to clean up and the next day I rewire the burner on the top of the range. Fire is a greater concern to me than storms; it is one of the most likely ways to lose a boat. We are still communicating with and making telephone calls through Victor India Sierra in Sydney, but by now we are a long way from help. I don't like to picture myself in a burning cabin trying to raise help on the radio with someone who may not speak English very well.

Our life raft is a Viking six-person double bottom model and has just been inspected and repacked by the Viking agent in Darwin. In the life raft are signal rockets, hand held flares, first-aid kit, sea-sick pills, can opener, six pints of water, food tins, fish hooks and line, flashlight, repair kit, and for me sugar pills. In addition are an EPRIB and a hand held water maker. The water maker is designed to provide enough fresh water to sustain life. If we have to abandon ship, we also will take along our deck-mounted orange bag of additional emergency supplies including space blankets, sun block lotion, a fish spear, five gallons of water, numerous cans of food, and additional flares. We will most certainly attempt to take along the handheld VHF. We keep it fully charged for just this possibility.

In the companionway, within reach of the cockpit, we keep a small orange bag with diabetic supplies. The location is such that even if there is a fire below deck this bag can be safely reached. A diabetic would have little chance on a life raft without these supplies. Crew members are encouraged to put any medicine important to them in this bag.

The next day in the Arafura Sea, several Indonesian or New Guinean fishing boats appear to be approaching us; and because of the remoteness of our location, we are concerned and break out our armaments. Never before have I felt more comfortable sitting with a loaded M-14, a loaded Alley Sweeper shotgun, and a loaded 38 caliber pistol. Our courses continue to converge and we are relieved when these good fisherman smile, wave, and go on about their business. I wonder if this elevation of heart rate is good exercise.

Some nights we have incidents of flying fish hitting the watch keeper or flying through hatches and flopping about inside the boat. Every morning there are a dozen or so on the deck. In tribute to Joshua Slocum who did this same passage almost a hundred years earlier, Bob Payne on several mornings collects, cleans (I hope), fries, and serves up flying fish for breakfast. They are really not bad; in fact, after a couple of weeks, one looks forward to Bob's breakfast. The important thing is to be sure he collects fresh flying fish and not ones that had been hiding under the life raft or somewhere else for several days. Bob's system is if he would even think about eating one it is probably fresh enough. Bob wants to make flying fish jerky out of those that are not fresh enough for breakfast.

At this point, we join the wake of Magellan and Cook as they came south to pick up the known trade winds to Africa and the Cape of Good Hope. As we have expected, we are approaching the reef pass into Cocos Keeling Islands in the dark. Our chart is not of a good scale for doing this at night and we call for instructions. The captain of the island freighter *C.V. O'Conner* answers and says he can see us on his radar. He talks us to a safe place to anchor for the night.

Early in the morning, a launch comes over from *C.V. O'Conner* with a copy of the chart we need compliments of "the old man." We move to the quarantined area and are quickly cleared by Customs and Immigrations.

There are two other yachts in the anchorage, one from Boston. The captain and owner is aboard with a lovely young, blond, blue-eyed, Dutch girl. Our Customs inspectors tell us there are a lot of wrinkles on that boat but none are on her. The captain, with all his wrinkles, comes over alone to ask us if we have any video tapes he can borrow or trade. They have only one movie, *Grumpy Old Men*, with Walter Mathau, and are tired of it. Unfortunately for them, we don't travel with a television or VCR. The captain doesn't invite us over, but we don't care; we've already seen the movie.

* * *

Cocos Keeling was first discovered by Captain William Keeling in 1609. In the early 1820's, a remarkable man named John Clunies-Ross from the Shetland Islands formed a partnership with a bizarre Englishman named Alexander Hare. Together they built the sailing ship *Borneo*. The first engagement of *Borneo* was to move Hare and his harem of 100 young Asian beauties and their children from Borneo to Cape Town. Thinking that was the last of his partner, Clunies-Ross returned to the Shetland Islands; and in 1827, he gathered his family and a group of young Scots to settle on Cocos Keeling. After a long and difficult voyage, *Borneo* anchored near where we moored and was greeted by Hare and his harem of 117 bare-breasted young women.

Clunies-Ross, undaunted, set out to build a copra plantation. The young Scot lads set out to get some of these girls away from Hare. Hare imported large quantities of rum for the young Scots to get their minds off his harem; that, of course, didn't work. Hare was jealous of these younger men; and when he had a chance, he departed for Borneo to start anew with the few girls he had left. Clunies-Ross was again left with the business. He developed a copra plantation which was owned by the Clunies-Ross family until 1982 when a financial reversal reduced their ownership to a homestead block on Home Island.

Beagle, with Charles Darwin, visited Cocos Keeling in 1835. *Spray*, with Joshua Slocum anchored near where we were in 1896 as did *Yankee*, with Irving and Electa Johnson in 1949.

* * *

Ashore we soon meet John Clunies-Ross VI. Bob, Ted, and I have dinner at the old Clunies-Ross mansion which is now a bed and breakfast run by an Australian woman and her daughter. It is an interesting meal. Our hostesses also are the cooks and waitresses and serve a course, take off their aprons, sit down and join us, put their aprons back on, clear the table, and prepare our next course. After dinner, John Clunies-Ross VI, his wife, and nephew join us for a couple of drinks and discuss our circumnavigation and the history of the island.

Two o'clock May 1, we depart Cocos Keeling for our 2,400 nautical mile sail to the Seychelles. The first day out of Cocos Keeling we receive radio reports and weatherfaxes from Australia indicating a cyclone near Diego Garcia. We track the storm and fortunately for us it reverses its direction and begins moving southwest –

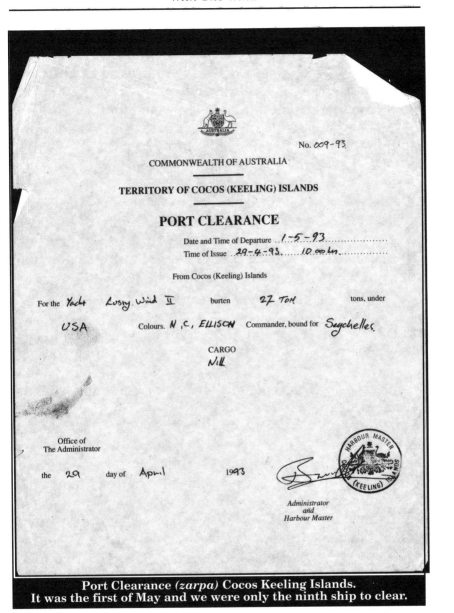

Port Clearance *(zarpa)* Cocos Keeling Islands.
It was the first of May and we were only the ninth ship to clear.

away from us. Here we experience real trade winds. For several days, wind is at an apparent 12 to 15 knots off our stern port quarter. We fly the spinnaker the whole way and do 175 nautical miles a day.

It is great to be out in the open sea on a broad reach in the "trades" with our old friends *Orion* and the *Southern Cross* keeping watch with us every night and assuring us we are on course. We also, of course, enjoy the rest of the magnificent sky and phosphorescence of night watches.

We are now passing 1,740 nautical miles north of latitude 39°05'S and longitude 95°33'E – the far side of the earth from Ft. Thomas, Kentucky, our home.

At sea, I try to call home or the office every two days to register our position in the event of our disappearance and to assure everyone things are all right. By now we are out of range of Victor India Sierra in Sydney and unable to contact other radiotelephone stations in Australia. I crawl into the lazarette and manually switch the wires to the more long range whip antenna but we are still out of range of Sydney. I then very easily make contact with Niner Victor Golf in Singapore to call home. I ask them to make a collect call. They don't make collect calls. I ask if I can make a credit card call. They don't accept credit cards; but if I gave them an address, they will send me a credit application and then, if approved, I can make calls and they will bill me. They assure me that if we have an emergency they would handle our communications immediately. Two days later after trying dozens of stations, I make clear-as-a-bell contact with Delta Alpha Papa in Hamburg, Germany, 5,400 nautical miles from us. I ask to make a collect call to the United States. They don't make collect or credit card calls. Today is Sunday; I can call back on Monday 8:30 a.m. to 5 p.m. Hamburg time to arrange credit. Monday I make contact with Zulu Sierra Charlie in Cape Town, South Africa. The accommodating operator makes the collect call and determines immediately that my transmission is garbled. By the time it is relayed from South Africa to New York and then to Ft. Thomas, it is garbled more so I talk to him and he relays the messages to Pat. This communication is less than satisfactory but greatly appreciated. It is difficult to say "Goodbye – I love you" to a guy. Another two days pass. I make contact with Golf Kilo Tango in Portishead, U.K., and the helpful operator makes a collect call getting our phone answering machine. The operator volunteers to leave a message that we are well, without charging us.

Meanwhile, Pat is home getting a baptism in business crisis. With all our communication difficulties, I am of little help.

Throughout all these difficult communications I listen to ham operators all over the world. I have two limitations with ham radio. First business is not allowed to be transacted and that's often the purpose of my call; secondly I only have a Novice license and I'm limited to just a few frequencies. It is reassuring to know this system is in place and we have the ability to use it in the event of an emergency when frequency restrictions don't apply.

We are now about a 100 miles south of Diego Garcia, our massive Navy and Air Force installation in the middle of the Indian Ocean. The original military significance was to give us a safe and permanent base to stage naval and air strikes against any aggression of the Soviet Union in the Indian Ocean region and to allow for B-52 strikes on the Soviet Union from the south. Today its significance is its proximity to the Middle East. The base was important during the Gulf War. With our high VHF antenna, we can hear the port controllers on their powerful transmitter. It is interesting to hear a young female voice obviously from Alabama or Mississippi passing instructions "Y'all be careful now, y'hear" to naval and supply ships coming and going. Yachts are not allowed to enter Diego Garcia except in a life or death emergency. I assume our armed forces are available for search and rescue.

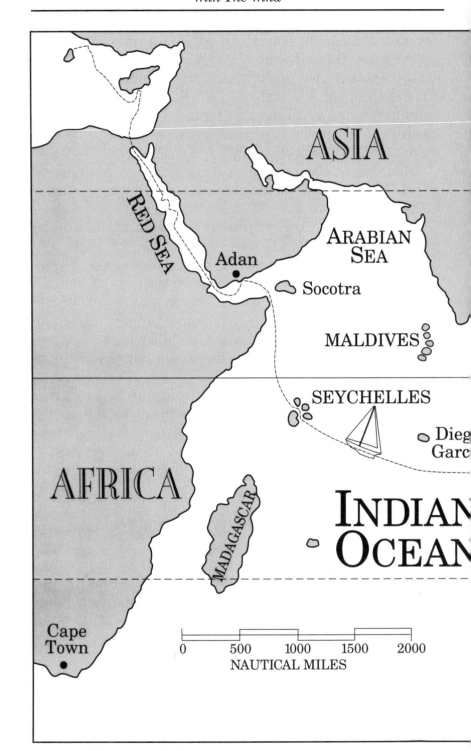

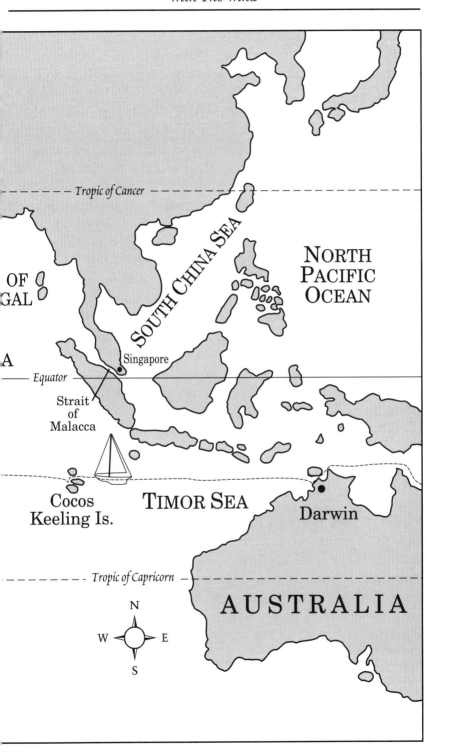

Tropic of Cancer

NORTH
PACIFIC
OCEAN

SOUTH CHINA SEA

OF
GAL

A

Singapore

Equator

Strait
of
Malacca

Cocos
Keeling Is.

TIMOR SEA

Darwin

Tropic of Capricorn

AUSTRALIA

N
W · E
S

We are west bound at the top of the trade wind circle and, of course, running with the wind directly behind us. In these conditions, a jibe is always a possibility and can be damaging to the rigging. I always give a long lecture to the crew at the beginning of their watch reminding them to be particularly mindful of a slight wind change and to know how to turn off the autopilot and change bearing to avoid a jibe. A few minutes after ending my speech, with Ted and Bob watching, I allow a jibe and for the second time break the bolts in the traveler car sending several associated blocks into the deep. This delays breakfast for an hour while we secure the boom, put new bolts into the car and find a substitute block. In the process of furling the main we develop what Bob Payne calls a spinnaker wrap inside the mast. The sail rolls up on a rod inside the mast very much like a window shade. The mainsail is eight years old and has been from Florida to Europe and back and by now 55% of the way around the world. It has stretched, is baggy, and does not furl well especially in our excitement. No problem – we just put the spinnaker back up.

The wind is gradually building; and before long, the wind over the boat, or the apparent wind, is up to 16 knots which is about the limit of the spinnaker. Everything is going well and I decide to let it go for a little longer. Pretty soon wind is up to 17 knots with gusts to 20. I had better get the crew up and the sail down before it blows apart. No time to put my thoughts into action. With a lot of ripping noise and flailing about the spinnaker disintegrates into a multitude of colored parts. I get Ted into the cockpit and I rush to the bow to begin pulling the sail down which is at least a two-man job. Journalist Payne arrives on deck a little later, delayed by getting the correct lens on his camera and a new roll of film. He begins taking pictures of my dilemma. "Don't worry" he says, "later you'll be glad I took these pictures." After Bob recovers his camera from where I had shoved it, he helps recover the sail. (These pictures are now of course among my favorites.)

Now we are under power and decide we have to get the main unfurled. Bob redeems himself by volunteering to go up the mast in the boatswain chair to pull the sail out of its cavity by hand while Ted and I alternately inch-by-inch furl and unfurl. With the sail finally out, we pole out the genoa on the port side and let the main out on the starboard side for good speed under wing and wing.

May 17, 5:45 a.m., we sight Frigate Island and by 10 a.m. pass through the wide reef opening into Victoria Harbor on the island of Mahé in the Seychelles. Not only is the pass wide, but we have the sun over our shoulder and Polaroids on. We are greeted by a launch with eight Customs and Immigrations officials who very quickly clear us. We motor into the harbor to moor off the Seychelles Yacht Club where again all courtesies are extended.

Son Andy who arrived the night before from Cincinnati and Paris is riding down a street in his rented *Moke* when he sees a moving mast with a Furuno Radio Direction Finder antenna over bayside buildings. He knows it is ours. When we dinghy into the yacht club, Andy is waiting for us and we are both very happy to see all is well.

* * *

Current thinking is that the Seychelles were first visited by Arab seaman in their *dhows* in the 9th century. It is documented that Portuguese visited these islands in their explorations of the Indian Ocean during the 16th century. The first occupants were pirates in the 18th century and the first settlers were the French in 1768. Napoleon later lost the Seychelles to England and they in turn gained their independence in 1976. Today the government is Communist, or at least high socialist, and a great deal of the economy is tourism.

The second most important part of the economy is espionage. On one mountain, the United States Government has a monstrous antenna farm listening in on the activities of this part of the world. Included in this antenna array is one of the GPS stations for controlling the 24 satellites that we use for navigation. On another mountain, the Russians have an equally large antenna farm listening in on our military activities in this part of the world including, I'm sure, that girl from Alabama in Diego Garcia. The English have espionage facilities only because they've been here since 1815. The French are here too trying to figure out what everybody else is up to. All of these governments provide substantial funds to the Seychelles government.

Also important is fashion photography, particularly by the French, on the beautiful beaches of these islands. Several of the soft porn *Emanuel* movies have been filmed on the beaches here.

Giant tortoises similar to those found in the Galápagos are found in the Seychelles and much is made of the Coco-de-mer, a unique double coconut

Ted Blackwood,
Young Interpreter,
Six Conartists,
Hussain in Jibla,
Yemen.
Photo by Andy Ellison

rt Control Tower
n Jiddah, Saudi
Arabia.
Photo by Andy Ellison

Abdulmonien
Abbas
Sokkar, at the
uez Yacht Club,
Suez, Egypt.
hoto by Andy Ellison

Transportation to shore off Bozuk Bükü, Turkey.

Lusty Wind II on the quay at Symi, Greece.

Sam and the Captain having breakfast ashore in Symi, Greece.

Lusty Wind II at anchor in Levitha, Greece.
Photo by Andy Ellison

tie, Molly, and Warren having za and coffee in norgós, Greece.

Monastery of
the Panayia
Khozviotissa near
Amorgós, Greece.
Photo by Andy Ellison

Pat on the path leading to the Monastery.

Passing through Corinth Canal, Greece.

Lusty Wind II
at anchor off
Napaktos
(Lepanto), Greece.

Valletta, Malta.

The Captain's
Galley Duties.
The stove is level
the boat, heeled.
Photo by Dick Pearson

Lusty Wind II
moored stern to a
Puerto Bañus.

"...the storm will go out to sea where it won't bother anybody."
Approaching Las Palmas, Canaries.

Photo by Charlie Mihalek

Nick with Marion a
Bill Littleford, ne
Vieques, Puerto Ri

Flying the spinnaker on
our Atlantic Crossing.
Photo by Charlie Jett

Man-O-War in the Southeast Trade
Photo by John Pen

with an appearance that brings to mind the female pelvic area. Coco-de-mer pictures hang on walls in restaurants and are printed on most postcards and T-shirts in Victoria.

* * *

Bob Payne regrettably leaves us in the Seychelles. After a day, we begin getting notes from and finally find Dave Townsend, an anesthesiologist and friend of our family from Salt Lake City.

When we register with the Port Authorities, we find the government charges a mooring fee, even though we are on our own anchor. The fee is roughly a $100 a day. We had certainly not heard of this charge but it must be common information among yachties as only six foreign yachts visited the Seychelles in 1992. We are the first boat for 1993. The yacht club is wonderful. The accommodating manager, an Indian gentleman, makes it a point to introduce us to all permanent members who are mostly electronic spies, high government officials, or expatriates from all over the world. The operators of the American antenna farm invite us up the mountain to their facility to have Satellite Burgers for lunch at their club. Another man in charge of the Seychelles sewers spends an afternoon over several beers explaining the whole system to us. I am mindful this conversation is costing $100 per day.

Just behind the yacht club is a sail loft where we take our spinnaker pieces. The loft is run by Elizabeth Goulding. Elizabeth, a wonderful English schoolmarm, was hired in the U.K. by the Seychelles' government to teach sailing to Seychelles youngsters. We all know Elizabeth's type – wherever she taught she would win the "teacher of the year" award. She understood immediately that sailing was one thing; but to have any benefits, skills and work ethic would have to be learned as well. Thus, the very clean and efficient loft is manned by local teenagers. They have the materials and talent to put our spinnaker back together and repair several tears in our stretched out main. It is great every day to see different age groups on different class boats learning to sail in the harbor with the older children teaching. Elizabeth is working towards, and I'm sure will succeed, a Seychelles' sailing team for the Olympics.

Andy and I change the oil and filters of the engine and generator and then prepare to motor to the fuel dock to top off our tanks. After a number of tries and as many searches for the reason, the engine will turn over but will not start. Near the port, there is a Volvo truck dealer and we borrow a young diesel mechanic. Fortunately this man learned his trade working on generators at the US communication base and speaks English. At least he knows all the words that relate to diesel engines. I don't learn quickly; so when he arrives at the boat, I explain to him what is wrong. He has never seen a Racor fuel filter but asks if it has a small plastic float. I tell him it has an aluminum float. He tells me he thinks it is plastic. I am sure he is wasting the time I am paying for, but he insists on taking apart the filter that I had just taken apart and cleaned. Sure enough, the little ball I thought was aluminum is plastic. Some burrs have developed in the body of the filter and these caused the ball to stick in the closed position starving the engine of fuel.

After paying 2,050 Seychelles rupees (US $400) port fees, and clearing Customs and Immigration (who needs to see receipts of payment of our port fees) we start northwest to catch the currents off the coast of Somalia to the Horn of Africa, the Gulf of Aden, the port of Adan, and the Red Sea.

* * *

The worldwide weather we have been experiencing is determined to a large extent by two laws of physics. The first is that wind blows from high pressure areas to low pressure areas. The second is the Coriolios Effect first described by the French Physicist, Gustave-Gaspard Coriolios. He said since the entire earth revolves once every 24 hours, the entire surface of the earth is turning at 1/24 of a revolution per hour. The rotational speed of the surface of the earth is different depending on the latitude. At the equator the surface has to travel 21,600 nautical miles in 24 hours or is traveling at 900 nautical miles per hour. At 10° north or south of the equator, the circumference of the earth is 21,272 and the speed is thus 886 nautical miles per hour. Thus if a person is on the equator and shoots a cannon due north, its eastbound inertia would be 900 miles an hour. As the surface over which it would be flying would be moving at slower and slower speeds, its point of impact would be to the right or east of the longitude from which it is fired. If the cannon is fired south from the equator; the point of impact would be left, but still east. If he is at latitude 10°N and fires that cannon south, the point of impact would be again to the right, but this time at a more western latitude. This is the reason the system which revolves over typical ocean center high pressures is clockwise in the northern hemisphere and counterclockwise in the southern hemisphere. Winds going from high towards low pressures bear to the right in the northern hemisphere and to the left in the southern hemisphere causing their clockwise or counterclockwise spin.

Likewise lows – hurricanes, gales, squalls, etc. – will rotate counterclockwise in the northern hemisphere and clockwise in the southern hemisphere. For the same reason, drains, such as toilets which flow inward like a low, spin counterclockwise in the northern hemisphere and clockwise in the southern hemisphere. Fill your bathroom sink with water, open the drain, and watch which way it goes. Land based toilets are generally built with water jets that work with this system and are built differently for the two hemispheres. Boat heads are built to accommodate each and go as they say, "with the flow." In the southern hemisphere, I'd been watching this phenomena and indeed drains and the head circulated clockwise. From about 5° North to 5° South there is not enough difference in the circumference of the earth to cause a noticeable coriolios effect. This is the same geometry, in the navigator's eye, that causes the sun to hang there at apparent noon, or the top of its perceived orbit.

As one travels from the equator to either pole, the reduction in circumference per degree traveled accelerates causing a more pronounced Coriolios Effect. This is partially why storms, other than tropical storms, are more severe in higher latitudes (closer to the poles) then they are in lower latitudes (closer to the equator). Tropical storms are fueled by convection not so much by the difference in the rotational speed of the earth's surface.

* * *

As we approach the equator the captain is below busily flushing the head to see if any difference can be found. The flow is almost straight down until we reach approximately 5°N at which time it is back to a very comforting counterclockwise flow.

We cross the equator and are heading north along the coast of Somalia towards the Horn of Africa. This passage which we are making at the end of May is best done between September and mid-October at the end of the Southwest Monsoon when the strength of the winds begins to subside in this part of the Indian Ocean. The worst time is May to June, when it is notorious for its high frequency of gales that combined with strong currents can produce extremely heavy seas at the Horn of Africa. Here we are in late May. We get frequent weather reports all indicating no problem. We have dodged another bullet and have a very peaceful broad reach between the Horn of Africa and the island of Socotra into the safety of the Gulf of Aden.

In the Gulf of Aden, we have our biggest fish day of the voyage. First Andy catches a seven-foot sailfish but lets it go. Second, Andy hooks a large Mahi Mahi but it gets away. Third, Dave catches, lands, and cooks for dinner a Yellowfin Tuna. Early the next morning, a large school of bottle nose dolphins welcomes us to the Arab world.

10

CHAPTER TEN

Running the Gauntlet

May 31, 1993 – July 30, 1993

Adan – Port Said, Egypt

It is 2 a.m. as we begin our approach to Adan Harbor. The channel twists through a number of junctions and turns although it is well marked. We are in the dark but with radar we are able to pick out all the buoys and we feel quite comfortable. We call the harbor master, who sits in a World War II pill-box overlooking the harbor. He gives us permission to enter. After making the last turn and approaching the harbor, we have difficulty reconciling the radar image with the chart. Land not on the chart appears on the radar. The harbor master's English is fairly good but he does not understand our questions. Now feeling decidedly uncomfortable, we ask and receive permission to pull out of the shipping channel, anchor for the night, to make our final approach in the morning. We drop anchor and quickly fall asleep at 3:30 a.m.

I am awakened a little after 8 a.m. the next morning by a port officer, who has obviously just come on duty and is not at all happy about our anchorage. When I get to the radio and explain, he tells us to pull up anchor immediately and go to the prescribed yacht anchorage.

Looking around we learn that the "new" island that appears on the radar is a fleet of abandoned fishing trawlers left by Russians who had stopped getting pay checks and went home. With great difficulty, I get the crew up; and we follow instructions.

Because Yemen has just shaken off English domination a few years ago and more recently, Soviet domination, I expect a great deal of bureaucracy. So I go first to Immigration and Customs where I find a man in what appears to be an abandoned office. It has neither a door to close nor a window to shut. A multitude of papers and assorted trash blow across the dirty floor. But to my pleasant surprise, he handles everything, including stamping passports, in a matter of minutes. I am then directed to the police station across the street where we fill out one form which is approved as quickly as it is completed. The last stop is the Port Captain's office which is somewhat more difficult to reach. The man in charge is very pleasant and takes no more than five minutes to complete all paperwork. We are the only yacht in the harbor and he says we may stay just where we are. In a place where one would assume *pratique* would be an all-day matter, we have all of our paperwork done including travel time in less than an hour.

During the 1990 uprising, an appropriately named yacht, *Innocent Bystander*, was anchored between Yemen Army and Navy installations. The Army and Navy were on different sides of the issue and firing at each other over the yacht. *Innocent Bystander* tried to make an unofficial departure and, as both sides felt it was to their advantage to have someone between them, they were shot at by both and sunk. The owners swam to a freighter and relative safety. It is not reassuring to sit on our boat just three years later and view our position between these same two military installations.

* * *

Adan is our introduction to the Muslim World. In the Arabic language the world Islam means submitting and a Muslim is one who submits. Muslims observe the five pillars of Islam: creed, performance of prayer, alms, fasting, and pilgrimage. In the observance of these pillars, Islam is a wonderful and peaceful religion. A growing number of Muslims recognize a sixth pillar originating after atrocities of the Crusaders – *jihad*, which means Holy War, or war against godless unbelievers such as Americans and Europeans. This growing minority of Muslims are the ones who shoot at boats, blow up tour buses, kidnap tourists, and take political prisoners. Unfortunately a yacht flying the American flag personifies the Godless unbelieving Westerner.

The earliest known people of this region lived more than 1,000 years before Christ. Their economy was based on agriculture and frankincense trade. The aroma of frankincense was highly valued everywhere in the civilized world and burnt as incense. Adan on the coast was an important stop on the sea route between the Spice Islands and Europe and was controlled by the Venetians; it was important until Vasco da Gama exposed the alternate route around Africa. Adan came under British influence about 1840 and was an important coaling stop in the British lifeline between England and India from the opening of the Suez Canal in 1869 to 1940.

The Yemen of today was formed in 1990 by a

merger of North Yemen with its Capital in San'a and Southern Yemen with its Capital in Adan. At the time of our visit, the military was fully integrated but most other functions of the government were still separate.

* * *

We are tired but manage several sorties into town. The scene is a dusty environment. Few buildings seem to be finished, and trash – particularly plastic bags – are abundant and blowing all over. We sheepishly take the trash we have accumulated since the Seychelles and find a dumpster to put it into. From the odor emanating from the dumpster, it surely contains a dead dog or goat. Later in the afternoon, we are found by Hussain, a cab driver with dyed red hair and fingernails painted red. Hussain makes it his business to take care of yachties passing through; and we find him to be fair in his pricing, knowledgeable of where to go to get anything we need, and all-in-all he is a tremendous help. When I ask Hussain why most buildings have reinforcing rods sticking out of their roof and walls, he explains buildings are not taxed until they are finished even though they may be occupied. This should have been obvious – only government buildings are completed.

It is June 1st, the birthday of Mohammed, and thus it is the Muslim Christmas. With Hussain's help, we motor over to the Adan Bunkering Company for fuel. Although the British have been gone for years the name Adan Bunkering Company had just been painted over the raised concrete letters on the building that spell British Bunkering Company. The barge we tie along side of is full of diesel fuel with a gasoline-powered pump to deliver the fuel to our boat. Before we take delivery, they take a fuel sample and test it. The fuel is probably the cleanest we have taken on during the entire trip and inexpensive at 89¢ per gallon payable in U.S. dollars only.

We meet Hussain again the next morning for a trip to the mountain villages of Jibla and Ta'izz. Jibla was founded in 1067 by Queen Arwa who ruled until her death in 1138 at the age of 92. Queen Arwa was a wise woman and spent the State budget for the common benefit. After 900 years, Jibla still prospers from her public works.

The provinces of Ibb and Ta'izz are amazing. They have many small villages perched up in the hills obviously for defense. They are surrounded by terraced fields never more than a few yards wide. In the gently slopping valleys, which must have been an unsafe place to live 900 years ago, there is now much new construction including a large Soviet sponsored truck factory.

Upon entering Jibla, we are approached by a number of aggressive girls, ages 7 to 10. These happy children speak English and are selling chewing gum which we buy. A few minutes later we go around the corner to find another group of young girls who in English are begging for chewing gum. We suspect a sting but give them all the gum we have just bought; they immediately run around the corner and give the gum back to their cohorts. The marketplace and food stalls in the village are a wonder to see. There couldn't have been but little change in 900 years. The Mosque of Arwa, built by the Queen, is open to the public except at prayer time. It is not prayer time and the priest – for a fee of $20 – lets us go through this Mosque. We have to promise not to tell what we see.

From Jibla, we drive to Ta'izz, a relatively young city that has an uninteresting appearance. The old part of the city is fascinating to walk through; but the most interesting place is a large ancient fortification on top of a hill dominating the city. The fort is now used by the army and is off limits. Hussain is nervous when we take pictures from his cab.

Early Thursday. We get the good Doctor David off to the airport for his flights to scheduled operations in Salt Lake City and Ted Blackwood off to his life of leisure in Ft. Lauderdale. Hussain returns from the airport to help Andy and me with some provisioning, sight-seeing, and clearing Police, Customs, Immigrations, and Harbor Authorities. Police, Customs, and Immigrations are a five-minute-snap; but at the Harbor Master's office, we are given what does not look to us to be an official bill for harbor fees of about $80. I stand my ground; and after much excited talking – including our suggesting we call the U.S. Consulate – the harbor master magnanimously waives the fee.

Andy and I depart at about 3 p.m.; and by about 3 a.m. the next morning, we are passing through the Bab al Mandab (Gates of Sorrow), the strait between Yemen and Djibouti at the southern end of the Red Sea. The name comes from dangerous currents and reefs at this strait.

The Red Sea is a major part of the Great Rift Valley, a fault in the continental crust of Africa and Asia. The Red Sea is the separation of Africa from Arabia caused by this continental drift.

In the Red Sea, weather for sailors is dominated by a low pressure system over the Asian continent causing a counterclockwise wind system which makes the predominate winds in the Red Sea out of the north or northwest. The Rift Valley channels the wind right down this sea which is not a pleasant thought for northbound sailors.

During the Northeast Monsoon, wind funnels across the Gulf of Aden and is turned by the mountains of the Great Rift Valley northwest into the southern part of the Red Sea until these winds are negated by the prevailing winds out of the north. The result is that from November through March the wind in the northern Red Sea is from the north and in the southern Red Sea from the south. From June through September during the Southwest Monsoon, the winds in the entire Red Sea are out of the north. Thus the least difficult time for northbound sailors is November through March. Here we are in June.

The currents of The Red Sea are also influenced by the low pressure of Asia and monsoons in the Indian Ocean. From November until March during the Northeast Monsoon, water is pushed by winds out of the southeast from the Arabian Gulf into the Gulf of Aden over the shallows of Bab al Mandab and then north into the Red Sea. From June through September when the Southwest Monsoon prevails, surface water is massaged by the wind caused by the Asian low and a southeast current prevails.

We are traveling in June and the current we find early in the Southwest Monsoon season is a quarter to a half of a knot southeast against us. The wind is always strong and will be and on our nose the rest of the way.

My perception of the Red Sea is that it would be virtually devoid of fish and wildlife, polluted by petroleum products, and extremely hot. My perceptions are all wrong. We see more fish and wildlife in the Red Sea than any other area in our circumnavigation. Pollution is negligible. Our other major surprise is that on the water it is never hot. At night it is cool enough to require a sweater or a jacket. The southeast flowing current is not made up in the Red Sea by large rivers or rainfall since all the surrounding area is desert. The water can't come through the Suez Canal as this narrow canal would require a current that no northbound ship could overcome; it thus comes from northbound currents in the depths of the Red Sea. These depths, a result of the continental drift, reach a cold 6,000 feet. The circulation of this cold water during the Southwest Monsoon and the infusion of new water during the Northeast Monsoon bring the rich nutrients which allow the abundant fish life to flourish and the marvelous but dangerous reefs of the Red Sea to develop. The reefs grow mostly along shore where the current does not cool the water. Of course, the salt content, necessary for reef growth, is high in the entire Red Sea.

Today with diesel powered merchant ships, the Red Sea is an important north and south-bound avenue of commerce. Prior to steam and diesel engines, commerce was ashore and done by camels – ships of the desert – because it was very difficult to sail ships back northbound.

With modern sailing rigs, the Red Sea even at the unfavorable time we have chosen can be sailed northbound by tacking back and forth. But this is slow business with a south-setting current. We are scheduled to pick up Katie and her college roommate Molly Peterson in Kas, Turkey, the second week of July and Pat, Sam, and Warren Wick (Katie and Molly's instructor of Classical Architecture from the University of Colorado) in Rhodes, Greece, the last week of July. So we do not have the time to claw our way up through this "hostile" environment. Our alternative is to use our cast-iron spinnaker (diesel engine) and plow, in the irons, the entire route with our nose directly into the wind and current. Sailboats are not powered like large merchant vessels; and although *Lusty Wind II* can do eight knots powering in a calm at an engine speed of 1,800 r.p.m., under these conditions, we are just able to make five knots, or about 120 nautical miles a day. At this engine speed, we burn three gallons of fuel per hour reducing our range from 1,100 nautical miles to about 600, or roughly half the length of the Red Sea.

The obstacles we face are numerous. They include 15-to-30-knot head winds, 1/4 to 1/2 knot of foul current, one of the busiest shipping lanes in the world with massive oil tankers and container ships, offshore oil rigs both on our charts and others under construction and not on the charts, sand storms which render radar useless, *jihad* on many shores, and reefs on all shores. One positive – we are, for the first time since the coast of Florida, in an area with Loran coverage and now have two electronic navigation systems operating. All the above makes the Cape of Good Hope not look so bad – but then, I've not sailed there before.

On our first day into the Red Sea, I am generating electricity, running the AC refrigeration, and making water. Then the watermaker starts making unusual noises and I shut it down. This noise has been covering up the noise the refrigerator compressor has been making; so I shut it down as well. During this process, a substantial amount of smoke starts drifting out around the electric panel. I shut the generator down; and with fire extinguisher in hand, carefully open the electric panel to find the large rotary switch, which selects the AC source from shore power, generator, or inverter, has had a melt down. I finally notice the generator is now producing 240 volts instead of 120. Our entire AC system including our ability to cook is *kaput*. However, I am able to run an extension cord directly from the inverter to the coffee pot; and thus, the most important part of this system is still operative. The inverter converts 12 volt battery power to 120 volts. We can still have coffee and use an electric frying pan carried for just this emergency.

After this excitement, I go up on deck for a little rest but discover we are in a sand storm. Andy who is on watch cannot see much beyond the bow of the boat. We hear the throbbing of huge diesel engines of ships but, of course, we can't see the ships. I go below, turn on the radar, and find the sand particles in the storm effectively filling the radar screen and no targets can be observed which means the big ships can't see us either. For about two hours while the storm persists, we move our course to very close to the edge of the navigable channel and with

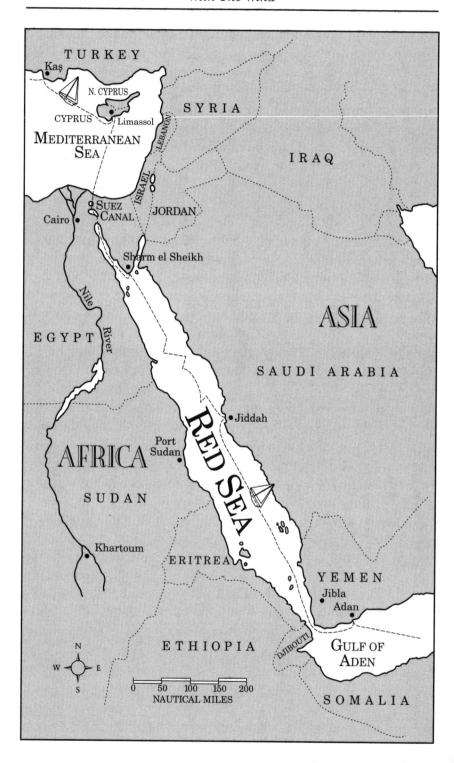

intense GPS and Loran navigation motor north with reefs on our immediate starboard side and massive invisible tankers and container ships far off on our port side – we hope.

The politics of the Red Sea largely dictate sailing plans. Yemen, where we have just had a pleasant and interesting stay, was during the early 1990's an unsafe stop for yachts. During that period, most yachts stop at the small country of Djibouti. Djibouti is a former French colony and still has substantial French Navy and Air Force installations. There are French supermarkets for the military and their dependents and they are available to provision by yachts; however, recent reports are that Muslim extremists can make anyone's stay border on unsafe and the government appears to discourage the visit of yachts.

The Red Sea province of Ethiopia is Eritrea. Eritrea is from time to time independent and has for many years been off limits to yachts. Some yachts are now visiting this coast and reporting it to be a wonderful cruising ground with a good reception from the government and the populace. This is however a very unstable political climate and not the kind of place that meets our criteria.

Saudi Arabia is unquestionably the safe country of the Middle East. Crime and terrorism are not tolerated. Unfortunately, neither is the visit of yachts or their anchoring in Saudi waters. If found in their waters without permission – which is next too impossible to obtain – the penalties are severe.

Port Sudan in the country of Sudan on the African shore, has long been a refueling, provisioning, and rest area for yachts in the Red Sea. Today the Sudan is a nation filled with *jihad* inspired political turmoil that brings on economic chaos, civil war, and refugee crises. Drought, famine and disease complete the scene. We heard reports on the Ham radio net that Muslim fundamentalists have not been hitting yachts, but have been shooting at them as they enter and leave the harbor. We also have heard that the government is getting extremely hard to deal with – as an example, international phone calls are not allowed from Port Sudan and use of a ship's single side-band radio is prohibited. To make a call, one has to take a bus or fly to the capital city Khartoum – a distance of a little over 400 miles, obtain government permission, and then make the call.

Egypt, particularly southern Egypt, is also a hot bed of *jihad* and generally considered unsafe. The assumed theory of the *jihad* is that money made from tourism is used to finance the military that supports the government and resists the fundamentalists. Their tact is to kidnap or kill tourists occasionally to reduce the flow of funds.

While all this is going on, my glucose meter stops working. I am now back to controlling blood sugar by how I feel – dangerous and not accurate, even for a diabetic with 33 years' experience.

International law requires all nations to admit and protect boats in an emergency. This international law is respected by almost all nations. On the VHF radio, we call the port authority of Jiddah, Saudi Arabia, and report we are running out of fuel and having problems with our generator. We ask if we may enter the port for fuel and repairs. We are told very politely that we may enter and will be directed to a service dock for fuel and repairs. We are also told that we will not be permitted to enter the country or get off the boat. We agree, although I am confident I can sweet-talk them into letting us enter the country after our arrival. We further report that we do not have a chart of Jiddah since we had not intended to stop there and will need to check from time-to-time during our approach. We are again politely told to check back as we feel necessary. We give our position and are given some instructions; but with the crackle of the radio, 20 knots of wind blowing in my ear, and difficult communication with the controller, it is hard to understand. He speaks English but his pronunciation is not easy for us to understand.

As we approach in the direction we think we should, we detect on the radar a large jetty protecting a harbor. The end of the jetty has a red marker and red light which, as we are in Buoyage Area A, indicate it should be on our left side as we enter the port – and we do so. As we approach the end of the jetty, we pass a Saudi Navy PT boat anchored but observe no personnel aboard. As we round the jetty and enter the port, we find a large artificial bay created by this massive jetty with the shore consisting of a huge petrol-chemical complex rivaling anything I've ever seen or even heard about. On the jetty and along the shore are 1,200 foot tankers bunkering up for delivery of refined petroleum products to a large portion of the world. I turn to Andy, "I'll bet we're not supposed to be here." We are at this point very tired and the sun is beginning to set. I'm not looking forward to moving around an unfamiliar port in the dark without a chart and I am looking out of the corner of my eye for a place we might anchor for the night. About this point we see a small work boat with several Arabs coming at us at high speed. I tell Andy, "We are about to find something out."

Aboard the boat, there are a number of smiling workers, one of whom speaks English. He informs us that we should leave this area immediately. We smile, wave, do a 180° turn, and start back to go around the red buoy. This time the PT boat we had previously passed comes around the end of the jetty at high speed. The canvas has been removed from the machine-gun on the bow and a sailor is strapping himself into it. Several sailors line both rails with rifles. They have been brought to life by their commander probably stimulated by an urgent call from the control tower of the petro-chemical complex. I don't know what "How in the _ _ _ _ did that boat get by you?" sounds like in Arabic, but I'm confident that's what they heard.

We are now dealing with angry sentries who have just been caught asleep. The PT boat comes up very close on our stern; and while several sailors scream at us, one attempts to write down the name of our vessel and the hailing port – I'm sure the U.S. flag is obvious. Our writing is, I'm sure, as strange to them as theirs is to us and they are having a great deal of difficulty. Upon completion, they pull up close along side; and again while most of the sailors scream and arm-pump their guns, the one who tried to write down the name of the boat appears to be trying to ask us a question. They have just obtained the name of the boat; so I assume they want my name and I carefully and slowly yell, "Nick Ellison." This brings a frenzy of excitement from the entire Saudi Navy crew. After a minute they calm down and ask the question again. I, of course, figure they didn't understand my answer and yell my name a second time, a little slower and louder, bringing another violent response.

Now quite fearful for our safety, I tell Andy to keep waving and smiling while I call harbor control and report our situation and position. The harbor control officer is sympathetic and says he will immediately send a pilot boat to intercede and to lead us to the service dock. He also tells us to continue traveling in the direction we are and that the pilot boat will be along in 15 to 20 minutes. As we proceed north, the PT boat stays off our starboard stern quarter and the sailors continue to scream for all they are worth. The machine-gun is pointing directly at us. I relay this information to harbor control. They advise us to continue north, the pilot boat is on its way. In a few minutes we see the red pilot boat. It is obvious someone is in radio communication with the PT boat as the screaming and hollering begins to abate. The pilot boat takes a position between us and the Navy while we continue steaming north. The PT boat follows the two of us all the way to the service dock and gives us one last major screaming fit before they turn and depart.

The crew of the pilot boat jumps ashore and assists us in tying up to the service dock directly behind a yacht hailing from Salzburg, Austria. We are immediately besieged by six Naval officers. We fill out the usual crew lists and forms. They do a thorough search of the entire boat, inventory our guns and ammunition but return them to us for safe keeping. They take all our liquor which is prohibited by their laws and ask if there is a locker we do not need access to where the liquor could be stowed. We indicate the locker under the galley sink so all the liquor is deposited there and then it is secured with a seal. These navy officers do not, however, notice there is a rear access to this locker from the aft head. The officers then take our boat registration papers and passports and we are instructed not to use any cameras while in port. Seals are put on all radios so we can't call. We are further told we need to engage a port agent to arrange for the generator repairs and any port services. We ask their recommendation and are told that in the morning they will contact Star Navigation, who will be our agent in port.

The service dock – which has no services – is directly under the new port control tower. This control tower would rival the Seattle Space Needle and is a magnificent piece of architecture. In a few minutes, a very dignified man in flowing white religious garb, glides across the huge concrete dock toward the boat in a surreal manner. This gentleman who is the Port Captain, with whom we talked on the radio. He welcomes us to Saudi Arabia and apologizes for all the difficulty. "If there is anything I can do, please let me know."

One of the officers, a young lieutenant, has been stationed in Ft. Lauderdale and his English is excellent. He is our contact and he will obtain anything we need. After the others leave, this officer asks us as the hour is late if he can get us anything for dinner. Andy says, "Do you have pizza?" This kind man returns in an hour with a large pizza in a Pizza Hut box, a two liter bottle of Pepsi, a two liter bottle of Diet Pepsi, and a stack of Pizza Hut napkins.

While we wait on deck for our pizza, a guard shack is brought to the dock and a young Saudi sailor with a machine-gun is placed as sentry.

After pizza and for me a big glass a wine sneaked through the back door of the sealed locker, we go to bed. During the night, the guard knocks on the boat every two hours and insists we both wake up and be seen. Like a teenager coming home late, I hold my wino breath.

Early the next morning Hussainin, our man from Star Navigation, arrives. Hussainin turns out to be pleasant and helpful. He brings a loaf of fresh bakery bread and an English newspaper. We tell Hussainin we need fuel, water, and a mechanic for the generator. We explain the problem is electrical and that the engine that drives the generator is working fine.

The following morning Hussainin arrives again with a loaf of fresh bakery bread and an English newspaper. Very shortly mechanics and electricians will come to give us an estimate on the repair of the generator. The group arrives and are Philippinos working for a company that normally does repairs on massive ships. I'm sure my generator looks like a toy to them. They turn it on, watch the gauges, and study wiring diagrams in the technical manual. The manual is, of course, in English and these mechanics and electricians only speak Spanish. In the process, the lead electrician turns absolutely white and makes a mad dash for the head where he blows breakfast. That's the first person I've ever seen get seasick tied to a dock. He apologizes and says he must leave immediately; however, his apprentice stays and cleans up the mess.

We meet Heinz and Riki, the crew of the Austrian yacht. Heinz is a young computer engineer and Riki is his delightful wife. Riki is the only bright spot in our stay.

Later in the afternoon, the electrician from the repair company comes back and from the dock and says the generator will have to be removed and the armature rewired; a process that will take two weeks and cost approximately $2,000. I tell him we do not have the time nor the funds and he, very politely, leaves.

The lieutenant in charge of us comes by several times to ask if he can be of help. We need to do some shopping and ask if he can drive us to town. He tells us to make a list of what we need and he will go get it. We tell him that won't work and we really need to shop ourselves. He consents to talk to his superiors.

Friday, June 11. It is another Muslim Holy Day; and for us, principally a day of rest. The Austrian Ambassador brings a basket of fruit to Heinz and Riki. They share some with us and we give them several cans of Dixie Chili and wish them bon-appetite.

The guards allow Heinz and Riki to take long walks on the dock. Andy assumes this privilege extends to him; so he goes out on the dock to play hacky-sack. The guard watches in great amazement, puts down his rifle, and joins in the game. Within a few minutes, two officers from the Navy base, speed up in a Mercedes, put a new guard on duty, and leave with Andy's friend. The guard is probably still scrubbing latrines at some Saudi Navy base.

Early in the afternoon, two of the navy officers come by and try to buy our three guns, especially our stainless steel M14. We know that could be a serious problem and refuse. These two then badger us out of three bottles of wine. They break and replaced the seal on the locker. Later in the day, we see them in a runabout – neither one could have hit the water with his hat. No one seems to notice – I think we have dodged another bullet.

During the day, Andy and I replace the rotary switch on the AC system regaining our use of 120 volt electricity, at least through the inverter. The generator, of course, is still out of operation and there is no shore power.

Observing Heinz and Riki's freedom, I carry our garbage to a refuse container and then have a closer look at the harbor control tower. My ulterior motive is to make contact with the Harbor Master and solicit his help in obtaining fuel and securing our release. I enter and find the building to be principally a Mosque and am immediately chased by several men in the white religious garb. I run back to the boat and to a guard who is obviously displeased.

It is Saturday morning. They say they will take us into town for groceries about 4 p.m. The lieutenant in charge arrives with a chauffeur-driven black Chevy Impala. The first stop is a bank to cash some travelers checks and call home. Our second stop is a walking tour of the ancient market of Jiddah. Our lieutenant escort gets upset if Andy or I become separated and he cannot keep a watchful eye on both of us. We understand and try to make his job easier. We then walk by a Kentucky Fried Chicken restaurant to some sort of Arab fast food restaurant, and the three of us have dinner. The lieutenant has taken Heinz and Riki on a similar trip and they have eaten at Kentucky Fried Chicken. Heinz told us "Kentucky Fried Chicken will not let Riki in since she is a woman; so we had to eat our 'chickens' outside."

We walk to a multilevel downtown shopping center with hundreds of small shops and several large stores, including a supermarket. It is the first real grocery store we have been in since Australia and certainly the first filled with stuff we can understand. It is wonderful to find Kellogg's Corn Flakes, Skippy Peanut Butter, and Campbell's Soup. We even find a box of Sunshine Oyster Crackers for our Dixie Chili. At the checkout counter, our guide gets us the 10% military discount. Just as we finish our shopping, all customers and employees are asked to leave the store. It is closed and the lights turned off for a one-hour prayer period. We wait in the mall as all other stores close. After the hour of rest, we visit several smaller shops including one like the nut shops in our shopping centers that specialize in dates. We buy small bags of several varieties. At the grocery store, our guide had steered us away from ice cream, dairy products, and meat products; we don't understand why but figure it out later when he takes us back after the prayer hour. It is to eliminate spoilage while we have waited.

The next morning after Hussainin arrives with his customary loaf of bread and newspaper, a large stainless steel water truck arrives and fills all four of our tanks with enough water left over to hose down the decks to get rid of the residue of salt from the sea and sand and dirt from the sand storms. There is still plenty of water; so we fill Heinz and Riki's tanks as well. We hope this makes it up to Riki for her not being allowed into the Kentucky Fried Chicken restaurant.

A little later a small barge is brought over to the boat, and 310 gallons of clean fresh diesel fuel is pumped aboard. A bit later Hussainin comes by to settle up his bill which is very modest except for a charge of $100 for water. He tell us we will probably not have to pay for the diesel fuel. After settling, Hussainin goes back to his car and returns with a bag containing a cake and ice cream.

Just before noon our passports and boat papers are returned to us. The guards tell us the fuel is compliments of the Saudi Government. Only in Saudi Arabia will diesel fuel be free and water 30 cents a gallon. Heinz, Riki, and the guard help with the dock lines and we are off – finally.

For the first day and a half, we motor-sail into 15 knots of head wind and a half knot of foul current.

Tuesday, June 15. The wind is up to 20-25 knots and we have slowed to four knots. I attempt to repair a pulley on the water pressure pump, but, too much vice pressure cracks it in two. I am able to epoxy it back together and have water pressure back on-line shortly after the epoxy dries.

During the night, we cross the Tropic of Cancer. It is Wednesday. The wind is down to 10 knots on our nose and our northern progress increases to five-and-a-half knots. We pass a merchant ship, *Tare Tare*, out of Malta and they ask us on the VHF if there is anything we need; we thank them and say, "All we really need is some wind out of the south."

As we approach the northern end of the Red Sea, where the Gulf of Acuba goes off to the right and the Gulf of Suez goes north, we hear substantial military traffic on the VHF. Soon we see a large number of ships representing the United Nations blockading access to Iraq through the Gulf of Acuba and Jordan. The navies engaged in this operation are the United States at the lead plus France, Italy, and Fiji. A U.S. Navy helicopter, just a few feet off the water, approaches us. Andy has his shirt off and is sitting with his back toward the helicopter and his long hair hanging down over his shoulders. I can see the expressions of disappointment and amusement from the four male aviators when he turns around and they find he isn't the topless redhead they have expected.

We approach Sharm el Sheikh at the southern end of the Sinai Peninsula at about six o'clock and come into a harbor surrounded by hotels and filled with various sailboats and dive boats. Sharm means inlet and Sheikh means king.

After anchoring, a man from an Egyptian sailboat dinghies over and helpfully explains that only Egyptian ships are allowed in this harbor and we will have to go around the point of land to the commercial harbor to anchor and clear Customs. He suggests we do that quickly before we are noticed by the officials. We take his advice and an hour later round into the commercial harbor and anchor. Because of the late hour, we will not be able to clear Customs and Immigrations until tomorrow. The harbor holds two other foreign yachts and a temporary Italian Navy base for several destroyers that were participating in the blockade. From all appearances, these destroyers were probably inherited by Mussolini when he took power. Several times while they are moving in the bay they lose power and have to be towed back to their base.

Friday, June 18. We quickly clear Customs and Immigrations and then walk to Sharm el Sheikh. I expect little more than a few Bedouins, camels, goats, and sheep at this tip of the Sinai Peninsula – "The Great and Terrible Wilderness" of the Bible.

*   *   *

Through the centuries, much activity has taken place here. In the 16th century B.C., the Egyptians crossed Sinai to conquer Palestine and Syria. Moses crossed in the 12th century B.C. after getting the Egyptian army drowned. In the 3rd century B.C., Alexander the Great marched the other way to conquer Egypt. During the first century, Mary, Joseph, and Jesus fled to Sinai to escape King Herod. The Arabs came across in the 7th century A.D. to bring Islam to Egypt and

Africa. In the 16th century, the Ottomans stormed across the Sinai to make Egypt and most of the shores of the Red Sea part of their empire. Of all these back and forth wars, the most recent is the Israeli occupation of the Sinai from 1979 through 1982. The Bedouins who live in the Sinai have watched all this give and take for over 36 centuries and have paid little attention.

During the Israeli occupation, the tourist attraction of the southern tip of the Sinai became apparent, and the Israelites began to develop the resort that we have just entered. In the last ten years, the economic value has become apparent to the Egyptians. A massive resort complex, including Sheridan Hotels, Hilton Hotels, Movinpik Hotels, and many condominiums have been developed. Ras Mohammed and numerous other reefs are among the greatest dive sites in the world and divers principally from Europe but also from all over the world come to this area. The Bedouins have finally taken note of an invasion and operate restaurants, camel rides, stores, and dive operations.

* * *

We hitch-hike to the tourist area and up the hill to the Hilton Hotel where we have deluxe cheeseburgers and a couple of good cold beers. After looking around, we walk back to the boat and stop at an Italian dive shop to make arrangements for a dive trip for Andy the next day.

When we return to the boat, we find the old man whom we are paying to watch our dinghy quite distraught as the starboard air tube in the dinghy has ruptured. Although he had tried to hold it up with some lines, the dinghy is half submerged in the water. I think we can get back to the boat with the two remaining tubes but the old man won't hear of it and he offers us a ride and tow for our dinghy. After getting the engine off, the dinghy aboard and the tube out, we find the rip much too large for repair. Andy suggests we fix it with a bung, and several hose clamps. I am sure this won't work but I agree to try. We put the bung into the tear – fat end first – and tighten two hose-clamps around the rubber. We put it all back and the dinghy is in operation – just a little down on the starboard side. Andy was right.

By cab, we go to Ras Mohammed at the southern most point of the Sinai Peninsula. We are struck by the great contrast between the barren desert and the profusion and variety of life on the reef. The water, however, at this turning point of the current is from the deep and very cold. This cold water is all the more startling because the air temperature ashore is 103°.

Monday, June 21. After some minor difficulties clearing out with officials, we weigh anchor a little after noon and sail on a beam reach around Ras Mohammed and then northeast into the Gulf of Suez ending our short sail with a 14-knot head wind.

During the evening, the wind grows to 25 to 30 knots and the seas are heavy. Our forward progress, hobby-horsing in these short seas against this wind is less than two knots. The autopilot is having difficulty holding course and swings us 25° to 30° to port and starboard. We hand steer and find nearly the same problem. The trouble is not the autopilot but the hydraulic steering. We bleed the system and top off the hydraulic fluid. We had been pumping air throughout the system and we are thus trying to steer with compressed air which doesn't work too well in a system designed for hydraulic fluid.

Steering problem solved. Flushing problem ahead. Marine heads are designed so that the user needs to put his face almost in the bowl while pumping the flush handle. At the bottom of the bowl is a rubber check valve designed to let whatever is in the bowl out without allowing sea water to flow back in. The design dictates that the forward stroke pumps the waste into the sea; and the return stroke pumps sea water through the rim of the bowl. The rubber check valve is held in place with a small brass rivet which has corroded to oblivion. On the second stroke, with my face in the bowl, a stream of the waste water spouts through the empty rivet hole and hits me right in the face. With one out of commission we discover the real reason two heads are better than one.

By morning, the winds are still at 25-30 knots and Andy calculates we have actually lost a little ground during his two hour watch. During the morning on the VHF radio, we hear several other sailboats trying to get out of this difficult situation. One has wandered into an oil refinery on the Sinai side and is getting a substantial amount of grief on the radio from the pilot of a large oil tanker – this yacht's anchorage is making his maneuvering difficult. Andy and I anchor just south of Ras Dib; and while Andy sleeps, I rebuild the aft head replacing the rubber check valve and its rivet. Ras means cape and we are out of the north wind for a short respite.

By Wednesday, June 23, the winds and waves have subsided. We weigh anchor and continue. As we approach the southern end of the Suez, two small boats are approaching us. We are called on the VHF radio by a person who identifies himself as the Suez Port Captain and who advises us that an official pilot boat is bringing us a pilot. He further says there is another boat ahead of it that is unofficial and we should not take its pilot aboard. We will know the correct ship because it is flying a large British flag. As we converge, there is an unofficial looking boat with a man on the bow ready to jump aboard *Lusty Wind II*. It is followed by another boat flying a British flag that is half as big as the boat. The first pilot comes along side and we tell him to get away since he is not our official pilot. Before we know it, Abdulmoniem Abbas Sokkar is aboard. Abdul explains to us we are not talking to the port authority because they do not talk to yachts; the other boat is telling us these lies so that we will hire them instead of him. Meanwhile "harbor control" is telling us we are making a big mistake. At that point, I feel I have at least a half chance of being wrong but decide to stick with the man who is already aboard – particularly as his boat is now racing back to Suez and nearly out of sight. Abdul attempts to ease our mind by explaining to us that he is the best pilot and agent and his pricing is very fair. He explains the other boat is operated by the self-proclaimed "Prince of the Red Sea" and the prince overcharges his clients. Somehow, all this is not making me feel any better. As a reference, Abdul offers Tania Aebi on *Varuna*. We checked *Maiden Voyage*, Tania's book, and find this is true.

Abdul guides us to the Suez Yacht Club operated by the Suez Canal Authority for the benefit of canal employees and transiting yachts. He then directs us to a buoy. As we approach, Abdul takes a line and lowers himself over our bow onto the buoy, which bobs aside. He is hanging by his hands on our lifelines with his toes pointed up to keep his slippers from falling into the water. I ask if I can help and he replies, "Oh, please do." Not being strong enough to lift him by myself, Andy has to leave the helm and come forward quickly to help me get Abdul aboard. Then Andy runs back to the helm to keep us from hitting any of the other yachts tied to buoys. Our second approach is more successful. Within a few minutes, we launch the dinghy to take a now grateful Abdul ashore with our passports and boat papers to begin working on all our Customs, Immigrations, and Canal transit paperwork.

A few hundred feet from us is the yacht club dinghy

dock. Over and over Abdul calls Andy from the dock. Each time I wake Andy and send him in, only to find that Abdul wants me. I finally ask Abdul why he calls Andy and not me; he smiles, hesitates, and tells me in so-many-words that "nick" in Arabic is not only a four-letter-word but the queen mother of four-letter-words. I guess that explains the hostile response by the crew of the Saudi Navy PT boat and probably explains why we were detained for five days.

Abdul turns out to be everything he promised, making shore arrangements for us, arranging for fuel, showing us where the best groceries are, and handling all our *pratique* and canal permission. Abdul's fee for all the above and several days' work is just about $60. Our agreement, in Arab fashion, is settled over a cup of tea, with no handle on the cup.

We have two choices for the roughly 75-mile overland trip from Suez to Cairo. The first is by public bus which will cost about $3 a person each way. The second choice is to hire a cab for the round trip. Abdul arranges this at a cost of about $80. Tour busses are occasionally targets of the *jihad* and not recommended.

Our cab waits in Cairo while we spend several hours in the Egyptian Museum, which is one of the greatest in the world. A number of years ago, Egypt was getting a bad name because of the hassling of tourists by people offering themselves as guides, etc. To counter this problem, the government developed Tourist Police who have special uniforms and are at all tourist areas to protect people from this annoyance. Unfortunately now the Tourist Police have brought the practice of hassling tourists to a science and we are besieged by these officers offering themselves as guides. They ask, "Where are you from"; and then say, "US number one" with their index finger up. We tell one we are from Denmark and he says, "Denmark number one" with his index finger up.

Before lunch, our cab takes us to Giza and the driver directs us to a wonderful Egyptian restaurant and some other friends of his who rent us camels for the trip up the hill to the pyramids.

*   *   *

The Giza pyramids rank as one of the Seven Wonders of the Ancient World. They have stood through 4,500 years, through the rise and fall of dynasties and conquerors.

The most interesting story for us has been realized in just the last few years. For years, no pattern of size or position can be ascertained for the three Giza pyramids. It is always a mystery why the first two pyramids are the largest and the last built is the smallest. In our modern cities each bank that builds an office tower builds it larger than the competitor before. So why, Egyptologists have asked, is the last one built the smallest? Only recently has a new theory been presented. The tomb areas of the pyramids have what were thought to be air shafts. The first clue to these mysteries was when it was discovered that the "air shaft" to the King's chamber in the pyramid of Cheaps gave the King's mummy a view of the constellation Orion as it comes high into the sky at the height that indicated to the Egyptians, as it does farmers today, the beginning of their planting season. The planting season, of course, symbolizes renewal of life. It was then noticed that the three pyramids represent the location and magnitude of the three stars that make up the belt of Orion. More study indicates remote ruins at the point of the right hand and left leg of Orion and that the river Nile and the Milky Way are both in proper relationship. It is fascinating to find this association to our old friend Orion of our Pacific, Indian Ocean, and past Atlantic crossings.

The wealth and splendor of the early Egyptian culture was largely to the same phenomena that made our northbound trip in the Red Sea so difficult and required the frankincense and spice trade to travel on land instead of the Red Sea. The Nile in these early times was not only a supply of fresh water and new soil for farm lands after every flood, but it was a near perfect transportation system. The winds out of the North caused by the low pressure over Siberia blew trading vessels with lanteen sails south up the Nile River. To return north merely required sails to be dropped. The current of the river would bring them back to the cities of the delta. Evidence has been found indicating this commerce flourished 1,500 years before the pyramids are built.

* * *

On our return to Suez, we find *Shadowfax* (the horse's name in J. R. Tolkien's *Lord of the Rings*) tied to a buoy at the yacht club. I have been reading newspaper articles from *The Islander*, a Sanibel, Florida, newspaper following *Shadowfax's* circumnavigation. We quickly meet Scott and Gretchen McPhee and their companion Sue. Scott and Gretchen are astounded to find someone who has read their articles. Gretchen helped pay for their trip by making black market T-shirts. The shirt of the moment is "Red Sea 93" – my favorite.

We go to the fuel dock for 290 gallons of clean fuel at 90¢ per gallon.

* * *

The first canal linking the Mediterranean and the Red Sea was built in 1800 B.C. It was an irrigation canal to irrigate farm land east of the delta with water from the Nile. During flood periods, this canal was navigable and was eventually extended to the Great Bitter Lake which was at that time connected by water to the Red Sea. The irrigation channel was improved by the Romans and became a small canal.

Several times during the 15th century, the Venetians who controlled the frankincense and spice trade proposed a canal but could not gain the cooperation of the Ottoman Empire which then controlled this area. By the 15th century, the irrigation canal was silted in and the Great Bitter Lake was no longer connected to the Red Sea.

In 1798, Napoleon visited Egypt and ordered a survey for a canal. Additional studies were made in 1834 and again in 1846. Finally in 1854, Ferdinand de Lesseps becomes interested and received permission from Mohammed Saíd to construct a canal. He formed the Compagnie Universelle du Canal Maritime de Suez and officially received the right to build a canal and operate it for 99 years. Construction began in 1859 and lasted ten years, four years more than the six projected. Costs were $100 million dollars. De Lesseps had many similar problems in the construction of the Suez Canal that as an old man he faced in the Panama Canal including a cholera epidemic which brought the construction to a complete halt. The French owned 52% of de Lesseps' company. Most of the rest was owned by Mohammed Saíd. The stock of Saíd was later sold to the British government to cover his heirs' financial excesses. By an international agreement of 1858, the canal is to be open to all nations in war and peace. The Anglo-Egyptian Treaty of 1936 gave Great Britain the right to maintain defense forces at the canal's approaches making the canal unavailable to the Axis Powers. The canal was continually operated until taken over by Nasser's Egyptian government in 1956. During border clashes, Israel invaded Egypt and the canal was closed again for about six months. During the Arab-Israel War of June 1967, the canal was closed and not reopened until 1975.

Six principal parts make up the Suez Canal – an important 87.5 nautical mile waterway.

- The first part is a 14.5 mile sea-level canal running from the north end of the Gulf of Suez to Little Bitter Lake. Ten miles north of the Suez there is a highway tunnel under the canal that was opened in 1980. The tunnel eliminated a swing bridge, a previous obstacle.
- The Little Bitter Lake was used to extend the canal seven-an-a half nautical miles with an almost 90° turn to the West.
- The Great Bitter Lake extended the canal 12.5 miles with a turn almost 90° back North. This 12.5 nautical-mile stretch has double lanes allowing ships to pass.
- The fourth part is a 10.5 nautical-mile canal connecting The Great Bitter Lake to Lake Timsah.
- Lake Timsah extends the canal three nautical miles.
- The northern most canal stretches 39.5 nautical miles to Port Said. Of the 39.5 miles, five have double lanes and there are two operating automobile ferries.

There is now an additional canal at the north end by-passing Port Said.

The original canal was built to a depth of 26 feet with a width at the bottom of 72 feet and at the surface of 230 feet. With recent improvements the canal now has a controlling depth of 64 feet. It is now 358 feet wide at the bottom and 919 feet wide at the surface. Tides are 1.5 feet at the Mediterranean end and 6 feet at the Gulf of Suez. The surface of the Red Sea is a little higher than the Mediterranean and thus the north-bound current is most affected by the tidal difference.

The first year of canal operation, 486 ships transited, or 1.5 per day; now 47 transit per day. With the recent improvements to the canal, super-tankers can transit empty but most cannot when fully loaded – thus, super-tankers can be seen riding high southbound but not northbound. The importance today of

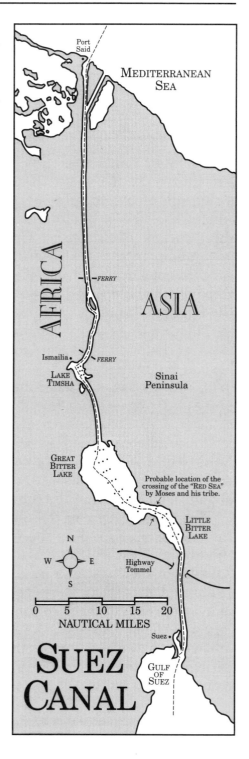

the canal is that 70% of all cargo is petroleum, which is vital to the economies of Western Europe. That cargo is the reason the canal has become a terrorism target.

* * *

The Suez Canal does not charge vessels of 300 tons or less but part of our settlement with Abdul includes payment of a $60 administrative fee to the Canal Authority. The only additional cost is $10 in tips and three cartons of cigarettes. This *bachsheesh*, or extortion, is common in the Arab world. Still this is an amazing bargain considering the alternative is a trip around the Cape of Good Hope. The Suez fee is half that charged by the Panama Canal.

Monday, June 28 is our prescribed day of transit. We wake at 5 a.m. to meet the Canal Pilot who is to be at the boat at 6 a.m. He arrives, in typical Egyptian fashion, at 9:30. Our pilot is very pleasant but speaks no English and makes little or no effort to communicate beyond pointing.

Our trip is timed to start immediately after a northbound convoy and we will wait in The Great Bitter Lake while a southbound convoy passes and another northbound convoy passes for us to follow. Our speed is about seven knots and the convoys are 13-14 knots.

The buoy system on the Suez Canal is green buoys on the east side and red on the west. The canal conforms to the rules of lateral buoyage, or buoyage of a channel parallel to the coast of a land mass. The rule is that the preferred direction of travel is clockwise. Since it is buoyage area A and the continent is interpreted to be the larger of the two, or Asia, the green buoys are on the right and red on the left for north-bound travelers. This is different from the Panama Canal where halfway is returning and halfway is going to sea.

After transiting 14.5 nautical miles of canal, we enter Little Bitter Lake. Between this lake and Great Bitter Lake is where archeologists now believe Moses and his tribe crossed the "Red Sea" and where the Egyptian army was drowned. These lakes could quickly dry and flood. Remember the Great Bitter Lake was once part of the Red Sea. For obvious reasons, the Egyptians have not erected historical markers.

In The Great Bitter Lake, our pilot directs us to a buoy out of the fairway and instructs us to tie to it. This stop coincides with the prayer hour and our pilot rolls a small prayer rug out on our deck. For most of the period, we politely wait while he prays facing Mecca. The buoy is red and on the west, or left hand of the canal.

We can see the northbound convoy coming into the Great Bitter Lake, we untie and allow them to pass. We slowly fall in behind to continue our transit. By 5 p.m., we arrive in Lake Timsah and anchor off the City of Ismailia. As we anchor, a small canal work boat approaches to pick up our pilot. We tip our pilot the customary $5 and several packs of American cigarettes. A very congenial Muslim "policeman," or priest-at-large, stands in the pilot boat. His greeting is, "How is Jesus for you today?"

He translates several instructions from our pilot including notice that we should stay on board and not visit the City of Ismailia. We are further instructed to give *backsheesh* to the entire crew including one crewmember whom we do not see and assume does not exist down in the engine room.

Tuesday, June 29. The pilot boat returns bringing us a new pilot and requiring *backsheesh* for everyone on board, again including the unseen Arab in the engine room. Our affable pilot speaks no English but somehow tells us he has four young daughters. He insists on my taking a picture of him with Andy to show to these girls. He can't write but tells us his address, which we can't begin to understand, and are thus unable to send the picture.

By 3:30 p.m. we are in Port Said with another pilot boat picking up our pilot, and requiring a tip and *backsheesh*. We are glad to get rid of all our cigarettes. By 5 p.m. we have escaped the gauntlet endured for the past 25 days and 1,466 nautical miles.

11

CHAPTER ELEVEN

Up the Middle Sea

July 30, 1993 – September 14, 1993

Port Said – Puerto Bañus, Spain

There are a few clouds in the sky our first morning in the Mediterranean which are the first we have seen since we had been in the Indian Ocean a month earlier. We are traveling north across the Levantine Sea and the winds are out of the west making for a very comfortable broad reach; it is a refreshing feeling to be sailing after motoring so long. The Levant refers to the Eastern Mediterranean and comes from the French verb to rise (the sun in its relation to France) as does unleavened bread (it doesn't rise). Our approach to Limassol, Cyprus, is shortly after midnight. Being in the Mediterranean, we have few reefs with which to concern ourselves; but rather than try to negotiate a new port in the dark, we anchor out and wait for morning.

After five hours rest, I have awakened, gotten Andy up, weighed anchor, and we are entering the yacht harbor at the Sheridan Hotel. As our cruising guide indicates, there is a quarantine berth and we tie up there. Andy goes back to sleep, and I fix a cup of coffee. On deck enjoying my coffee, I suddenly notice two uniformed Custom officials looking us over from a second story balcony. One spreads his arms and with a big smile says, "Welcome to Cyprus." This official reception is unlike any since Australia and it is made even more significant by our recent trials through the Arab world. I tell these officers I will be right up to clear; they smiled again and say, "Take your time – enjoy your coffee and this beautiful Cyprus morning."

After quickly handling *pratique* and registering with the marina office, I awaken Andy again to take the boat to our assigned spot. We are now about to make a Mediterranean mooring – a maneuver feared by us and other American sailors accustomed to tying up alongside finger piers. In the Mediterranean, though, sailors drop anchor and back to a pier with boats only a fender away to both port and starboard. The theory is the anchor keeps the stern of the boat from hitting the dock and the two stern lines keep the boat from going back out to sea. The whole deal is complicated by some boats spreading out three anchors which overlap and tangle with those of their neighbors. It's thus advantageous not to stay too long so other people's anchor lines are not on top of yours when departing. In tourist harbors, most crews put out one anchor and allow the bow of their boat to swing a bit when the wind blows.

Our assigned spot is next to an elegant motor yacht and the owner is on deck to keep us from doing any damage. All boaters in the Mediterranean know that Americans cannot back sailboats, and this is, of course, an important part of the arrangement. As we expect, things are not going well. We find ourselves unable to back in a straight line into the narrow space. Our neighbor is yelling, "Go faster, go faster, let out rode, let out rode. Trust your engine and transmission; they'll stop you before you hit the dock." Since it is his boat we are likely to scrape, I follow his advice and find much to my amazement with adequate sternway I can steer and maneuver. I just need to remember to turn to port to go to starboard. Meanwhile, Andy is forward paying out just enough chain. Our new neighbor is quickly on the dock to secure our stern lines and all turns out well.

We spend our first day back in the western world cashing travelers checks, renting a car, and making arrangements with mechanics for all the necessary repairs to our generator, refrigerator, and watermaker. We are directed to Tony, an excellent mechanic, who reschedules other jobs to work on our generator. The only blemish on the day is when this navigator side-swipes a Pepsi truck with the rental car. Andy sees great justice in this as the rental agency thinks he is too young to drive.

To our pleasant surprise, the generator coils are fine and do not need rewinding. The problem is a defective diode and a new one costs less than a dollar. With Tony's charge of $150 this is much less than the $2,000 quoted in Jiddah. From Egypt, we ordered a new 120 volt compressor for the refrigeration and a new motor for the watermaker. When the parts arrive, Tony installs the watermaker motor and recommends a refrigeration mechanic who installs the new compressor. We also purchase a new dinghy – our old one, *Sam*, is now leaking badly.

* * *

The Mediterranean, or sea in the middle of land, was formed from the Great Tethys Sea which eons ago encircled the Eastern Hemisphere. When Europe and Africa slid toward each other and

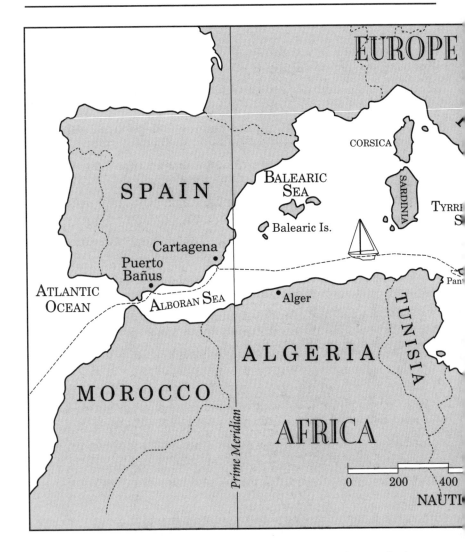

joined at Gibraltar, an enclosed sea was formed. As most of the area south of this sea is desert and the area north is just a short distance from the European Continental Divide, little water flows into this sea, actually only about one-third of what is lost through evaporation. In time the land bridge between Spain and Morocco eroded away and a

great flood of water entered. Today, because of evaporation exceeding the water from rivers, there is a six foot difference in the Mediterranean and the higher level of the Atlantic causing a constant inflow of surface water through the Strait of Gibraltar. This flow is a little stronger in the summer months when the evaporation is greater.

The Aegean Sea has a slight current moving south as the water from the Danube River and the plains of Russia flow into the Black Sea and then through the Bosporus, the Marmara Denizi, and the Dardanelles into the Mediterranean. This is the source of much of the Mediterranean makeup water.

The Mediterranean has almost no tide. The small area of this sea is only slightly influenced by the gravitational pull of the sun and the moon. The tidal fluctuation of the Atlantic Ocean only affects the rate of flow of the current inbound at Gibraltar and has no other measurable effect on the Mediterranean.

Wind in the Mediterranean, particularly in the summer months, is predominately from the Northwest. This is again a result of the Coriolios Effect and our old nemesis, the low pressure system over Siberia turning counter clockwise.

* * *

After a broad reach on our northeast course from Port Said to Cyprus, we find the wind almost always comes from the direction we were going. Odysseus, without a diesel engine, took nearly 10 years to get back to Itháki; and based on our experience I would say he had a fair passage. Odysseus believed these contrary winds to have been caused by Aeolus' opening a bag of winds and letting them out; if he had had a toilet, he might have correctly understood the Coriolios Effect. This wind that plagued Odysseus and us in the Aegean is called by the Turkish name *meltimi*.

These winds are part of the same system caused by the predominant low over Siberia – the same low that made northbound travel in the Red Sea difficult.

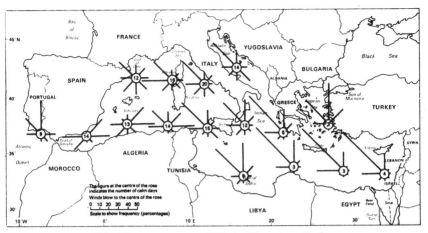

Mediterranean Pilot Chart – July

Lines radiating out of circles indicate percentage
of the time wind is out of each direction.
Number in the circle is percentage of calm days.

The pilot chart for the month of July illustrates our
summer time sailing difficulties. It indicates we should
have good sailing from Itháki to Malta and from Tunis
to Spain – we do not. As in "down east", down and up
relate to the wind for sailors who, of course, are always at
sea level. We are to spend three months sailing up this
middle sea.

* * *

The Mediterranean, if not the cradle of civilization, is certainly the cradle of Western Civilization.
It has been swept back and forth by merchants and
conquerors for 3,000 years or more. These were the
peaceful Minoans, Phoenician traders, Persian
invaders, Greek and Carthagean rivals, Alexander

the Great, Romans, Viking raiders, Venetian merchants, Muslim and Christian rivals, English and French rivals, Hitler and Mussolini, and now the United States Navy's Sixth Fleet.

The major problem that faces the people of the Mediterranean Sea today is pollution. With the current generally moving east it is difficult to get all the individual nations bordering this sea to treat sewage which the current will sweep to their neighbors. There is little recirculation of the water to the open ocean and the problem just gets worse. Since the major outlet is evaporation almost all the pollution remains. It is estimated the water in the sea is only renewed every 80 years. We can only hope in the future economic and political cooperation plus technology will reverse this disastrous trend.

* * *

We depart Limassal but it is a departure marred by steering difficulties. The problem is low hydraulic fluid; we add fluid and are soon at sea. Obviously we have a leak somewhere. Until I repair it, I must remember to top off the system at every opportunity.

After a trip of a day and a half, we sail past the outpost Greek Island of Kastellóizon to the Turkish city of Kas. Kas is principally a tourist stop and it appears no one is awake at 6 a.m. Fortunately we find a spot on the quay, make our turn, drop our anchor, and start backing in. My shouting directions at Andy who is busy paying out anchor chain and fending off on our port and starboard awakes a wino who stumbles up from his sleep to help us with our stern lines. All-in-all the maneuver works pleasantly well – we don't even arouse the occupants of the boats on either side. The wino and Andy go back to sleep and I put on a pot of coffee, retie our lines, then sit down to enjoy the cool morning quiet before taking care of Turkish *pratique*.

After simple clearance procedures, I return to the boat to find Katie and Molly aboard. They already have Andy up and are exchanging travel stories. I sense the nature of these stories change on my return. Katie and Molly flew to Istanbul and have taken a bunch of bus rides with stops along the Turkish Aegean coast. Their mission is to study and sketch Greek and Roman ruins for an independent study course that they had arranged through the University of Colorado. Somehow they have been able to arrange for their instructor, Warren Wick, to join us later in Ródhos (Rhodes) and further supervise their studies. As Katie's father, I am a bit shaken to hear that, rather than spend nine dollars to rent hotel rooms, they paid two dollars to gain permission to sleep on the roof. Katie has my new glucose meter and generator governor solenoid with her and I will gladly pay the other seven dollars to keep everybody and everything safe.

This southern coast of Turkey, the Turquoise Coast, can best be described as being like the foothills of the Colorado Rockies. But on the Turquoise Coast, the ocean laps against them and they additionally are sprinkled with Lycean, Greek, Roman, and Byzantine ruins. Kas is an exceptionally beautiful city especially with the Lycean tombs that are carved into the hills and are now flood-lit at night. Many buildings are covered with bougainvillea.

In the morning with the *meltimi* blowing strongly from the northwest, a family on a charter boat comes into the harbor and attempts a Mediterranean moor on the portside of the boat to our portside. They don't allow for enough scope and their anchor doesn't hold. The captain is yelling, "Pull on the anchor line" which only reduces their scope and makes matters worse. Before they know it, they are being pressed by the wind against the bows of three moored boats. The best part of the whole show for me is their teenage daughter in a bikini lying on the swim platform trying with her feet to hold their boat off one of the three they were lying against. The boat is obviously tangled up in the anchor lines of the three victim boats; and with the strong wind there appears to be no solution. It is all I can muster to keep from adding to the captain's woe by video taping the whole procedure; I know how he surely felt. In the middle of all this, the Dutch captain of the boat to our port, who in several days has spoken no English, raises both of his arms, says, "No good" and goes below. In due time, a Turkish navy patrol boat comes along, ties lines on the bow and stern of the vessel, and pulls her free sideways. The patrol boat then releases the line on the stern, backs the charter boat into its slip, and properly places the anchor. They've done this before.

By 2:30 p.m., the wind has dropped to almost none. We clear out of Turkey and depart for Ródhos. By 5 p.m. the *meltimi* is on our nose at 16 knots; the sea rough, and the ride slow and wet. The next morning, the wind is out of the east at 20 knots and I am reluctant to enter crowded Ródhos to attempt a Mediterranean mooring in this wind. The excitement of the day before is a strong influence. After studying the chart, I pick Bozuk Bükü, Turkey, to wait for the winds to die down.

Bozuk Bükü is not a port of entry; and since we have cleared out of Turkey, our stay is not legal. It looks to be a small enough place not to bother with *pratique* and that turns out to be the case. There is a restaurant at the end of the quiet bay with several moorings for customers. A cute little girl age six or seven rows out to a mooring and assists us in tying up. She then rows us ashore so we can make reservations for dinner at the Lorina Restaurant owned and operated by her family.

During the afternoon, Andy hikes to the top of the hill to take pictures and Molly, Katie, and I take the dinghy to see ruins of a byzantine fortification at the entrance to the harbor. Later in the afternoon, we watch the little girl's mother use a large wooden paddle to take loaves of bread out of a stone hearth 100 feet away from the restaurant. The aroma in the light breeze is too much. We dinghy ashore and sit down for a beer. Katie makes admiring comments about the bread and we are quickly served a loaf with a pound of butter – which all too quickly disappears – plus more cold Turkish beer. The next day the winds are down and my plan is to reach Ródhos by 11 o'clock, the time boats will be leaving this crowded harbor. We weigh anchor, depart Bozuk Bükü at 8 a.m., and motor into Mandraki Harbor at 10:45. Just as we come in, a boat is leaving a space just east of the entrance. As the wind is up a bit, we decide to come in bow first using our stern anchor to hold our bow off the quay. With the help of a passing policeman, we tie up.

Anchoring bow to has advantages – much better control on approach (one doesn't need so much control going out), more privacy in the cockpit, less likelihood of damaging the boat's rudder on rocks just below the quay, and easier launching of the dinghy from the stern davits. Disadvantages – the boat stands out like the bird on the *New Yorker* cover and it is more difficult for us to climb over the bow than the stern. A dedicated stern anchor is helpful.

The Greek word *mandrake* means flock of sheep; and

the diminutive *mandraki*, a small flock symbolizing the protected grouping of boats in the harbor. For me, it raises goose bumps to realize we have just tied to a wall in a harbor built in 400 B.C., or at least 80 generations back. Of significance also to me is that Mandraki marks the completion of my personal trip around the world since I first visited Ródhos in 1960 and remember walking down this very quay.

Quickly I clear with Customs and Immigration and walk to the hotel where Pat and Sam have reservations. I want to see if there is any news of their arrival. We find a fax indicating they are now in Athínia (Athens) and would be at Ródhos tomorrow. We cancel their reservations and head back to the boat for some serious cleaning before the "Admiral's" arrival.

* * *

The Colossus of Ródhos, a bronze statue of Helios the Sun God, and one of the seven wonders of the Ancient World, was built about 200 B.C. and was 120 feet tall. Soon after its completion the colossus was destroyed by an earthquake and 80 years later sold as scrap. It is believed one leg of the Colossus stood on the east side of the entrance very near where we were tied and the other on the west. Boats are required to sail under the legs; boats as large as *Lusty Wind II* had to lower their masts so not to "startle" the bronze Colossus while coming or going.

The history of Ródhos is full of ups and downs as one conqueror upset another. The most significant group was the Knights of St. John. These knights' stated mission was caring for pilgrims; their work was financed by personal wealth plus pirating of the Turks. The knights considered crusaders to be pilgrims. They both cared for the sick and the injured and fought their enemies. After the crusaders were driven from Jerusalem, the knights moved to Cyprus and then in 1309 settled in Ródhos. During their 213-year stay they built the fortifications that are now the great tourist attraction and economic engine of the island. The crusades and activities of the Knights of St. John were supported by western nations to protect the spice trade which before DeGama had to pass through the otherwise Muslim Levant.

The location of the knights so close to Asia Minor was of course an annoyance to the Ottoman Turks – a bit like the Russians in Cuba. The Turks under Sultan Suleiman The Magnificent laid siege to Ródhos in 1522, a year after Magellan was killed in the Philippines. Six-hundred and fifty Knights of St. John with 6,700 soldiers held 100,000 Turks off for three months. The siege was eventually successful for the Turks partially because the fields and wells of Ródhos kept this hoard supplied. The knights' defense was so valiant that Suleiman allowed those still living to withdraw in honor. Ottoman rule lasted 390 years. This was followed by the rule of the Italians, the Germans, and finally the Greeks.

My first visit to Ródhos in 1960 found a quiet, sleepy place. There were few restaurants and one had to look around a bit to find a postcard. Now 32 years later Ródhos is awash with tourists and related activities. Three or four large cruise boats (it's great to watch a 500 foot cruise boat drop anchor and back to the quay) are in port at almost any time and hundreds of hotels and condominiums

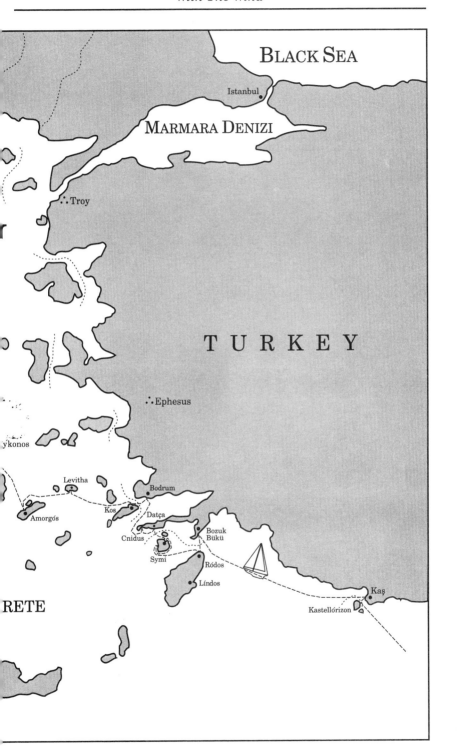

promote tourism from all over the world. The tourist shops, restaurants, and discos are too numerous to count. There is even a bungy jumping franchise, flood-lit and operated all night. However, the magnificence of the fortifications, the old town, Lindos to the south, and the history of it all is so great it shines past all the hoopla.

* * *

The day after Pat and Sam's arrival, Katie and Molly are scheduled to meet Warren Wick at the west side of the entrance to Mandraki. He is on time and joins our crew which is now seven – not at all crowded considering we are cruising, not passage making, and will be at sea only several hours at a time.

We spend the next several days touring Ródhos and Lindos. I spend some time every day trying to find a German named Klaus who is reported to be an expert on hydraulics. On our second day, I am talking to a woman on the boat next to ours; and when I find she is German, "Do you know where I can find Klaus the hydraulic mechanic?" It turned out she was *Frau* Klaus.

Klaus rearranges his schedule and spends most of the next day with me working on the hydraulics. Several areas are wet with hydraulic fluid; so we rebuild joints in the vicinity. Actually this fluid was probably spilled by me in the many times I have refilled and bled the system. Klaus thinks the problem is a defective valve near the hand-steering pump and rebuilds it. He tells me it should be replaced as soon as possible since its aluminum case has suffered some electrolysis.

Just after lunch we attempt to depart and discover why our stern anchor is holding so well. It is hopelessly caught under a large chain on the bottom of the harbor. Andy dives three times in 10 feet of murky water: first to find the anchor, second to put a shackle on the crown, and third to attach a line to pull it out from under the heavy chain.

By dinnertime, we are anchored alone in the harbor of Panormittis on the island of Symi. This beautiful peaceful harbor is dominated by a large monastery. Reading several historic markers, we learn this monastery had been a hot bed of anti-German guerrillas during the occupation of the Aegean Islands during World War II.

In the morning we sail for the crowded town of Symi and arrive late in the morning. On our departure, the ferry coming from Ródhos rocks us in her wake and a knife falls in the galley nearly stabbing Pat's foot. Ships are responsible for damage caused by their wake; however, Pat holds me responsible. The lesson – the watch keeper should warn those below of any impending unusual movement of the vessel.

Symi is an absolute delight with small buildings that seem to climb right off the quay and up the sides of the hills. The pastel blues, ambers, creams, and roses with a liberal sprinkling of abandoned buildings is one of the most delightful settings of our trip. Restaurants and tourist shops abound all around the quay and are a bustle of activity when the tourists from Ródhos stream off the ferries. In the afternoon after the last ferry departs, Symi is back to a very quiet pleasant state to be savored by the local populace, a few tourists, and yachties.

The next day we depart for Datça, Turkey and I plan to use the Nimos Passage which is a narrow channel between Symi and the Island of Nimos and a shortcut to Datça. We check our cruising guide. "With a strong *meltemi* blowing into the channel, the depth at the trough in any swell may be reduced by about one meter. Just look straight ahead and not at the variegated sea bottom passing under the keel." The cruising guide doesn't mention crashing rocks, like Jason on *Argo* encountered, so we proceed. When we get to the channel, the wind is 30 knots on our nose; I do as the cruising guide suggests and we are soon through the worst of it and making a successful Mediterranean "bow to" mooring just in front of an open bar at the quay a bit east of the town of Datça.

Datça is built on the original site of Cnidus but there is little to see. The town is new and uninteresting. It is however a port of entry; and after securing the boat, I walked into town for *pratique*. First I had no clearance papers from any point of departure in Greece. I have gone to the police station which handles *pratique* in Symi and have been told what I understood to be "No problem." The second problem is my original entry papers from Kas show Andy and me as crew members but we now have in addition Katie, Molly, Pat, Sam, and Warren. I think these Turkish officials must believe I am running an illegal non-tax-paying charter service. After hours of discussing all of my transgressions, I am called to a special meeting of the Mayor, the Chief of Police, and the Customs Official. A small payment which turns out to be about $20 to each of the three would allow my problems to be overlooked. I pay the $60. We celebrate our agreement with Turkish coffee. Frankly the $60 is easier to swallow.

After the coffee, I am told as it is Saturday and it is impossible to finish the paper work, I should be at the Customs office on Monday at 8 a.m. Monday I arrive at 8 a.m. and am told to come back at 10. I return at 10 and am told to return again at 2 p.m. At 2 I get our cruising permit and we are very quickly off to Cnidus, motoring into the wind for 23 nautical miles. The delay is an obvious ploy to help the local merchants. One tries for three days to sell Pat a rug – he gave up just before 2 p.m. Historians theorize that the Dorian capital was moved from the present site of Datça to the current site of Cnidus because of easier defense and a better position to monopolize Aegean maritime trade; these historians obviously had never tried to clear customs at Datça.

The principal deity of Cnidus is Aphrodite (from the Greek meaning foam-born), the Goddess of Desire who rose naked from the foam of the sea. A temple with large nude statue of Aphrodite and is the earliest known sculpture of a nude woman in the Greek world. One sailor is reported to have crept into the shrine and passionately kissed the statue on the thigh causing a dark stain. Other stories relate that the shrine had a back door so visitors could view Aphrodite's fantastic fanny. Times change but not seamen.

Cnidus, on a peninsula, has two harbors, one to the northwest and one to the southeast. There was once a canal connecting the two, making arrival and departure in either direction easy for sailing vessels without engines. St. Paul waited out a strong *meltimi* here on his way to his trial before Caesar. The canal is now mostly silted in.

My method has been to arrive late in the morning to seize the moorings of early risers. We depart Cnidus at 6:45 Wednesday morning and arrive at the Bodrum Marina (where there is plenty of room) just before noon. For once we are not motoring into the wind; there is a lull in the *meltemi*.

* * *

Bodrum was originally know as Halicarnassus and was part of the Dorian confederacy including Cnidus and Ródhos. Before his death, Mausoleus, a powerful ruler in the third century B.C., began construction of a massive tomb which was to become one of the seven wonders of the ancient world. (This tomb gave the English language the word mausoleum.) Bodrum became known as the

Greenwich Village of Turkey early in this century when a number of artists and writers were exiled there by the Turks. One, Travot Sakir Kabaagac, became known as "The Fisherman of Halicarnassus." The knights of St. John built the Castle of St. Peter which was completed the same year Columbus sailed to America.

* * *

Thursday we rent a car and drive 80 land miles north of Bodrum to Ephesus. This ancient city was the finest of the seven cities that were the pride of Rome in Asia Minor, built at a natural harbor on the mouth of the Kucuk Menderes River. The city, originally Greek then Roman, thrived as a commercial center. In time the harbor was silted in by the river and the water was then four miles from the ancient quays and was the reason the city was abandoned. The Kucuk Menderes river winds through a rich agricultural valley and gives us the English word meander. Fortunately for us there were no other major centers of population in the area and thus no economic reason to "mine" the ruins for building stones and stones to grind for mortar. This left one of the greatest Greek and Roman cities quite intact.

It is to Ephesus that St. John brought Mary after he was charged with her safety by Jesus just before he was crucified. John feared the Romans then occupying Ephesus and hid Mary in a small house up in the wooded hills above the city where she lived the rest of her life. A foundation has been identified as Mary's home. A shrine has been built and we have a special feeling of reverence, not often experienced by us, at this site.

Friday evening, Katie, Andy, Molly, and Warren announce they are going to a disco in Bodrum. I go to bed about 10 p.m. and 1 a.m. Pat, frantic, wakes me. Katie,

Molly, and Warren have returned, but not Andy. She is afraid the Kurds, militant *jihad* Muslims of East Turkey, will get him. I tell her the Kurds don't want Andy. At 4 a.m., Pat is shaking me again. Andy is still not back. I dress and get Katie up to help me find the disco and recover Andy. The four-mile night walk is an eye opener to this seasoned traveler. During the day in Bodrum, there are tourists but they are mostly families or older couples. At night the scene changes dramatically. Foreigners, principally from the age of 17 to 21, not hundreds, but thousands are on the street. Any combination a person can conjure up is there: boys and girls holding hands and kissing, boys holding hands and kissing. There are several groups consisting of a girl with five guys. Where do all these people spend their day? University students on summer breaks come to Turkey because it is not a member of the European Economic Community and is thus substantially less expensive. As we walk up a narrow street and approach the disco, the music, which we can just hear from the boat, is deafening. We turn the corner and see the building, the bricks are pulsing with the beat. I notice an attractive Turkish girl on the dance floor and on second glance see she is dancing with Andy. He sees his father and sister at 5 a.m., drops the girl (to her astonishment), comes over, grins at me, and says, "Let's have one more and we'll all go." "We aren't all going, just Katie, you, and me," I tell him. "We aren't having "one more."

The sun is up. It is time to leave Bodrum for Kos back in Greece. Since I want to arrive in Kos by late morning, we need an early start. Before 8 a.m. I am up and ready to dinghy across the harbor to Customs and Immigration. I decide justice must be served so I awake Andy to help. The only place we can find for the dinghy is near the ferry dock. I tell Andy to stay aboard and hold on while I clear out. The clearing out process goes well until I get to the

Harbor Master. He insists on seeing a boat operator's license before allowing me to depart. I try to explain that in the United States boat captains do not have licenses. He cannot imagine this is true. A supervisor is summoned and when a German yachtsman who speaks Turkish and English translates that I do not have a license and adds that I do obviously have experience as I have sailed most of the way around the world. The supervisor finally issues my exit permit. The German probably saved me a $20 tip. I return to find the dinghy and Andy gone. Looking out at the harbor I can see the dinghy floating back toward the marina with Andy asleep, one leg hanging into the water. At that moment a passenger of a passing ferry snaps pictures of my son and the dinghy. The ferry pilot blows his whistle and Andy wakes up. After regaining his senses, he comes back for me.

We were finally off, motoring into the wind for Kos. Our pilot book warns us of odors in the Kos harbor as a result of an over-worked sewer system. Either this has been rectified or the wind is in the right direction, for we notice no odor at all and have a delightful stay. The island is the birthplace of Hippocrates and one of the tourist sites is a large tree under which the Tourist Bureau says he taught. But even an amateur arboriculturist knows that the tree is not nearly old enough for this to be true. The entrance to the harbor is dominated by yet another castle built by the Knights of St. John. Our spot on the quay is directly across from a number of restaurants, bars, and discos all operating until dawn. Fortunately we have moored bow to and the captain's quarters aft are somewhat protected from the nightly noise.

Our neighbors in both Bodrum and Kos are Paul Visser and his wife aboard *Aaltje* out of Amsterdam. Paul is professor of Art at Universiteit van Amsterdam and finances his summer cruising by painting. *Aaltje* flies the European Economic Community flag in lieu of the

Netherland's flag. Paul, who would have been a boy during World War II, felt nationalism has cost too many too much.

A ferry has arrived in Kos this morning from Piriévs (Piracus) with Brian Balderson aboard. He is an Irish classmate of Katies from Fort Thomas. Tonight we are going to a Mexican Restaurant and find we are served by a young waitress from Iceland. Here we are – seven Americans and an Irishman served by a Icelander at a Mexican restaurant in Greece.

Sam and I go for a swim on the beach just west of town. There is no dress code and many women are topless. Sam's thirteen-year-old eyes are wide open. In 1935 Julius Fleischman, also from Cincinnati, sailed around the world. In his book, *Footprints in the Sea*, he made much ado about exposed breasts in the South Pacific and the Spice Islands. Fifty-eight years later we miss all that, but Mr. Fleischman would have been envious if he had seen all these perky young Scandinavian girls in summertime Greece. Again, times change, but not sailors.

After two days, we are ready to go, but the Harbor Master warns us there are 60-knot winds out of the northeast and very choppy seas outside the harbor. We visit his office several times a day to study weather maps and finally depart. Winds were down to 20-25 knots, but the ride still wet.

Paul Visser recommends a stop on the sparsely inhabited island of Levitha. This small island is occupied only by a lighthouse keeper, a fisherman, a sheep farmer, and their families. We do not find good holding in the anchorage; so it takes several tries to get the anchor down, the scope right, and our stern tied to a stone ashore. After we are all settled, we notice the only other boat in the bay is the same Dutch boat that was to our starboard in Kas three weeks earlier. I notice the master has been watching our attempts at anchorage. I raise my arms and say, "No Good." He remembers us, for he has his wife come up on deck from the galley where she has been preparing dinner and tells her a long story. He finishes by raising his arms and saying, "No good."

The sheep farmer and his family operate a *taverna*, or informal restaurant, in their farmhouse a short walk up the hill from the bay. It is not an inexpensive or pretentious meal, but it is marvelous.

We depart Levitha in the late morning and, as expected, motor into the wind to Katapola, Amorgós, arriving late in the afternoon. Amorgós is off the main tourist route and not visited by many yachts. Even though our arrival is late in the day, we find a convenient spot on the quay opposite many *tavernas* and shops.

Typical of islands in the Cyclades, the *chora*, capital, is secure from pirates and raiders on top of the hill. The *chora* at Amorgós is beautiful with several small sidewalk cafes and bars. As there aren't many tourists in Amorgós, the frequency of restaurants and bars is in proper scale, and one does not have the feeling of being in Disney World. This *chora* is a place of windmills, whitewashed houses, bougainvillea, stone paved streets, and numerous small Greek Orthodox Churches.

A few miles along the east coast of the island, is the Holy Monastery of the Panayia Khozoviotissa. The ride is only four miles, but the most frightening four miles of our circumnavigation. The bus has a very short wheel base (no reserve buoyancy) and the reason became obvious; as it goes around bends the front and rear quarters of the bus both breathtakingly hang over cliffs of several hundred feet. Andy says, "This ride redefines hairpin curves." Without a word being spoken, the bus driver knows where all the passengers are going and stops for us at the beginning of the long trail leading to the monastery.

This monastery is built on a spectacular cliff and is suspended between the sky and the sea below. The building is one-room deep and four-stories high. Construction was begun in the eleventh century and it is dedicated to the Virgin Mary. The monastery is a long hard up-and-down climb; we read later in the guidebook that one should remember to bring drinking water. I wonder how to say "diabetic" and "sugar" in Greek. We enter the monastery at the bottom level and find a large table full of skirts. What are these monks up to? We climb a winding narrow staircase three stories to a reception room where we are greeted by one of the brothers. I enter first and find a table with candy, small glasses of schnapps, and large glasses of water. After a shot of schnapps and a piece of candy for my now low blood sugar level, I go for some water. Sam enters second and being both thirsty and polite, goes for a small glass of "water" rather than the large – to the horror of the monk who is not quick enough to stop him. I don't think Sam will ever drink again. Pat enters third, out of breath from her climb, again to the horror of the monk. She is wearing slacks which reveal her figure and this is not something for him to see. While the monk turns his eyes to the ceiling to avoid temptation, he politely instructs Pat to climb back down the steps and put one of the skirts on over her slacks before returning.

This amazing edifice was the inspiration to LeCorbusier. He is well-known for the design of the famous Notre-Dame-du-Haut, at Ronchamp, in France which has a resemblance to this monastery.

Monday morning, we depart Amargós for Míkonos. We motor the entire way and anchor at Ornos (simply meaning bay) a two-mile walk or bus ride from the city. Míkonos is a low-lying rocky barren island without high hills to safely locate a *chora*. The planners of the city of Míkonos made their street patterns a maze to confuse pirates. This made it easy to trap and capture them. This reputation made Míkonos as safe as any *chora* on a hill. Míkonos today is a tourist mecca and is the Greek Islands' answer to Key West or Fire Island. The unusual street pattern still works – Sam becomes lost for an hour of panic. Like Ródhos, the history of Míkonos shines through all the restaurants, bars, discos, tourist shops, and vacationing hairdressers.

Near Míkonos is the ancient island city of Delos. Yachts are prohibited from anchoring at Delos for fear the dropping anchors will damage undiscovered antiquities on the sea floor. There are, however, plenty of tripper boats to ferry sight-seers from Míkonos.

* * *

Delos was for a while the political and religious center of the ancient world and mythology has it that Apollo and Artemis were born here. Delos' importance was at first economic. It is the best anchorage between Europe and Asia on the trade route of the time. Delos was also on the east-west trade route between mainland Greece and the Dodecanese. What would otherwise be an open roadstead was shielded by Míkonos to the east and from the *meltimi* by Rinia to the northwest. Like Cnidus, the harbor can be entered or departed from either the northwest or the southeast. The Dorians were partly inspired to move their main city to Cnidus to gain this same economic advantage. Here the trade was first, followed by the temples. As Ernle Bradford in *The Greek Islands* says, "Merchants, then as now, are eager to purchase security in both worlds." The prosperity of Delos began after the defeat of the Persians in 478 B.C. It became a "free port" amassing immense wealth and power. The Romans came in 200 B.C. In 88 B.C., the Mithridates sacked Delos, knocked down all the monuments and killed nearly all of its population. By 3 A.D., Delos' economic influence was finished. The island was put up for sale, but there were no takers. Like Ephidus, there were no nearby population centers and the ruins were not mined for building stones and mortar; it is therefore quite intact and another sight to behold. We are fortunate to have Warren, an instructor of classical architecture, as our personal tour guide.

* * *

We depart Míkonos for the island of Kithnos and arrive just at lunch time. The anchorage at Loutrá, the main village, is crowded and we can see Ornos Ay Irini to the south and east – a beautiful bay with a small village and no boats. We drop anchor and cannot believe our good fortune of being the only boat in this setting. Later in the afternoon, a couple of other boats arrive but depart after their crews take a short swim. At about 5 p.m. in the afternoon, we find out why we were alone in the bay as the serenity of the scene is ruptured. Four of the buildings in the little village were merely fronts for massive speakers. I look up "crank it up" in the dictionary and find a picture of Ay Irini. Local entrepreneurs have purchased the entire village and turned it into a disco. First a trickle then a pilgrimage of young locals and tourists arrive from all over the island. The music did not pause or the volume decrease until 5 a.m. During the night, there is a breeze out of the northwest, but *Lusty Wind II* lies off her anchor to the northwest with her stern held into the wind by the amplifiers and speakers of Ay Irini.

Two hours after the music stops, we depart Ay Irini to arrive we hoped in Piraiéus by 3 p.m. We have two big treats: first we are able to sail most of the way and second we see our first overcast sky since waiting out Cyclone Roger in Australia four months earlier. We arrive at 3 p.m. and easily find Zea Marina. We are directed to a slip on the breakwater and, now experienced, successfully complete a bow-to Mediterranean moor.

* * *

In 493 B.C., Athinai (Athens), by then a major Mediterranean Sea Power, moved its harbor from the open bay of Palaión to Piraiéus Harbor and two smaller harbors also at Piraeus. They are now Zea Marina and Munydia Marina. Ancient Roman maps show the Zea and Munydia with essentially the same shape as they are now except for the breakwater we are tied to. It now nearly doubles Zea's size. The Zea harbor was an important Athenian Navy installation. Ship sheds for navy vessels were built all around the original harbor and separated from other ship sheds by rows of columns. The remains of these sheds and their columns can still be seen running into the water in the inner part of this yacht harbor.

* * *

Our mooring is next to a sleek and classic-looking yacht named *Kismot*. *Kismot* began her career as a Yugoslavian fast patrol boat and was requisitioned by Marshall Tito to be turned into an elegant private yacht. After the death of Tito, she was sold and is maintained in "Bristol" condition by its current owner. The captain is very watchful of our approach and seeing our American flag probably is not surprized we come in bow to. He is a big help to us by giving referrals for fuel and provisioning.

The next morning Katie, Molly, Warren, and Brian rent a car and leave to tour the Peloponnesian Peninsula and eventually to fly home. Our crew has now been reduced from 8 to 4 and it is quiet. We spend the day cleaning and working on the boat.

August 15th, Pat, Andy, and Sam depart for New York and Cincinnati. Now alone on the boat, it is much too quiet but a new crew is on their way. I soon find John West and Dick Brauhgam trying to determine if this bow-to sailboat is *Lusty Wind II*. John is an old friend from Northern Kentucky and now a lawyer in Lexington. Dick is a professor of Sociology at the University of Kentucky. The next day, we hear a cab screech to a stop and find Dick Pearson in the back seat fumbling for change. Late the next morning we depart Zea and sail by the island of Salamís, to the Aegean terminus of the Corinth Canal. The island of Salamís is where Themistodes the Greek outwitted Xerxes, ending Persian dominance of the Levant, in 480 B.C.

* * *

The Corinth Canal is about 3 nautical miles long and 80 feet wide. The cut is 273 feet from a 250-foot high lime stone hilltop to 23 feet below the water. The Greeks and Romans had a road called the *dhiolkos* to drag their ships across the isthmus at this same point. Octavian, in pursuit of Anthony after the battle of Actium, had his ships dragged across on this road. Several times Greeks and Romans worked out schemes for a canal and work was actually begun by Nero. Even Napoleon had some plans for a canal; and it was eventually built by the French but not finished till 1893. The canal was damaged by German bombing during World War II but repaired and improved afterward.

* * *

Our cruising guide indicates an obstacle of chain ferries at either end of the canal. These ferries use a large chain stretched across the canal and pull themselves back and forth with a wildcat powered by a diesel engine on the ferry. If a yacht passes too close behind one of these ferries she can get fouled in the chain. I couldn't imagine why a yacht would pass so close behind these ferries; but when I see the 80-foot width of the canal, I understand the problem. The administration area is at the Aegean side and we tie to a quay to make our arrangements and pay our fees. The cost is $230 which makes this canal, which is 6 percent of the length of the Panama Canal and 3 percent of the Suez Canal, the most expensive of the three. Also it only saves us 250 miles on our trip from Piraeus to Itháki instead of saving us a trip around Cape Horn or the Cape of Good Hope like the other canals.

Canal traffic is one way; so after waiting for several Aegean bound ships to come through, the red signal flag came down, the blue flag was raised, and we began our transit. Fortunately for us the chain ferries have been replaced by mobile hydraulic-lifting road bridges at both ends. These hydraulic bridges drop down into the water to let yachts or small boats pass over. They even can be moved to the side of the canal for vessels with a deeper draft. Dropping bridges are like reefs and clearance cannot be verified until it is too late. There is a current of one to two knots in the canal flowing either way depending on the wind direction – usually and of course in our case from the north.

We reach the southern end too late to enter the yacht

harbor at Kórinthos (Corinth); so we motor to Loutrakiou Bay and anchor for dinner and the night. Before dinner, we recover the main sail from another "spinnaker twist" inside the mast. This twist occurred as we furled the baggy sail just before the canal. The next afternoon we are at Navpaktos on the north shore of Gulf of Corinth.

* * *

Navpaktos is an ancient walled city; most of the buildings inside the walls are intact. The walled area goes all the way to the top of the hill affording wonderful views from the summit. In the 16th century, Navpaktos was known as Lepanto and the Gulf of Corinth was known as the Gulf of Lepanto. In 1571 the western world heard that our old friend Suleiman "The Magnificent" was assembling the largest naval fleet ever known. Wary of the intentions of the Turks, the European powers jointly put together a fleet under the command of 24-year old Don Juan of Austria. Suleiman had 400 ships and 120,000 sailors; the western Europeans assembled 300 ships with 80,000 sailors. The ships were only somewhat different from those that fought at Salamís 2,000 years earlier except that they now had cannons aboard. Don Juan sailed his fleet down the Gulf of Lepanto and found Suleiman's fleet stretched across the gulf at Lepanto. The ensuing battle was the largest naval engagement the world had seen and the size was not exceeded until the Battle of Layte Gulf in 1944, 373 years later; the western world, of course, won that one as well. Don Juan's forces had 8,000 killed and 16,000 wounded and the Turks' had 25,000 killed and probably as many as 40,000 were wounded. The Turkish fleet was destroyed and they no longer had an impact on the Mediterranean Sea. One of the 16,000 Westerners wounded was Cervantes, later of *Don Quote* fame, whose left hand was crippled in the battle. Cervantes was thereafter known as *Manco* (the maimed one) *de Lepanto*.

* * *

We leave in early morning in very light air to motor and motor-sail to Itháki (Ithaca), the legendary home of Odysseus. I remember coming into Itháki, in January of 1960 on a ferryboat bound from Brindisi, Italy, to Piraeus. The beauty and charm of this port and island had a big impact; and I resolved then to return. We spend several days touring including visiting what is believed to be the foundation of Odysseus' home. Most of our crew gets a bit of food poisoning. After departing we motor against 15 knots of wind through the Ionian Sea to Valletta, Malta.

The principal dangerous weather in this region is a wind called the *gregale*. It is a gale-force wind that forms in the Bakians and reaches out across the Ionian Sea to the coast of Africa. In 69 A.D., the galley carrying St. Paul to his trial in Rome was thrown onto the rocks at Malta during a *gregale*. Paul was saved by the centurion of the Roman guards.

As we approach Valletta, Malta, in the early morning of August 26, we hear a Mayday on the VHF radio. A yacht several hours away has exploded, is on fire, and all the crew are in the water. We listen as a Maltese fisherman, trying to rescue the crew, has a heart attack and dies. A number of other, closer, fishing boats and rescue vessels are on the way. A bit shaken by this, we find the yacht harbor, make our bow-to moor unaided, and very quickly handle all *pratique*.

* * *

After being driven from Ródhos in 1523, the Knights of St. John found themselves without a home base. For seven years the Order wandered around looking for a suitable home. In 1530 they finally convinced Charles V of Spain to allow them to lease the island of Malta which he owned (this is the same Charles V who sponsored Magellan and Enrique de Malacca's voyage of 1519-1521). The largest single portion of the knights was French, and Charles was at the time at war with France. He was somewhat satisfied with the knights' pledge to neutrality; however rather than give or sell this island to potential enemies, he gave the knights a lease with the rent of a falcon a year. If in the United States a person owned property next to his church and leased that property for a dollar a year, this would be called "nominal rent." In Europe under the same circumstances, the rent would be called a "Maltese Falcon." The small sum the Fat Man agreed to pay Sam Spade for information leading to the jeweled gold falcon was also a "Maltese Falcon."

Malta is not a lush fertile place; however this suited the knights well. The greatest feature Malta had was excellent harbors for their fleet and the barren countryside could not support besieging enemies. For 35 years, the knights resumed their pirating activities; and with the Turkish plunder, built massive fortifications. Suleiman, now an old man, was constantly annoyed by the knights' pirating activities - the same knights he had let go at Ródhos.

In May of 1565, six years before the battle of Lepanto, Suleiman sent an armada of 180 vessels and 31,000 men to lay siege on Malta where 641 knights resided with 8,000 paid soldiers. Before the

Turks could put one longboat ashore, the knights, remembering Ródhos, poisoned every well on the island and brought all domestic animals within their forts. The resulting "Great Siege" is the fiercest ever known. European support was almost non-existent likely because the spice trade was by then coming around the Cape of Good Hope and the knight's protection in the Levant no longer as important. It's interesting how the religious crusaders were no longer necessary after the spice trade shifted. After three-and-a-half months of siege in which the Turks captured almost all of the knights' fortifications, the Turks had had enough, knew bad weather was coming, and returned in shame to Istanbul. Six years later in the battle of Lepanto, the Turks suffered another crushing loss and were finished as a sea power.

After the opening of the Suez Canal and until the beginning of World War II, Malta was, as were Adan and Gibraltar, an important coaling stop in the British Lifeline between England and India. Now for awhile the wealth would flow to London.

Malta has suffered two of the major sieges of world history. The second was in 1942 and 1943 when the Germans and Italians feared Malta would be used by the allies in their coming attempts to cross into Sicily; so they had their air forces bomb Malta to deny the allies this strategic base. This small community was bombed more than London. If the allies had intended to use Malta as a stepping stone, this siege was successful.

* * *

Saturday evening. We are invited to dinner at the home of Rene and Beverly Randon. Rene is a lawyer in Valetta and a member of an old and prominent Maltese family. Beverly is from the United States and is a friend of a law partner of John West. The Randons' marvelous old home has an enclosed courtyard in front, massive doors and high ceilings. The interior is filled with art, antiques, and books. A two-story loggia across the back overlooks Balluta Bay. After dinner on the porch, we walk into the village of St. Julienne where a huge church festival was taking place. The festival is complete with fireworks over the water. The respect Rene and Beverly have from the people on the street make their standing in the community obvious.

The remainder of our activities in Malta include a long tour of Mdina (pronounced M Dina), a medieval fortification in the center of the island. Mdina is one third the size of the walled area of Ródhos but has only three restaurants and one gift shop. Mdina reminds me of Ródhos in 1960.

We have some crew changes. Dick Braughan returns to Lexington but is replaced by Jon Kiehnau. Jon is a friend of Dick Pearson and is with *Money Magazine* in New York City.

John West has developed a toothache and is having difficulty finding a dentist. I am now working on the steering and tell John I have some dental equipment and medication and will be glad to help. He immediately departs in his quest for a dentist. After John is gone, I notice I have a greasy vise-grip in my right hand.

We leave Malta in the morning, and after a short stop on the Italian island of Pantelleria, we negotiate the Strait of Sicily into the Tyrrhenian Sea. Pantelleria was also besieged during World War II but in this case it was by allied bombers in their efforts to deny it as a base for the Germans and Italians as Sicily was invaded.

The weather we encounter along the coast of Tunisia and Algeria should have been from the south allowing a broad reach, but it is from the east instead. This area of the Mediterranean is normally dominated by a dry, dusty wind, the *scirocco*, known locally as "the breath of the Sahara." These winds are caused by lows in the western Sahara which with their counterclockwise turning blow the hot dusty air northward. When the depressions are particularly low and the wind is severe, they are called a *simoon*, an Arab word for poison wind. We thus should have had an aggressive and maybe unpleasant broad reach all the way to Puerto Bañus. Instead, as one might imagine, the wind, at about 15 knots, is coming out of the west, the direction we are traveling.

The boat is again having a great difficulty in steering particularly against these head winds. Just as in the Red Sea, we are yawing 20° to 25° in each direction. We find again we have a substantial amount of air in the steering system and we are using hydraulic fluid at such a rate that we will run out quickly. We take everything out of the lazarette, remove the floor boards, and, *voilá*, find the steering cylinder has a leaking seal which by now is leaking at a substantial rate. It is obvious we can soon lose our main steering system. *Lusty Wind II* is equipped with emergency steering system, but this requires a helmsman to stand with a tiller on the stern of the boat and work hard for his entire watch with no operating autopilot. Except for political considerations, the wise thing would be to pick a port in Algeria to attempt repairs. In a life-threatening emergency, this is certainly what we would do. Instead, we fashion a Tupperware container under the leak and every four hours I climb into the lazarette with a turkey baster, harvest the hydraulic fluid from the Tupperware, and pour it back into the steering system. This works relatively well and keeps our autopilot in operation, but there is a growing volume of air in the system and considerable yawing of the boat.

Engineer Pearson estimates our collection procedures are 80% efficient and calculates that we do not have enough hydraulic fluid to reach Puerto Bañus. To add to our problems, a cooling line on the engine ruptures; but it is easy to replace after allowing the engine to cool for about an hour. While the engine is in question, I eye Palma, Mallorca, as this port northeast of our course will be an easy sail. We pass through a front where conditions get pretty choppy, we find ourselves in calm seas with light air. With reduced steering activity, the rate of hydraulic fluid loss decreases substantially.

September 6. We cross the Prime Meridian, or 0° longitude. The GPS switchs from East of Greenwich, where we have been since just before Fiji, to West. Before 1884, astronomers from many nations used a Prime Meridian usually crossing through each ones principal observatory. A conference in Washington, in 1884, settled on Greenwich, much to the consternation of the French who, of course, considered the only logical point to be the Paris observatory.

We alter our course to Cartagena, Spain, to purchase more hydraulic fluid. My experience has been when the going gets rough not to stop anywhere with an airport nearby. So with this in mind and in fear of losing crew, I tell them there is no airport at Cartagena. This ancient port was founded by traders from Carthage during the 3rd century B.C. It is now the headquarters for the Spanish navy. While we are here, World War II diesel-electric subs depart every morning, for patrols, from sub-pens tunneled into the rock. The fuel dock is back between two piers, crowded with the fishing fleet. Sailboats with long deep keels and one prop don't turn well and our maneuvers bring the work of about 200 fisherman to a halt. Our eventual success brings many smiles and waves.

After a day of rest and buying all the hydraulic fluid available at two local truck stops, we proceed through the Alboran Sea to Puerto Bañus. We arrive late in the evening on Friday, September 30, and spend the night at the fuel dock. This fuel dock represents the completion of the around-the-world sail of *Lusty Wind II* as we had purchased fuel there before crossing the Atlantic in January, 1988. The marina kindly assigns us slip C-78 where we were five years earlier.

Puerto Bañus is a major attraction along the Costa del Sol of southern Spain. Andalusia, the providence, is all that Spain brings to mind: white-washed buildings draped with orange blossoms and bougainvillea; the flamingo dance; snow-capped mountains; fields of olives, oranges, and tomatoes; beaches; and a lot of sun. When I first visited this area in 1960, I thumbed all day for a ride, was passed by only three cars, and eventually took a bus. Today one cannot cross the road because of the traffic. Puerto Bañus itself is an artificial port built by the Spanish government in 1970. This is not what most yachties are looking for. It is expensive, glitzy, and crowded with tourists. Puerto Bañus' appeal is security, excellent on-site mechanics, and lots of excitement. I know a mechanic, Pepito Ogalla, from our previous trip and make arrangements for him to watch *Lusty Wind II* while I am home waiting out the Atlantic hurricane season. Pepe, his father, and Rafael Cazallas had taken care of *Lusty Wind II* in 1987-1988. Also Rafael sailed with us on our first home bound passage from Puerto Bañus to Las Palmas.

After cleaning the boat and getting the crew off, I spend several days making additional arrangements to leave the boat for six months. Wolfgang Thone, the Hood Sail agent, is engaged to build a new main sail. I collect complete information to be sure to get the correct new steering cylinder seals.

12

CHAPTER TWELVE

Hasenpfeffer and Capers

January 3, 1994 – February 18, 1994

Puerto Bañus – Tortola, British Virgin Islands

The most dangerous time for sailors to cross the southern North Atlantic Ocean is June through November when they are most likely to encounter tropical storms. These storms originate over Tropical Africa and the ITC near the Cape Verde Islands and they build crossing the Atlantic to become very powerful and dangerous as they approach the West Indies. For this reason, our planned crossing of the Atlantic is in January and early February when these dangerous storms are almost nonexistent and sailing conditions are near ideal. I will remember these words as we approach the Canary Islands in the middle of January. My strategic wait allows me three-and-a-half months, including Christmas and New Years, at home. Columbus, of course, completed this passage with much luck in October, the peak of the hurricane season.

After twelve hours of flying and walking airports, I arrive exhausted at Puerto Bañus and find *Lusty Wind II* as I left her. To avoid the possibility of losing a precious possession – new steering system seals and spares for the hydraulic steering, and a spare microphone for the VHF – I have transported them in my carry-on baggage. On board, the VHF is still working – we haven't had any rain since Australia.

Too early the next morning Pepe Ogalla and his apprentice arrive to spend most of their day servicing the generator and engine. Pepe takes the steering hydraulic cylinder to his shop so he can install the new seals more carefully. During the day, sailmaker Wolfgang Thone arrives with my repaired and strengthened genoa and the new mainsail he has built during my absence. While Wolfgang and I bend on the main we notice some cracks in welds at the boom gooseneck. This is a point of major stress, particularly in a gibe, and a fracture can cause substantial personal injury, boat damage, and, of course, the loss of use of the main. Wolfgang recommends an aluminum welder who comes right away to take a look. He tells us the cracks are not at an important point and that the gooseneck is secure. Since I am getting this important advice in Spanish translated by a German from a welder who doesn't sail, I feel a bit unsettled especially since we are about to embark on a blue-water voyage with fuel for one third of the way.

January 6th is the day after the 12th day of Christmas and the start of a long weekend holiday. In Spain this is the day when children get gifts. In keeping with the season, my day of quiet ends in the late afternoon with the arrival of "Three Wise Men"; John West, Jim Kegley, and Charlie Mihalek, all lawyers from Lexington, Kentucky, who have flown to Madrid and have driven to Southern Spain to be my crew for the passage to the Canary Islands. Is having a crew of three lawyers showing proper respect for the sea?

Dinnertime. We go to the restaurant *La Caracola del Puerto* and have salt haddock served by Ehicque Coldsba, the owner. *Tescado en Sal* is almost any fish baked in a thick crust of coarse salt which seals in the juices and produces a succulent, firm, but surprisingly not salty, marvelous main course. During dinner Charlie Mihalek mentions he would like to experience some challenging weather. Dinner is followed by a bottle of Napoleon brandy and a big night on Puerto Bañus. The next morning proves these four Kentuckians are a little long in the tooth for all this and can ill afford the loss of brain cells.

Friday. A weathered looking brigantine from St. Petersburg, Russia, named *Avos* sails into port. *Avos*, in Russian, means something like, "I don't know how to get there but I'm going anyway." A new entrepreneur from St. Petersburg constructed this vessel from an abandoned hull and the vessel is making a trip from St. Petersburg to Viet Nam to publicize his new shipyard. The captain is the son-in-law of the builder; but the ship is run by the builder's daughter, or at least it appears this way because she speaks English and is, for this reason also, more fun to talk with than her husband. The name of her father's firm is Gladkov and Sons. I tell her that in the United States a similar firm would be named Gladkov and Sons and Daughter. She gets a look on her face that spells trouble for her father and brothers when she returns. She and her husband are interested in the construction of and equipment on *Lusty Wind II*.

After two days of provisioning, we depart the fuel dock of Puerto Bañus and experience, as to be expected, short choppy seas and headwinds. By midnight, we are just south of Point Europa at the southern tip of Gibraltar.

Weather patterns in the Strait of Gibraltar cause difficult conditions, particularly for vessels leaving the

Mediterranean. Westbound sailors find the permanent foul current of approximately two knots is strongest in the center and weakest at the edges. In shallow water, particularly along the north, or Spanish coast, the current reduces substantially. Because of mountains on both sides, winds are channeled only from east or west. Winds blowing from the west are locally called *poniente*; and winds blowing from the east are called *levanter* (again from the French verb to rise).

Without the use of our powerful diesel engine, we would need to postpone our departure to wait out this *poniente*. Fortunately the wind is with the current and the seas are not steep. In a *levanter*, with a strong wind opposing the current, the seas can be very choppy and the ride wet and uncomfortable, particularly for an eastbound vessel. We experienced these conditions during July 1987, on our eastbound passage through the Strait to Puerto Bañus. To find less current and avoid the shipping lanes, we hold close to the Spanish shore until we are well past *Punta de Tarifa* on the Spanish coast and *Cap Spartel* on the Moroccan, or African coast. We then turn southwest.

As evaporation increases the salt content in the Mediterranean, the water becomes more dense and sinks. This lower level water is then pushed out as a low level westbound current through the Strait. During World War II, German submarines floated into the Mediterranean below the surface on the upper eastbound current we are experiencing and returned to the Atlantic in the lower westbound current. In both directions they drifted, not using engines, to avoid detection by British destroyers patrolling out of Gibraltar.

Before Mediterranean traders ventured outside this sea, Gibraltar and the mountains of Morocco were known as the Pillars of Hercules. Greek legend holds that Hercules placed these rocks and crossed the distance with a scroll saying, "No More Beyond." It is said Hercules intended this as a warning to sailors not to enter the fearsome Atlantic.

We are now in the North Atlantic, which *Lusty Wind II* has crossed before in both directions, and are again following Columbus' wake of August 1492 and Slocum's of late August and early September 1895. Magellan began his last voyage southbound in these waters in September 1519; and in August 1522, his ship, *Victoria*, with only 13 of her original crew of 230, passed north against the system. They were confused because they had just found out they had lost a day on their circumnavigation.

The conditions for sailing in the Atlantic are dominated by a high pressure known as the Azores High in the center of this ocean. This high pressure north of the equator causes the predominate winds to be in a clockwise circular motion, again because of the Coriolios Effect. These winds over aeons have massaged the water and cause currents also to travel clockwise. The North Atlantic is thus like a huge clockwise carousel. Sailing yachts generally get on to the north for an eastbound crossing during the months of June and July as this time of year avoids frequent gales and low temperatures of the winter months. Westbound yachts travel south avoiding the months of June through November to elude destructive hurricanes.

* * *

The North Atlantic clockwise turning carousel contributed to one of the world's classic trade routes. In the early 19th century, sailing merchant vessels loaded manufactured goods in New England or Northern Europe and sailed with the system to West Africa where the goods were sold. Slaves were loaded aboard and transported, with the system, to the islands of the Caribbean or the southern states of the United States where inexpensive labor was needed to raise sugar cane in the Caribbean and cotton and tobacco in the South. The ships were then loaded with sugar or rum (which is one of sugar's by-products) in the Caribbean or cotton and tobacco in the southern states which were then transported to and sold in New England or Northern Europe to complete the unjust, inhumane but efficient circle. Whenever it is possible, captains of diesel powered merchant vessels try to take advantage of currents and winds but not anywhere near the extent captains of sailing vessels needed to do.

* * *

The best time to travel from Gibraltar to the Canary Islands is May to October; but that does not mesh with the remainder of the crossing to the Caribbean unless a sailor wants to wait in the Canaries until late December or early January. *World Cruising Routes* by Jimmy Cornell warns that boats sailing to the Canaries after October may meet with strong winds and rough seas. In our previous trip during January 1988, we found Cornell's advice, as usual, to be correct. As on our previous trip, we are experiencing light air and are motor-sailing as we begin our trek.

In his 1895 passage through these waters, Slocum was chased by Moroccan pirates. Remember he had just been advised to take this route to avoid pirates. He was under full sail in brisk winds and the pirates were gaining on him. While Slocum was below getting his gun, his boom broke at the gooseneck. After securing the boom and sail, he noticed the pirates had lost their mast and were falling behind. Again he beat the odds.

As we recall this not-quite-reassuring tale, our bilge

pump light begins coming on frequently followed by the engine warning light and buzzer. We notice our diesel engine is overheating. Quickly we bring the engine to idle and the warning light and buzzer go off. When we look into the engine room, we find the cooling pump is, even at idle speed, spraying salt water all over – not good for electrical connections. We shut the engine down to cool before attempting repairs.

In the light air, we are doing just over two knots but making progress. A quick study of our charts indicates Casablanca, Safi, and Agadir in Morocco are potential ports if we cannot effect a repair at sea. We are just past Casablanca but it is the best choice because of its size and it has an international airport in case we need to get parts quickly; of course, I don't mention the airport to my crew members.

It is obvious we need to rebuild the pump. I locate the rebuild kit and wait for the engine to cool. In sloppy seas, we use half our effort just keeping small and large parts and tools out of the bilge, but we are able to close the seacock, remove the hoses and belt, and finally the pump. After we disassemble the pump, it is apparent the problem is a worn shaft which has damaged the seals. The rebuild kit has seals but no replacement shaft. I assume the shaft has been wearing a long time; so new seals should last at least until we arrive in the Canary Islands. We put everything back together, start the engine, watch the pump carefully, and find a successful repair with no leaks has been made. We then call home, through Golf Kilo Tango, Portishead, England, on the single sideband radio and ask Pat to contact Westerbeke dealers in both Cincinnati and Ft. Lauderdale to ship parts independently to Las Palmas in the Canaries. This way we should have at least one complete replacement pump enabling us to continue on our voyage across the Atlantic. Within an hour of starting the engine, it begins overheating again; and we find the worn shaft has now destroyed our spare seals and the pump is again spraying salt water all over the bilge and engine room compartment.

The good news – or so we think – is the winds are now picking up and we are making nearly six knots under sail toward Las Palmas. Our faithful captain has a brainstorm – the air-conditioning compressors are cooled by 120-volt Marsh pumps. We are wearing sweat shirts and jackets and certainly do not need air conditioning. I close the seacocks, remove the largest of the two pumps, lash it into position, and connect the hoses from the seacock and engine to the pump. I then wire a cut-off piece of heavy extension cord to the pump so it can be plugged into our 120-volt system powered by the inverter. This arrangement acts as both switch and power source. I have to remember though that when the engine is not running I must not run the pump. If I do, seawater will fill the muffler and the engine may not start. After cooling the fresh water that circulates through the engine, the seawater is mixed with the exhaust to cool the muffler and exhaust pipes before it exits with the exhaust; if the engine is not running, there is no exhaust to push the seawater out and the muffler will fill and cause exhaust back pressure. After the job is complete, we open the seacocks, start the engine, and quickly plug in the pump. Much to our satisfaction, it operates perfectly. However, with the winds building, we don't need the engine. Since I am not absolutely confident of the short plastic nipples on the pump and on my plumbing repairs, I close the seacock.

With the weather worsening, we reef the genoa and main. Again, this weather system is "out to sea where it won't bother anyone." I recall our passage in these same waters six years earlier plus the warnings of Jimmy Cornell. As the seas reach 10 feet and the wind over 30 knots, I remember the last passage when the rope halyard of the genoa parted and sent the sail into the sea for a dangerous and difficult recovery. Then crewmember Pat Klocke, the president of our hometown bank, asked me to cut the sail free saying he will lend me – notice he did not say give or even lend interest free – money for a new sail. That night Pat wrote in his journal, "Dear Lord, if I'm ever tempted to go on a trip like this again, let me remember tonight." Had we freshened the nip of the halyard the problem probably would not have occurred.

Even though all rope halyards on *Lusty Wind II* have now been replaced by wire and rope halyards – wire at the principal point of fraying – I do not want to repeat the previous incident. This time we furl the genoa, engage the starboard running backstay, unfurl the heavy staysail, and reduce the main to a balancing size. By now, winds are at 40 knots and seas 15 feet and steep. *Lusty Wind II* is handling these conditions with reassuring stability and we are making good time toward Las Palmas without the use of our somewhat crippled engine. The wind is on our starboard stern quarter and at least I don't have to worry too much about a gibe and any resulting damage to our questionable gooseneck. In this, our second gale of the circumnavigation, the single side-band is working and a call from a French yacht going to Martinique confirms our VHF is also working.

On our last trip, we were running short of fuel by this point and were in heavy weather; so we altered our course to the lee of Lanzarote to buy fuel and wait out the bad weather. This time we have plenty of fuel and we tenaciously, without any advice or consent from the crew, continue on to Las Palmas. We are running late and this crew has flights to meet. I also have a new crew eagerly waiting our arrival.

Stuff is all over. Books, gear, anything loose is on the sole and nobody has any inclination to pick up. Nana, my maternal grandmother, had told me her scratched silver was more valuable than new as it had patina which came from use and love. *Lusty Wind II* is gaining patina as we are knocked hard by wave after wave.

During our last night at sea on this passage, I am awakened by watchkeeper Charlie Mihalek. Winds are sustained at 45 to 50 knots gusting to 60 (remember 60 knots is 69 land miles per hour), and we are experiencing steep seas of at least 20 feet. Oooooooooh Baby! Winds of 41 to 47 knots are classed as a Strong Gale and as Force 9 on the Beaufort Scale of 0 to 12. Beyond 9 is a Storm with 48 to 55 knots; Violent Storm, 56 to 63; and a Hurricane is Force 12 with winds over 63 knots. By morning, sea conditions hit the designation "Strong Gale" on the Beaufort Scale:

"High waves; dense streaks of foam along the direction of the wind; crest of waves begin to topple, tumble, and roll over; spray may reduce visibility."

Our sail plan of using the heavy staysail and a balancing amount of the main in severe weather is working well and, all considered, our vessel is stable. She is in her element – a lusty wind.

During the day conditions continue to deteriorate. I notice the clew of the staysail is fraying and I'm afraid it will fail – it does not but it will require repair.

By 5 p.m., we are approaching Las Palmas and are in the lee of the northeast corner of this island. We are still in a "Violent Storm," Force 11 – between 56 and 63 knots. Fortunately the seas, although choppy, are not high because we are in the lee of Gran Canaria. A low point in the profile of the island causes the wind to be even more severe because it is funneled between two hills.

The port entrance is directly into the wind; so we can't sail in. Now for the test – we turn on our otherwise faithful diesel engine and plug in the extension cord for the salt water pump. It takes substantial r.p.m.'s to make any headway against this strong wind and these choppy seas. Almost immediately the engine overheats and my quick plan is to drop the Bruce anchor now that the water is shallow enough, let the engine cool, then proceed again until it overheats, drop anchor, and continue this pattern. The Bruce anchor grabs quickly; and while I am checking the security of the anchor line with John West, we begin getting calls directed to "the American yacht just anchored near the harbor entrance." As I am busy with our ground tackle, I ask Jim Kegley to handle the call. It is Rafael del Castillo Morales, *Capitan de la Marina*, who is spending his Sunday trying to relax in his condo high on the hill while watching this storm ravage his harbor. Our VHF again will not broadcast so we resort to the handheld VHF. Jim informs the Port Captain we have lost our engine and cannot enter. Senor Morales says he will dispatch a rescue vessel to tow us in. Even though we can handle this ourselves, I am quite pleased to hear the news – Force 11 is a serious matter. Fortunately, there is very little traffic coming or going and our position, except for the storm, is safe. If our ground tackle fails, we will be swept toward the rocks and shore south of the port; but our engine would be under these less strenuous conditions (not into the wind), and be able to give us the leeway we will need to drift on out to sea. If that wouldn't work, a sail will provide the necessary leeway if we are quick enough. None of these contingencies are reassuring.

We begin rigging a tow line; and within 20 minutes, two red rescue vessels come out of the harbor to our aid. The larger approaches us tossing its own tow line. The other, being smaller, circles to be of potential assistance or to pick up anyone who might fall overboard in the excitement. With calm gestures, the non-English-speaking Spanish crew indicates we should pull up our anchor, but we find our windless is jammed. Without a word, these seamen understand, take the tension off the anchor line by pulling us forward a bit, and patiently wait while John West and I clear the jam and weigh anchor. After pulling us into the calm and security of the harbor – "any port in a storm" – the rescue vessel slacks our line and backs to come alongside to our port. We put out fenders, tie a bow line, a stern line and spring lines between the two vessels, whereupon we are taken to the yacht harbor, and very gently laid against the dock to starboard. My crew quickly transfers fenders and lines then ties spring lines, bow lines, and stern lines to the dock.

When the rescue boat insists on using its own tow line, I assume it is to strengthen their legal basis for charging us a substantial fee. We thank the rescue vessel and I am quite pleased when they tell me our rescue was a true emergency and there will be no charge.

Next time I think I'll sail on from the Mediterranean to the Canaries and leave the boat there for a few months. This will, according to Jimmy Cornell, avoid these gales.

While settling in, one of my crew members looks into the bilge and tells me the engine cooling seacock is closed. I tell him I know that. I closed it after we shut the engine down. It's a lie. The truth is I "screwed up" one of my best acts of seamanship – replacing the engine saltwater pump with the air-conditioning saltwater pump – by not reopening the seacock.

We are quickly found by Charlie Jett, a banker; Henry Couzens, a builder; and Paul Harbour, a retired IBM engineer, all three also from Lexington. Considering the weather, they have been quite anxious for us. Charlie and Paul have substantial Thistle sailing experience; however, only I have been offshore. I've never seen three crew members, John, Jim, and Charlie, pack their bags and get off a boat so fast. They reason they should stay in a hotel so they can get up and make their 8 a.m. flight to

Madrid the next morning. This, of course, is the principal reason I do not duck out of the weather at Lanzerote.

The following article is translated from the morning edition of *La Provincia*, the Las Palmas' newspaper:

"The sea forced his law on the capital of Grand Canaria. On the Avendia Maritima dangerous situations are present for the morning traffic facing unusual high waves that takes possession of the highways full length beating the avenue with such force that not even the oldest residents of the area can remember happening before. It is a result of a wind storm with speeds near hurricane level that involved the whole archipelago forcing the security and civil protection forces of the state to be at maximum alert and the rescue by sea and air of two boats and their crews on the high seas."

We wonder if one of the two rescued is us. During the night a freighter, *Sea Lion*, is torn off her mooring; and when the crew can't start her engines, she is blown onto the rocks.

* * *

The Canary Islands are 58 nautical miles off the coast of Africa and just 5° north of the Tropic of Cancer. They thus are in an area warmed all year by the sun. Because they are in the cool Gulf Stream, which on the eastern side of the Atlantic is southbound, the weather is what the citizens of San Diego call "spring year round."

Romans first visited the Canary Islands during the first century bringing back dogs which gave the island their Roman root name. The birds were later named after the islands and much later stool pigeons after the birds. Early in the 15th century the islands were taken over and settled by the Spanish.

In Columbus' epic voyage, *Pinta* had rudder problems and she stopped at Las Palmas for repairs while *Santa María* and *Niña*, with Columbus, proceeded to Gomera, another of the Canary Islands. Columbus later backtracked to Las Palmas fearing *Pinta* was avoiding the trip. All three went back to Gomera before starting their crossing.

Gran Canaria and its principal port, Las Palmas, share with the island of Tenerife and the port of Santa Cruz the claim of being the principal commercial port. Magellan stopped at Tenerife before finding the Strait of Magellan and crossing the Pacific. Las Palmas is however the Capital of this Spanish Province. Condominiums have been developed along the shore, particularly the southern shore, of Gran Canaria to a near disastrous extent. But the resulting English, German, Scandinavian, Swiss, and Spanish tourists necessitated building huge supermarkets which make this a wonderful provisioning stop before crossing to the west.

* * *

A group of sailboats in the harbor have been getting ready for leg two of the Europe Round-the-world Rally. Leg one was from Gibraltar and leg two is to Barbados. One boat, *Serenity II*, is from Cincinnati. The owner, Jerry Wernke, is understandably too busy preparing for departure to spend much time with us but crewmember Bruce French, from Northern Kentucky, is able to come aboard and compare notes. Bruce, just starting his journey, is talking of where he will go; and I, of what we will do when we get home.

Most of our supplies are purchased at Cruz Mayor, a supermarket a few miles south of the city. Fresh fruits and meat are from at El Corte Inglés, a department store in Las Palmas with a wonderfully large food store in the basement. In the back of this store, are several specialty shops; one has a large wood cow over it; another, a large wood pig; the next, a wood fish; and the last, six wood chickens. We need 32 skinless, boneless chicken breasts packed in eight packages of four each for our freezer. This will give us eight chicken meals for our estimated 18-day voyage to the Virgin Islands. Of course, we are provisioning for 24 days. The counter under the chickens has wonderful-looking breasts; and with a puzzled looking clerk and some language difficulty, all is finally accomplished and the chicken breasts are stowed in our freezer.

We get word both water pumps are being shipped DHL and I check daily at their office for both. We learn through DHL's computer that the pump from Cincinnati was delivered to the DHL hub at the Cincinnati/Northern Kentucky International Airport and the pump ordered from Florida was air-shipped to the Cincinnati hub. They are side-by-side on a shelf awaiting shipment to Brussels, Madrid, and eventually Las Palmas. Unfortunately Cincinnati is having record cold weather with deep snow and the airport is closed. We finally get word that the parts are in Madrid. To be shipped to the Canary Islands, where Customs is controlled by the military, requires bills of lading from the suppliers specifying the price and use of the parts. The bills of lading need to be sent to Madrid, attached to the packages, and then sent to Las Palmas so both packages and bills of lading arrive at the same time. Meanwhile we have the staysail repaired, clean the boat, install the spare VHF microphone, and wait.

The weather in the Canaries has improved dramatically

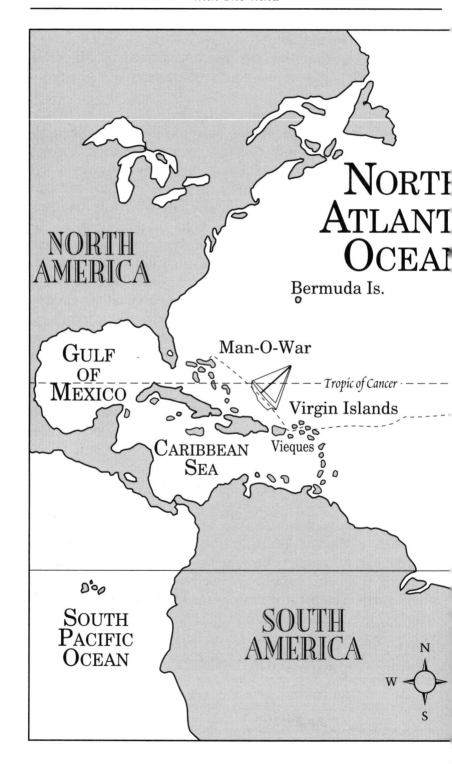

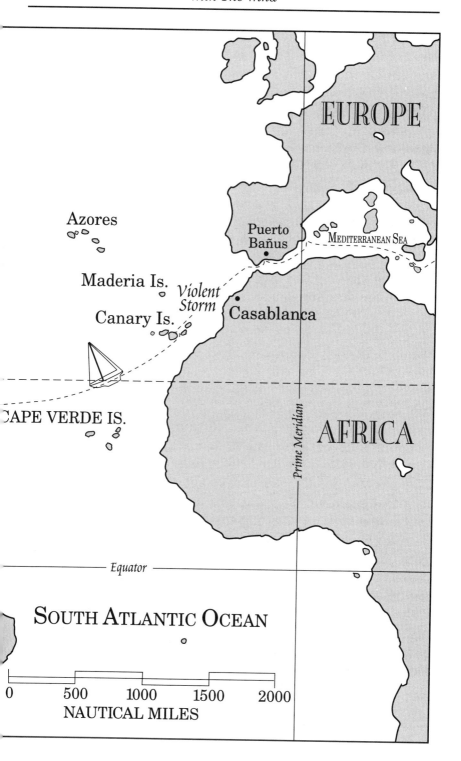

EUROPE

Azores

Maderia Is.

Canary Is.

Puerto
Bañus

MEDITERRANEAN SEA

*Violent
Storm*

Casablanca

CAPE VERDE IS.

Prime Meridian

AFRICA

Equator

SOUTH ATLANTIC OCEAN

0   500   1000   1500   2000
NAUTICAL MILES

and we have an excellent window to depart for our Atlantic crossing. My crew is nervous about potential late arrival in the Virgin Islands. The solution is for me to get up early in the morning, fly to Madrid, collect the packages, pass duty free through Customs, put them into my small suitcase, go back to the airport, and take a domestic flight back to Las Palmas. The DHL agent in Las Palmas makes arrangements and the station manager meets me and takes me in his BMW to the DHL warehouse where I get the parts, and pass through Customs. He then takes me back to the airport. I return to Las Palmas in the early afternoon. It takes some doing, but I have bypassed Canary Island customs.

Some small differences in the new pumps require two trips to a machine shop in the middle of the red-light district of this old seaport. All crew members insist on accompanying me both times, just to look, of course. While I install the pump and everything is apart, we learn the fuel dock will be closed for the next few days. I need to complete the job quickly so we can motor to the fuel dock before it closes.

We get to sea by 1 p.m., January 27, and a school of porpoises escorts us out of the Canaries. Our voyage starts aggressively with 12-foot seas and a broad reach on 25-knot winds. By the end of the day these subside to four-foot seas and pleasant 18-knot winds.

Charlie Jett is sleeping in the forward stateroom well before the mast. In heavy seas, he has great difficulty getting to the head; so he has improvised with a wide-mouth bottle and secure lid. Henry Couzens is sleeping in the salon. The first evening out Henry is asleep and Charlie, just off watch, is carrying a glass of water to his stateroom to drink while reading himself to sleep. The boat takes an unusual lurch and Charlie's glass of water sloshes all over Henry who immediately wakes up, jumps up, and asks excitedly, "What is that liquid, Charlie?"

Doing a deck check early the next morning, I find a squid washed aboard by the seas. I have never had a squid on deck before and toss the carcass back to sea before any Slocum students consider *calamari* for breakfast.

Winds are out of the west, or Africa, at an apparent six knots and seas are two feet. We motor-sail at low rpm's with the spinnaker and are doing seven knots. The bad news – the sails, rigging, deck, bimini, dodger, and cockpit are coated with Sahara dust bringing back memories of the Red Sea.

On Charlie's watch, we cross longitude 22.5° west giving him a five-hour watch. This is the first time the long watch is necessary since the Indian Ocean. Our navigation is by GPS with confirmation by watching the compass and the direction of the path of the sun. On this westbound passage, just following the sun will get us a landfall. At night we have the Southern Cross just above the horizon to port and Orion almost directly above – both comforting signs.

Sunday morning, January 30th. Charlie and Henry prepare and deliver an Episcopal Church service. The two members of the congregation, one of which arrives late, greatly appreciate the service. It is a warm feeling hearing the familiar liturgy that I remember from my youth.

* * *

Columbus was a Mediterranean sailor with some enlightenment, probably from his brother Bartolomé of Lisbon. Most Mediterranean sailors navigated following loxodromes, or rhumb lines, drawn on charts with the bearings indicated on them. We see these loxodromes, or rhumb lines, running in odd directions on reproductions of ancient charts. These lines show bearings (expressed as 32 points of the compass or 11°15' each) which take into account magnetic variation and the effects of current. The short distances in the Mediterranean almost guaranteed a reasonable landfall. Columbus was familiar with early celestial navigation; however, he did not have great confidence in its accuracy. At one point when latitude calculations with his quadrant did not come close to his dead reckoning position, Columbus stopped using the quadrant. Basically, Columbus followed the ship's compass to his landfall. He meanwhile eyeballed the sun and stars just as early South Pacific navigators had done and we on *Lusty Wind II* have done. Of course, we also have GPS which we trust implicitly.

* * *

To reciprocate for the great church service Henry and Charlie have given, the Captain is fixing a big bacon and egg breakfast and Paul has volunteered to cook dinner admitting to us that he has never cooked before. Paul and I study several menus and he decides to do chicken and capers. Henry and I both want to help but Paul insists on doing it himself. When dinner is served, the first thing we notice is Paul has forgotten the capers. No matter, it looks good. Looks are deceiving. The chicken seems quite overdone and has an unusual taste. We go ahead and eat, but we quiz Paul to see what magic ingredient he may have used.

The next day winds are down and coming around to our stern. In order not to use too much fuel this early in the trip, we attempt to pole out the spinnaker for more efficient down-wind sailing. Henry is on watch and I have

Charlie on the foreguy and Paul on the afterguy attempting to position the pole correctly. I look up and reassess my position directly under the heavy spinnaker pole. I step back a few feet and continue supervising the operation at which point the mast fitting of the pole fractures and it crashes down where I have just been standing. The next Episcopal service could well have been for me.

That evening we cross the Tropic of Cancer for the third time during the circumnavigation. The wind is picking up and the weather getting squally. By using the radar to watch these squalls, we have more than ample time to drop the spinnaker.

Sailing guides tell us that the trade winds, out of the east and crossing the southern North Atlantic, are normally between latitude 15° and 20° North; unfortunately to get to these steady trades requires traveling southwest, not directly towards our destination. Jimmy Cornell advises us that between December and March trade winds can blow at 22 to 27 knots for days on end accompanied by correspondingly high swells. With boat speeds of seven to eight knots, this makes wind speed across the deck 15 to 20 knots, very close to ideal sailing except for the increased chance of a gibe with the wind almost directly behind the boat. Cornell further tells us that nearly everybody experiences at least one several-day calm on this run. These calms can last from hours to days and are usually followed by a burst of trades with many squalls.

With a relatively inexperienced crew for this passage and with my continued concern over the cracks in the gooseneck, I use conservative sailing tactics. For example, I do not let the boom out as downwind conditions might otherwise dictate so that a gibe will not swing the boom so far and thus develop less force. These conservative tactics unfortunately reduce our daily run from an anticipated 160 to 170 nautical miles to 135 to 145 nautical miles.

We are looking for the trades to carry us westward just south of Columbus' wake across the Atlantic. The first clue of the trades is winds out of the east and we begin experiencing this near the Tropic of Cancer. The second classic sign is to watch for small puffy clouds, like those from a steam engine, which were also the sign for early sailors. Admiral Nelson turned west when the butter melted. The modern test is to get weather maps on the weatherfax; unfortunately we are too far from Norfolk, Virginia, to get the U.S. maps. We are receiving Spanish and French maps; however, they do not show enough distance into the Atlantic to give us any assurance. At 21°N we are 60 miles from the top of the 15° to 20°N typical range of the trade winds but the winds are good for westward course; so we turn to just a shade south of due west. Over several days we gradually reduce our latitude to assure proper location. If the winds decrease and we are too far north, we will be able to motor south. Otherwise we might save a day on the passage.

The difficult part of planning this passage is that it is 2,800 nautical miles, more than the distance from New York to San Francisco, and our fuel capacity is about 1,100 miles. A good amount of the fuel will be used early in the trip to get to the trade winds which in theory will carry us to our destination – that is, if we find these trades. As a last ditch, there is enough current in the Atlantic to get boats across in about 80 days. Steve Callahan lost *Napoleon Sole* after leaving the Canary Islands, in 1982, and was *"Adrift"* for 76 days. Callahan, incidentally, made a quadrant with three pencils and three rubber bands, and generally knew his latitude. Callahan's epic crossing is not my idea of part of a life-long dream.

Just after we make our turn, the winds build. As I am

gathering the energy to take down the spinnaker, it blows into many pieces – again. By the next morning apparent winds are 20 knots over our starboard aft quarter with true wind speed of 28 knots. We are making good speed but rolling awfully. Sailors call this a death roll. Our rigging plan was to have a big boom to stretch the main way out and reduce the roll; however our conservative sailing tactics do not allow us to use this advantage.

It is Paul's turn to cook his second dinner, and it becomes a massive juggling act in the rolling seas. This is not just his second meal of this passage, but the second of his lifetime. Paul cooks a chicken and cheese casserole. He remembers the cheese but again way over-cooks the chicken. And he's still using some odd ingredient. But again we eat it all.

During the evening, a black bird with webbed feet comes aboard for a rest and to entertain us. The crew thinks maybe a landfall is imminent; but this is a sea bird, not a land bird. In his log, Columbus mentions many times in his log visits from sea birds who live and have their young at sea and are never on land. Columbus knew the difference; and when land birds began to appear, he had a sense of how far he was from land, but not the direction to the land. What confused him was that he was traveling 150 miles north of the Greater Antilles, within the range of these birds, but he was still 700 or 800 miles east of his landfall on Samana Cay in the Bahamas.

The wind slacks off to an apparent 12 knots, or 17 to 18 knots of true wind. We are still rolling unmercifully. It has been estimated that on this passage sailboats roll three million times between the Canary Islands and the Caribbean. This is a conservative estimate. On our previous trip, the one-inch slide of the aft stateroom mattress wore all the varnish off the boards below.

Charlie Jett is not missing a cooking turn or a watch but he has a bad case of *mal de mer*. We call Charlie's doctor in Lexington via Whiskey Oscar Mike in Ft. Lauderdale to find if Charlie can take Tigan (for seasickness) with his other medication. We get permission and Charlie is soon feeling better.

Henry, a master chef, has worked out a recipe for chicken stew using only one pot (to save water and cleanup). That sounds great; and in the afternoon, I take four chicken breasts out of the freezer to thaw. The chicken is frozen but I notice the freezer is not as cold as it should be. I make a mental note to run the compressors a little longer. At 6, Henry starts his stew. The first step is cubing the chicken. I watch and learn. Henry examines the meat and proclaims, "This isn't chicken."

"Sure it is, Henry" I say and gave him the whole story about the six wood chickens over the counter at El Corte Inglés in Las Palmas.

"Well, it isn't chicken." He says. "It's *Hasenpfeffer* – rabbit." *Hasenpfeffer*, it turns out, is a favorite meal in the Canaries both with the locals and the German tourists and it is usually sold at the poultry counter. The good news is we still have 24.

I'm glad Paul forgot the capers. *Hasenpfeffer* with capers would not have been an appetizing presentation. Henry's *Hasenpfeffer* stew is delightful.

The next morning winds are dying and we begin motor-sailing at low rpm's to conserve fuel. In my fuel planning at the start of a passage, I establish a threshold low speed usually five-and-a-half knots and motor-sail to increase speed when the wind will not give us the five-and-a-half. I monitor fuel usage; and if it appears we are using too much to reach our destination safely, I reduce the threshold. It saves fuel but the trip takes longer. We have used considerable fuel in the early days and still have 1,500 miles to go. I reduce the threshold to five knots and our day's run is 128 nautical miles.

I am considering the pros and cons of turning south. Historically there is certainly more chance of wind to the south, but we will waste at least a day getting there. Charlie comes on deck feeling much better and suggests we are way too far north and should travel south. If I weren't such an even tempered, warm-hearted Captain, I would take away Charlie's Tigan to bring an end to his insolence. I tell Charlie I have been thinking about this all day and have just about decided to do it. That way if it turns out to be a good idea, I will get credit. We turn southwest. Two days later we reach 18.5°N and find essentially the same winds we have to the north. Of course, I tell Charlie he had a bad idea.

The first day after turning east the winds increase, blowing out our genoa in a 30 plus knot gust. It takes us a while to bag the sail and bend on genoa number two.

A large pod of orkas, or killer whales, are playing around the boat. Orkas and other whales can be dangerous to small boats in the blue-water. They have been known to pound them until they eventually cause hull damage and sometimes a sinking as with the Robertsons and Baileys. These orkas are up to 20 feet long and heavy enough to do damage. Our hull is a heavy inch-and-a-half thick below the water line and we probably could survive a pounding, but I don't want to find out. The current theory is that whales sleep on the surface; and when one is accidentally hit by a sailboat, it is interpreted by the pod as an attack and they counter attack. Sailors used to turn off their depth finder when out of soundings; however, it is now suggested that the pinging of the depth finder will awaken whales and possibly avoid these attacks – we follow this advice. I assume this pinging also gives nuclear subs something to note in their logs.

It is apparent both the 120 volt and the engine drive

refrigeration systems are failing and we are still 1,000 miles or, at our speed, six-and-one-half days from the Virgin Islands.

By popular request we again have *Hasenpfeffer* stew – this time with fresh baked bread. For me it is a wonderful birthday dinner. All meals are now frozen food to be used before spoiling. The freezer will be as cool as a refrigerator for a few days, but it will be canned food for the duration unless we catch fish.

Winds return and by noon we are doing seven knots. Charlie reminds me that he made the right decision turning south. Again, being easy going and warm-hearted particularly at sea, I don't show Charlie the NAM weatherfaxes out of Norfolk, Virginia, showing good winds all the way to 22°N.

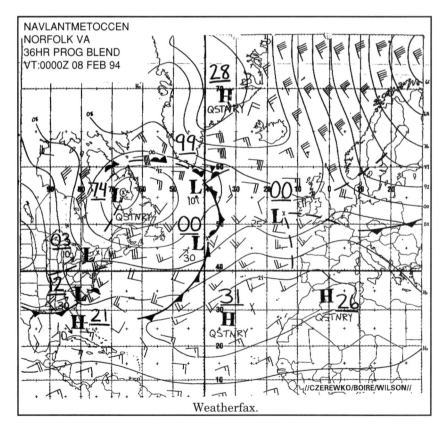

Weatherfax.

Friday, February 11. We are becoming accustomed to warm beer and soft drinks and have eaten the last of the frozen foods. Twelve possibly spoiled *Hasenpfeffers* are thrown overboard. Some fish is probably wondering what that was.

Speed is improving, slowed only by our reducing sail during occasional squalls. Now that we have lost our spinnaker and genoa number one and are using our old genoa number two, we are being even more conservative. We will slow down considerably if we lose our last headsail and we have not become that accustomed to warm beer and canned food.

This afternoon, the Captain decides to go fishing. I put the lure out and soon reel in a dolphin. Paul makes a case that he has actually caught it with the gaff. Henry and Paul prepare a large dinner early as we, of course, have no ice or refrigeration.

Sunday morning the 9 a.m. Episcopal Church service is postponed until 11 a.m. while Paul – half the congregation – sleeps. He says he is exhausted after gaffing that fish.

At sunset I see another marvelous "green flash." We are now at 18° 24' and the wind is down to five or six knots, which is just about our boat speed under power. By midnight on February 15, I calculate we have 215 nautical miles to go with 80 plus gallons of fuel, or enough for 293 nautical miles. In my log entry, I congratulate myself on excellent fuel planning.

By 2 in the afternoon on February 16, we can see St. Martin on the radar. By 4 p.m., it is visible with the naked eye. In honor of the occasion, Henry does a wonderful job with canned chicken chow mein. Or is it *Hasenpfeffer* chow mein?

Feb. 17. Dawn. We are approaching the Salt Island Passage and we must remember we are back in Bouyage region B and "Red Right Return." We sail between Salt

Island and Peter Island then across Sir Francis Drake Channel with one lonely porpoise leading the way. Just before 7 a.m., we tie up at Nanny Cay Marina near Roadtown, Tortola, British Virgin Islands, and are met at the dock by Johnny Hassan of Johnny's Maritime Services. We have reservations and Johnny has been expecting us but he is on the dock early because Dodge Morgan is also expected in today. Morgan, alone, of course, is bringing his new boat, *Winds of Time*, to the Caribbean for some cruising.

Our crew spends a busy day clearing Customs, taking our guns to the police station, cleaning, and getting the boat otherwise ship-shape. The next morning, after a final cleanup, I have Johnny make arrangements to service the engine and generator, repair the refrigeration system, and repair genoa number one and the spinnaker. We then leave for flights home.

Columbus took 36 days to cover the 3,100 nautical miles from Gomera to Samana Cay. He said in his log:

> "Gutiérrez has already acquired all the wood and water necessary for the voyage, which I estimate will last 21 days. However, to be on the safe side, in case of contrary winds or currents, I ordered Gutiérrez to prepare for a voyage of 28 days. I anticipate no problem in replenishing our supplies when we reach the Indies."

Columbus also had provisioned for one-third more days than he anticipated.

When I return home, some people think we had completed the circumnavigation because we're back in familiar waters. I'm a director of Star Bank of Kentucky N.A.; and when I show up at my first meeting in a long time, a fellow director makes a motion to pass a resolution to congratulate me and welcome me back – the motion dies for the lack of a second.

13

CHAPTER THIRTEEN

"...when the Long Trick's Over"
March 18, 1994 – March 31, 1994
Tortola – Man-O-War Cay

I arrive in Tortola, British Virgin Islands, after a month at home, turn on the refrigeration system, unpack my gear, and spend a little time cleaning the boat. I'm soon off to the cafe at Nanny Cay for a cheeseburger and a beer. While self-consciously sitting alone, I look up and do a classic double-take as Dodge Morgan walks in alone for his lunch. Dodge Morgan achieved fame and honors particularly among sailors when he sailed *American Promise,* in 1985 and 1986, non-stop around the world single-handedly – breaking records all the way. Dodge's trip was eastbound, mostly in the high southern latitudes, and took 150 days. I introduce myself, tell him about our trip so far, and my vow not to write a book. We share more beer and discuss our trips. Dodge tells me that I should write a book; and he is right, it's almost as much fun as the voyage. I run back to *Lusty Wind II* to get my copy of his book for his autograph. Later I ask Manny, Dodge's wife for her autographs, too – Pat and I understand her part in the trip as well as anybody. Manny is thrilled and says I am the first ever to ask.

Both refrigeration systems are working perfectly. Milton Felex who works for Johnny's Marine Services has serviced the engine and generator and he helps me take the boat to the lift to be hauled out for the bottom to be cleaned and inspected. When Felex and I return with the boat, we find a sailboat with an orange hull has taken the slip assigned to us. Felex tells the man on the boat that he is in our slip and politely asks him to move. The man replies, "I won't and what do you think of that?" I take the mike and tell him I think he is a jerk on an orange boat. At that point I was perfectly satisfied to radio a request for another slip assignment.

* * *

Columbus sighted the Virgin Islands on his second voyage in 1493 and named them for the 11,000 virgins of St. Ursula. Through the 16th, 17th, and 18th centuries, these islands were traded back and forth between six European countries that were jockeying for economic power, military position, and pride. Intertwined with this constant changing political status were pirates and their bases plus insurrections by poorly treated slaves on European-owned sugar plantations.

The British Virgin Islands, the eastern half of the Virgin Islands, are where the British gained control in 1672. Today the British Virgin Islands are linked to the British Commonwealth. Laws are made and administered locally, but the Queen still appoints the figurehead Governor.

* * *

On Monday, Ross Brown, a retired telephone executive joins me. The next day Jack Gartner, an architect, Bill Vermillion, and Pat Klocke, both bankers, arrive. Bill and Pat were at that directors' meeting and, of course, neither offered to second the motion to welcome me back. All four crew members are from Northern Kentucky. During the day we buy eight days of provisions for our anticipated six-day trip to Man-O-War. Late in the evening we collect our guns and clear out through Customs and Immigration.

March 23. Wednesday. We depart Nanny Cay at 7:30 a.m. and motor in light air through The Narrows to Cruz Bay on St. John to clear into The United States. We then motor across Pillsbury Sound to Red Hook on St. Thomas, where we have lunch and take on fuel. On our departure from Red Hook, Jack Gartner's hat blows off. We have a "Man-overboard" drill and recover the hat. Jack puts it back on and it blows overboard again with another drill bringing our procedure to near perfection. We then motor through St. James Cut and make our course for Isabel Segunda, Vieques, Puerto Rico.

We are motor-sailing in light air when the engine comes to an uncomfortable sounding stop. We have motored over a submerged fishnet. Bill Vermillion and Pat Klocke have their swimsuits on and are quickly in the water with knives to remove the net now entangled in our prop. While they work, we are under sail at about two knots. I am eyeing the chart to see where the wind might help us find an anchorage if their attempts are unsuccessful. Bankers are trained to tie a person up, not set anything free; but they soon have our prop clear of the net and we are on our way.

* * *

The name Vieques comes from an old Indian word bieques meaning, like *motu*, a small island. This island was discovered in 1524 by the Spanish Captain Cristóbal de Mendoza. The British and the French had occupied and abandoned the island at various times until the Spanish finally annexed it to Puerto Rico in 1854.

During the Spanish-American War, the American gunboat *Yale* arrived and a detachment landed. The Spanish commander explained he could not surrender the island without firing a shot; whereupon the Americans gracefully allowed him to fire off a valley before establishing their control. In 1940, our government realized that the Nazis could overwhelm the British. So just in case, construction was begun on a naval base at the west end of the island to provide a haven for a possibly routed British Navy. To create a major port, construction was begun on a sea-wall stretching from Culebra south to Vieques and then west to Roosevelt Roads on Puerto Rico. After Pearl Harbor, it was evident that concentrated naval bases were not necessarily a good thing; so work was stopped. Our navy is now building a new concentrated base at Roosevelt Roads to replace the soon-to-be-abandoned Guantánamo. The military presence on Vieques is of major importance with the navy controlling 70 percent of the land. Much of this island has been used for air and sea target bombardment.

* * *

As we approach Isabel Segunda, a woman is watching for us. She has a harbor view and is a close friend of Bill and Marion Littleford, my aunt and uncle. Bill and

Marion live a large portion of the year in their home near the highest point of the island. This home is what we dream of. It consists of just a few informal rooms around a porch and breezeway and has views covering 360 degrees. Where the circle is not dominated by ocean vistas, it is to adjacent small native farms.

Uncle Bill is a vital part of this circumnavigation because he and Aunt Peach, my mother's sister and his first wife, kindled my desire to sail. Bill and Peach often chartered boats in the Virgin Islands and owned one on Long Island Sound. After hearing their stories, I dreamed of someday sailing myself.

On getting notice of our arrival, Bill and Marion meet us at the waterfront. I borrow Ross Brown's baseball cap with a ponytail sewn in the back. I know Uncle Bill is glad to see me, but he cannot look directly at me after noticing the ponytail. Once Bill realizes the ponytail is attached to the hat and not his nephew, we can't get it away from him. It is a little embarrassing to my crew to see Bill and Marion climb from the dinghy to *Lusty Wind II* with more speed and agility than any of us. Soon a rowboat arrives with Chuck Webster, engaged by Bill, to watch our boat while we all go to dinner. We drive to their home running several horses off the road on the drive up the hill. After cocktails, hors d'oeuvres, and a marvelous sunset, we have dinner at a restaurant on the south side of the island and then return to the boat.

By 10:30 a.m., we depart for our last passage of the circumnavigation. By 1 p.m. we are through the San Juan Pass between Puerto Rico and Culebra and sailing in trade winds. We pass over the Puerto Rico Trench, 28,232 feet (5.3 miles) deep and the deepest known point in the Atlantic Ocean. The sailors' guru, Jimmy Cornell, tells us the best time to make this passage is November to May and the dangerous time, because of tropical storms, is June to November. We are here, by plan, at the best time.

This is ideal with trade winds and nearly a knot of current going our way, marred only by occasional short calms or light wind requiring motoring or motor-sailing. The hazard, which has almost been eliminated by GPS navigation, is drifting too far to the west and wrecking on submerged banks such as Navadad Bank, Silver Bank, and Mouchoir Bank.

Several times we are escorted by orkas who stay with us several hours each time. Traveling north, we cross the Tropic of Cancer for the fourth time of the circumnavigation near the point where Columbus spent his last apprehensive night at sea before landing at what is believed to have been Samana Cay. *Lusty Wind II*'s performance reminds me of Melville: "She jogged her way like a veteran old-sea-pacer as she is."

Tuesday, March 19. We sight Elbow Cay in the Abacos, Bahamas, at 6:05 a.m. I am on watch and alone on deck when I see the Elbow Cay light; I quietly say, "Land ho." By 9:30 we are through the reef-strewn south Man-O-War Pass, with the sun over my shoulder for once and my heart, as usual, in my throat the entire way. We motor to Marsh Harbor to clear into the Bahamas. A young man named Cassius Cunningham cheerfully clears us in. When he learns this is the last stop on an around-the-world trip, he asks if I write a book to include him – so here you are, Cassuis Cunningham.

The Abacos have been our sailing home for nearly 20 years. My mother's childhood friends in Ft. Thomas, Alice and Jane Robinson, with their father and my Grandfather's friend, Skipper Robinson, settled for the winter months in these islands just after World War II. Prior to buying *Lusty Wind*, we chartered many times in this easy and rewarding cruising ground. *Lusty Wind* and Lusty *Wind II* have both been based at Man-O-War Marina in the Abacos a goodly portion of the time.

* * *

The first recorded European discovery of these islands was by Ponce de León in 1513. There is some reason to believe Europeans visited the Abacos years before Columbus. Caves have been found on Great Abaco with what appear to be early Indian drawings of galleons showing royal crests on the mainsail that predate Columbus by 42 years. One expert who examined the cave drawings says, "Fresh is good for fish, but not for petrogyphs." They do, however, illustrate the probability of early visits. Many Portuguese and other sailors never returned. Early sailors could have been lost at sea, could possibly have returned with either no significance given to their stories, or they could have buried the evidence to keep enemies from gaining the advantage of this knowledge.

Over the next two centuries, many galleons sank in the waters of the Abacos. Later pirates used the Abacos as a base to raid the shipping between the Carolinas and England or New England. After the Revolutionary War, loyalists from New England and the Carolinas escaped anticipated prosecution by fleeing to the still British Bahamas. They eked out a living by fishing and farming. Occasionally their hard-earned improvements were smashed by hurricanes. A few made their living by turning off lighthouses and salvaging ships that subsequently found themselves wrecked on the barrier reef. Tourism and winter homes of wealthy Americans have led the descendants of these loyalists into prosperity. Skipper Robinson would be amazed to find many homes with satellite dishes and the children and grandchildren of friends he made in the Abacos now spending vacations skiing in Colorado, Utah, and Switzerland and flying to Super Bowl games. These same loyalists attempted to block the independence of the Bahamas and tried to secede from the early independent nation.

* * *

For several days before our arrival, we have been preparing to dress *Lusty Wind II* for her return to Man-O-War. We have the courtesy flags of all the 23 nations and territories we visited starting with the Bahamas and ending with Puerto Rico strung from the masthead to the bow. We have signal flags spelling out "AROUND-THE-WORLD" strung from the masthead to the stern. In the word "world" we use our third repeater flag for the "O" and the second repeater flag for the "R." Not having a sixth repeater flag, Pat "Betsy" Klocke is pressed into service with a needle, thread, scissors, yellow T-shirt, and blue T-shirt to make a second "D," or delta flag. As we are crossing Abaco Sound, a gust of wind comes up and blows the flags loose at their connection at the stern. This must be why flag etiquette instructs sailors not to dress ships underway.

Did we sail the Seven Seas? Before venturing out of the Mediterranean, sailors talked of seven seas, the Mediterranean, Red, China, West African, East African, Indian, and the Persian Gulf. When Columbus, Magellan, and de Gama expanded the known world, it became evident there were more oceans than they had believed, and the expression Seven Seas dropped out of use. At the end of the last century, Rudyard Kipling resurrected the phrase naming a book of poems *The Seven Seas*. Today sailors consider the Seven Seas to be the Arctic, Antarctic, North Atlantic, South Atlantic, North Pacific, South Pacific, and Indian. Thus we cross four of these Seven

Seas. The National Geographic Society doesn't recognize the Antarctic Ocean. Considering *National Geographic* as the authority, we have crossed four oceans of six. If one counts bodies of water called seas, we cross the Caribbean, Kero, Coral, Arafura, Timor, Arabian, Red, Mediterranean, Levantine, Agean, Ionian, Tyrrhenian, and Alborun; but there are many more.

In our passage, we have crossed the Equator twice, the International Date Line once, the Prime Meridian once, and the Tropic of Cancer and the Tropic of Capricorn four times each. We have visited four of six continents.

By the definition of the *Guinness Book of Records*, a world circumnavigation requires passing through a pair of antipodal points. We accomplished this first on April 27, 1993, in the Indian Ocean just before reaching the Cocos Keeling Islands. Our wake had four pairs of antipodal points.

As well as we have been able to ascertain, *Lusty Wind II* is the first boat from Kentucky to sail around the world. A challenger to this record would be U.S.S. *Kentucky*, a battleship, which circumnavigated with Teddy Roosevelt's Great White Fleet in 1907-1908. This battleship is not actually from Kentucky, but close. During her circumnavigation, there were twenty-four court marshals all for an offense I understand – crew stealing the captain's liquor. Now the new U.S.S. *Kentucky*, a Trident submarine, is probably continually circling the globe.

Statistics rattle in my head; lists of ports, of provisions, of storms and sunsets and repairs – how many repairs have we made on this trip?

I feel the rush that comes with completing a long, hard task, the wave of pride and relief that accompanies the birth of healthly children, the Christmas morning grin that won't go away.

We charge through Man-O-War pass with 14 flags

flying nearly straight out from the masthead in 25 knots of wind, turn northeast with the tradewinds and into the Man-O-War harbor. We are surprised to see a crowd gathered at our slip. Scott Eldon, who is now the Man-O-War Marina manager, and John Allen Fulmer, who lived across Vernon Lane in Ft. Thomas when I was growing up, are there to help with the dock lines. Marcell Albury, Betsy Fulmer, and Ro Gardner are also among the group with their congratulations. Scott reminds us it is March 31 and our reservation isn't until April 1st. "Don't worry," he says, "I'll work it out."

While we are being congratulated, I notice Lincoln Albury, who has maintained *Lusty Wind II* for years, varnishing a boat a few slips away. Lincoln is a man of few words and is avoiding the crowd. After everyone leaves to allow us to get settled, I watch Lincoln put down his brush, clean his hands and walk over to shake mine.

Fiberglass, teak, aluminum, and stainless steel are supposed to be inanimate items; but if Lincoln and I had checked her water line we would find *Lusty Wind II* riding a little higher in the water than usual – and so she should.

> I must down to the seas again,
>   to the vagrant gypsies' life,
> To the gull's way and the whale's way
>   where the wind's like a wetted knife;
> And all I ask is a merry yarn
>   from a laughing fellow-rover,
> And quiet sleep and a sweet dream
>   when the long trick's over.

> *Sea-fever* (Third Stanza)
> John Masefield

AFT

Voyage Statistics

Beginning: November 9, 1991   Man-O-War Cay,
Abaco, Bahamas

End: March 31, 1994   Man-O-War Cay

Legs:		**Nautical Miles**	**Statute Miles**
Man-O-War Cay – Ft. Lauderdale	Nov. 1991	250	288
Ft. Lauderdale – Brisbane, Australia	Apr.-Sep. 1992	10,640	12,250
Brisbane – Puerto Bañus, Spain	Feb.-Sep. 1993	11,703	13,474
Puerto Bañus – Tortola, BVI	Jan.-Feb. 1994	3,568	4,108
Tortola – Man-O-War Cay	Mar. 1994	880	1,013
Total		27,041	31,133

Duration:	2 years 5 months
Nautical Miles:	27,041
Statute Miles:	31,133
Weeks on Board:	61
Weeks at Sea:	25
Weeks in Port:	36

Countries: 19
Ports: 63
Average Daily Run: 163nm 187sm
Fuel Used: 4,454 gallons
Engine Hours: 2,830
Generator Hours: 750

Lusty Wind II Specifications

Make & Model: Mason 53 Center Cockpit
                        (Shoal Draft)
Type: Auxiliary Cutter
Length: 53' 6" (16.31 meters)
LWL: 39' 8½" (12.10 meters)
Beam: 14'10" (4.52 meters)
Displacement: 54,000 lbs. (29.77 metric tons)
Ballast: Lead 16,000 lbs.
Draft: 6'5" (1.91 meters) Salt Water
                        6' 6½" (1.96 meters)
                        Fresh Water
Freeboard: 3' 6" (1.04 meters)
Theoretical Hull Speed: 8.75 knots
Mast Height: 63' (19.20 meters)
                        from waterline
                        71' (21.65 meters) with antennas

Sail Area:
    Genoa (135%)   840 sq. ft.
    Staysail   193 sq. ft.
    Main   681 sq. ft.
    Cruising Spinnaker 1,850 sq. ft.
    Storm Trysail   169 sq. ft.
Fuel Capacity-tanks: 283 gallons
Fuel Capacity-Jerry cans: 90 gallons
Range Under Power   1,260 nautical miles
Water Capacity: 340 gallons

Equipment:

Life raft	Viking-6UK Double bottom
Furling	Forespar, Profurl and Hyde
Engine	Westerbeke W100
Generator	Westerbeke WMD 8kW
Mast	Forespar
VHF Radio	Stevens-SEA 156
VHF Handheld Radio	ICOM-ICM11
SSB Radio	Furuno-FX4001
EPIRB-406	ACR-RLB-24 Category II
EPIRB-Type B	ACR-RLB-21
Weatherfax/Navtex	Furuno-FAX 208A
Compass	Ritchie-Globemaster
Sextant	Tamaya-NAVTECH MS-733
GPS	Furuno-GP-1500
Loran/GPS	Northstar-800/8000
Radar	Furuno-FR805D
ADF	Furuno-FD171
Sailing Instruments	B&G-Hydra 330
Autopilot	Robertson-AP200DL Sail
Refrigeration	Rich Beers, Inc.
Galley Range	Sea Ward 3142 (120 volt)
Watermaker	Village Marine-MPW 400 (17 gallons per hour)
Built:	July 1985 to February 1986
Commissioned:	March to June 1986
Maiden Voyage:	June 1986 (Ft. Lauderdale – Man-O-War)
Designer:	Al Mason / PAE Design Group
Builder:	Pacific Asian Enterprises Dana Point, CA. Joe Meglen, Jeff Leishman, Dan Streech
Construction Yard:	Ta-Shing Yacht Building Co., Ltd., Tainan, Taiwan
Dealer:	Pilot Yachts, Ft. Lauderdale, FL Rich Gopfert

Subcontractors:

Electronics Unlimited, Inc -
John Day, Darrell Hawkins,
Mike Spyros and Ron Muller
Jim Marshall Canvass -
Jim and Lynn Marshall
Maritime Marine Inc. -
Malcolm Parton
Michael Jaramillo, Carpenter
Mike the Welda - Mike LaMarre
Rich Beers Marine, Inc. -
Rich Beers & Kevin McCarthy
Riggers Loft, Inc. -
Doug Schweers

Emergency Equipment

Life Vests Type I (12)	Jack Lines
Six-Person Life raft	Fire Extinguishers (4)
Flares	Automatic Fire Extinguisher
Signal Mirror	Trauma Kit
Electric Horn	Medicine Cabinet
Air Horn	Cockpit Manual Bilge Pump
EPIRB Type 406	Cabin Manual Bilge Pump
EPIRB Type B	Engine Drive Bilge Pump
Portable VHF	Axe
Butcher Knife	Bungs
Solar Stills (2)	Hydraulic Cable Cutter
Emergency Tiller	Handheld Water-maker
Strobes (6)	Emergency VHF Antenna
Horseshoe Buoy	Flashlights
Life Sling	Sea Anchor
MOB Pole	Emergency Hatch Covers (3)
Safety Harnesses (6)	Emergency Port Covers (4)
Searchlight	Emergency Water (10 Gal)

Fire Procedures

1. With electric fire, shut off master electric switches before extinguishing fire (ship's service & start batteries below aft settee bench and navigation batteries below forward settee bench). Do not turn off start battery with engine or generator running.
2. Remove gasoline or other flammable materials from area of fire if this can be done safely.
3. If possible, shut off fuel supply from tanks (port & starboard under salon sole and aft under aft stateroom bunk).
4. Fire extinguishers should be aimed at base of fire, not at smoke.
5. Burning materials should be jettisoned if possible.
6. Reduce air supply by maneuvering boat or closing off the area of fire.
7. After extinguishing fire, cool area with sea water.

Storm Procedures

1. Put on life preservers and have safety harness ready. At night wear strobes.
2. Pump bilge.
3. Remove dorades; replace cover plates.
4. Install forward weather boards.
5. Secure ports and hatches.
6. Be sure jack lines are in place and secure.
7. Put knives in galley rack into drawers.
8. Secure top tool drawers in boatswain's locker.
9. Secure all gear above and below decks.
10. Put storm trisail in track and secure.
11. Have sea anchor and rode accessible.
12. Disconnect navigation & radio antennas, power supply and ground in electrical storm if appropriate, at minimum, disconnect Northstar Loran/GPS.

Man Overboard Procedures

1. Give five short blasts with horn (red button on steering column) and yell "MAN OVERBOARD." Keep watch on MOB or last known position.
2. Reduce sail or power.
3. Throw horseshoe, man overboard pole, and several cushions overboard. Horseshoe and man overboard pole are connected by 30' of line.
4. Assign first and, if possible, the second on deck to continue to watch MOB or last known position. Have second on deck note position from GPS and bearing from compass. Press "event" button on GPS.
5. Throw additional objects that will float to ensure the path back to the MOB can be retraced.
6. If under sail – disengage autopilot – once hands are on deck, head into wind, and furl sails – after checking for lines overboard, start engine.
7. Locate MOB under power. Be careful not to run MOB down.
8. When MOB is sighted, deploy "lifesling" located on port stern to retrieve MOB. See instructions on Lifesling case.
9. Circle MOB until contact is made.
10. Shift to neutral – MOB puts lifesling on – DO NOT TOW MOB.
11. Pull MOB slowly alongside boat by hand.
12. Only in the event a child or injured person is overboard should someone go in after him – only then with a life vest and line secured to vessel.
13. Recovery should be affected amidships on lee side (wind on other side) where vessel's movement and freeboard are at a minimum.
14. Free halyards – spinnaker and auxiliary main – both with red markings are long enough to reach a MOB alongside and may be used for recovery.

15. If MOB is not recovered very quickly, see distress communications.
16. The best MOB procedure is to prevent a MOB. Never urinate over the side. Have a safety harness handy in cockpit to be used when out on deck. No fishing at night. No one is allowed out of cockpit unless someone else is in the cockpit. ABSOLUTELY NO EXCEPTIONS.

Distress Communications Procedure

SPEAK: SLOWLY – CLEARLY – CALMLY

1. Select VHF Channel 16 or SSB 2182 kHz.
2. Press microphone button and say:
   "MAYDAY – MAYDAY – MAYDAY".
3. Say: "This is
   WHISKEY TANGO UNIFORM 9602 – LUSTY WIND II,
   WHISKEY TANGO UNIFORM 9602 – LUSTY WIND II,
   WHISKEY TANGO UNIFORM 9602 – LUSTY WIND II,
   MAYDAY – LUSTY WIND II."
4. Tell where you are (position or what navigational aids or landmarks are near).
5. Tell if the EPIRB has been deployed.
6. State the nature of your distress.
7. Give number of souls aboard and condition of any injured.
8. Estimate present seaworthiness of the boat and intent of boarding life raft.
9. Describe boat: LENGTH 53 FEET (16 meters) AUXILIARY SAILING VESSEL, WHITE HULL, ONE MAST.

10. Say: "I WILL BE LISTENING ON VHF CHANNEL 16, SSB 2182 kHz," or other appropriate frequency.

11. End message by saying:
"MAYDAY – THIS IS THE SAILING VESSEL LUSTY WIND II – WHISKEY TANGO UNIFORM 9602 – OVER."

12. Release microphone button and listen: Someone should answer. IF SOMEONE DOES NOT, REPEAT CALL, BEGINNING AT ITEM NO. 2 ABOVE. If there is still no answer, switch to Amver Frequencies (Upper side-band), channel 424, 601, 816, 1205, 1625, and 2206 Radio Telephone channels or Ham Radio (Lower Side Band) try Ham net frequencies on 14,300 to 14,320kHz. (Ham License KC4CUC)

13. To transmit automatic distress signal on the Furuno SSB radio press "SEND" then "START" to activate the alarm generator. A signal will continue to transmit until power is discontinued.

14. Mayday is reserved for life-threatening emergencies. If the emergency is not life-threatening, use "PAHN PAHN – PAHN PAHN – PAHN PAHN" (Rhymes with DON).

15. After contact on VHF channel 16, you may be asked to switch to VHF channel 22 or SSB 2182 kHz to 2670 kHz.

16. If emergency call is heard, clear radio, render any assistance possible and maintain log of radio messages. Use "MAYDAY RELAY – MAYDAY RELAY – MAYDAY RELAY" to report another vessel in distress.

17. Keep ship's batteries charged above 12.5 volts and batteries of handheld VHF charged for radio operation in the event of emergency.

Life Raft Procedures

1. Life raft is located on deck just forward of the mast.
2. Remove life raft canister from chocks by releasing pelican hook or snatch block at either end of securing strap. Do not release painter line from the vessel, but pull 10' out of canister.
3. Do not throw the canister overboard until you are ready to board the life raft. It is best to stay aboard the vessel as long as possible.
4. It is imperative to take the EPIRB Type 406, located on bulkhead between the salon and galley. The EPRIB Type 406 notifies authorities of the location and name of the vessel with worldwide range. Also important is charged handheld VHF (in nav. desk) and boat flare kit (in locker aft of dinette).
5. Throw canister overboard - when the remaining 20' of the painter is pulled either by wind or waves or by hand, the CO_2 is discharged and the life raft inflates and blows the canister off. The painter still holds raft to the boat. Life raft may be pulled back aboard and inflated with the pump through the yellow/white check valves situated on the two tubes inside the life raft if necessary.
6. When all are aboard the life raft, there is a knife on the canopy arch to cut the painter free of the sinking boat. Do not cut the life raft free earlier than necessary. The boat may not sink.
7. The securing strap has a Berwin MK8 hydrostatic release valve which will release the life raft when the boat is 10' below water surface if not released manually.
8. Turn on the EPIRB. If you are in the area where you would anticipate response within 48 hours, turn on both EPIRBs to assure one is transmitting. In a more remote area, turn on the Type 406 (from boat) then, in 72 hours, turn on the Type B (in life raft). Each should provide 80 hours coverage, for a total of 152 hours.

9. Each person should receive four cups of water, one quart, per day. There is thus enough water in the life raft for ½ day for six persons. In the Orange Bag there is enough water for an additional three days. There is enough water for another three days in the five gal. emergency water bottle located under the seat in the Foreward Stateroom. The handheld watermaker in the life raft is capable of making one cup of water in 15 minutes. The two solar stills should produce one gal. per day or enough water for four persons. DO NOT DRINK SEA WATER OR URINE.

10. Handheld Watermaker Instructions: For first two minutes pump water overboard. Pump handle at a comfortable rate of speed – about 40 strokes per minute. You will get more water if you stop temporarily then repeat the above procedure. If the unit is hard to pump either the strainer is clogged or the water is unusually cold or salty. Pump at least 15 minutes each day.

11. The life raft contains the following:

Instructions	Droque
Parachute Rockets	Bellows
Handheld Flares	Can Opener
Hand-held Watermaker	Knife
First-aid Kit	Repair Kit
Solar Still (2 qts./day)	Whistle
Fish Hooks & Line	EPRIB Type B
Batteries & Bulb	Sunblock Lotion
Magneto Flashlight	Seasick Pills
6 pts. Water	Flashlight
Food Tins	Sugar Pills
Paddles	Bailer
Hard Candy	Signal Card
Rescue Line	

12. There is an orange bag of additional emergency supplies which should be strapped to the mast on ocean passages. The bag contains the following:

Sun Block Lotion	Fish Hooks & Line
Space Blanket/Bag (6)	Spear Sling
2nd Solar Still	Can Opener

The following should be put in the bag at beginning of an ocean passage:

Water (two $2\frac{1}{2}$ gal.)   Food (see #14)   Flares

13. If time permits, other things to take are:

5 Gal. Emergency Water	Medical Supplies
Food (see #14)	Handheld VHF
Clothes	Books

14. Attempt to choose food low in salt. Best foods are low salt canned soup, low salt peanut butter, and low salt V-8 juice.

15. Any crew member needing special medical supplies should inform the master before departure and make necessary provisions for the life raft.

Watch Instructions

1. STAY AWAKE AND ALERT – it is important for the watchkeeper to stay awake. Do not lie down. Stand or sit. And if you feel you cannot stay awake – Please notify the captain.
2. STAY IN COCKPIT – you may leave cockpit to go below for a few (five) minutes at a time to check navigation, use the head, fix coffee, soft drinks, snacks, etc. Do not go out on deck unless it is necessary and then not without someone else in the cockpit.
3. AVOID COLLISION – if any ship, land, or shore beacons, flotsam or jetsam, whales, fishnets, etc. come within five miles of the boat, notify the captain. The horizon is 15 miles, so five miles is 33% of the distance to the horizon. Remember to keep a lookout 360°. White flares in starboard winch handle locker are to alert to collision course.
4. NOTICE WEATHER – if there is appearance of squalls, thunderstorms, a shift of more than 10° in the wind direction or five knots in wind speed, if heeling angle exceeds 26° – notify the captain. If it rains, see that hatches and ports are secure.
5. LOCATION – know location, course of the vessel, and any navigational hazards at the beginning of watch.
6. HEADING CHANGE – if the heading of the boat changes more than 5° – notify the captain. Notify on less of a change in restricted waters.
7. DEPTH – if water depth changes more than instructed – notify the captain.
8. SAILS – if sails will not fill, appear to be tearing, or if a halyard, sheet or furling line parts, let the captain know.

9. ENGINE – if engine temperature exceeds 180°, oil pressure drops below 50 lb., vibration begins, or color or volume of exhaust changes – notify the captain.

10. BILGE – if bilge pump lights come on more than occasionally – notify the captain.

11. GPS – if the GPS loses signal for more than 30 minutes – notify the captain. If navigation is restricted – notify the captain immediately. This is indicated by "Off" being displayed on the B&G and an alarm on the autopilot.

12. NOTICES – occasionally check the Weatherfax for Navtex "Notice to Mariners." If any notice is important – notify the captain.

13. DISTRESS SIGNALS – if you observe distress signals – Mayday or Pahn Pahn on the radio, red or white flares, orange signals – notify the captain.

14. OTHER – any other important occurrences such as fire, unusual vibrations, unusual odors, bilge water, important VHF traffic, anything else you don't understand – notify the captain.

15. If necessary push red horn button five times to alert captain and crew.

Remember – the key word is WATCH. Reading, earphones, or other distractions are prohibited.

Provisioning List

The following were the planned dinners for an estimated thirty days at sea from Ft. Lauderdale to Tahiti:

4 chicken and capers
4 chicken and cheese casserole
4 fried chicken
3 steak
4 hamburger
6 spaghetti
3 Dixie Chili three-ways
3 canned ham
3 canned beef stew
3 canned chicken chow mein
3 canned salmon
? fresh fish

The following was our provisioning list:

60 skinless, boneless chicken breasts
12 steaks
36 hamburgers
6 large canned hams
8 small canned hams
3 large canned stew
3 large canned chicken chow mein
8 pks. chow mein noodles
12 cans salmon
6 cans Hunts spaghetti sauce
6 lbs. ground beef
60 cans Dixie Chili
3 jars Tabasco sauce
4 blocks Philadelphia Cream Cheese
12 boxes spaghetti
6 boxes Shake and Bake
6 boxes frozen peas
6 boxes frozen asparagus
6 cans green beans

6 cans corn
6 cans carrots
6 cans new potatoes
6 boxes instant potatoes
14 cans macaroni and cheese
6 boxes rice
4 cans peaches
4 cans applesauce
6 cans sliced pineapple
4 cans apricots
1 jar capers
8 cans cheddar cheese soup
8 cans low salt cream of mushroom soup
6 packs Lipton French onion soup
8 cans low salt vegetable soup
8 cans clam chowder
2 boxes oyster crackers
8 cans low salt chicken noodle soup
   assorted bouillon cubes
24 cans tuna
24 cans chicken
6 bunches garlic
   salt, pepper, herbs & spices
6 cans roast beef hash
6 cans Spam
14 jars peanut butter
10 jars low salt peanut butter
12 jars jelly
6 jars pickles
2 jars steak sauce
6 jars mustard
3 jars ketchup
12 jars mayonnaise
6 jars salad dressing
8 bags flour
4 bags sugar

24 pks. yeast
480 slices of cheese
4 bags grated cheese
8 lbs. block cheese
4 packaged bologna
4 packaged pickle loaf
4 packaged turkey slices
18 candy bars
6 boxes crackers
36 tubes Pringles potato chips
12 boxes Snyder's pretzels
6 jars no salt peanuts
12 boxes cookies
6 bags tortilla chips
3 bags fish crackers
3 jars salsa
3 jars Mazola oil
1 jar olive oil
1 jar low sodium soy sauce
14 boxes cereal
12 boxes powdered milk
1 gal. frozen strawberries
3 boxes ice cream
2 frozen desserts
12 large cans low salt V8 Juice
24 bottles spring water
24 cans ground coffee
1 box tea bags
4 cases beer
12 bottles white wine
4 cases soft drinks
120 pks. Crystal Light

BIBLIOGRAPHY

AEBI, Tania, *Maiden Voyage*, Balantine Books,
New York, 1989. ISBN 0-345-368762
ALLEN, Philip, ed. *The Atlantic Crossing Guide*,
Adlard Coles, London, 1983. ISBN 0-393-03283-3
ARAB REPUBLIC OF EGYPT, Ministry of Information,
The Suez Canal, Cairo, 1994.
BAILEY, Maurice and Marilyn, *Staying Alive*,
David McKay, Inc., New York, 1977.
ISBN 0-679-50752-3
BEAGLEHOLE, J.C., *The Life of Captain James Cook*,
Stanford University Press, Stanford, CA, 1974.
ISBN 0-8047-0848-7
BRADFORD, Ernle, *The Great Seige*,
Harcourt Brace &World, Inc., New York, 1962.
BRASSEY, Mrs. Thomas, *Around the World in the Yacht
Sunbeam*, Henry Holt Co. New York, 1879.
BROWN, Alexander Crosby, *Horizon's Rim*, Dodd,
Mead & Company, New York, 1935.
BUTCH, David, *Navigation Rules*, Paradise Cay
Publications, Middletown, CA. ISBN 0-939837-14-5
CALLAHAN, Steve, *Adrift*, Houghton Mifflin Co.,
Boston, Mass., 1986. ISBN 0-395-38206-8
CHAPMAN, Charles, *Piloting, Seamanship and Small
Boat Handling,* Motor Boating and Sailing,
New York, 1994. ISBN 0-688-1683-3
CHICHESTER Francis, *Gipsy Moth Circles the World*,
Coward-McCann, Inc., New York, 1967.
COLFELT, David, *100 Magic Miles of the Great Barrier
Reef*, Windward Publications Pty. Ltd.,
Berry N.S.W. Australia, 1985. ISBN 0-9590830-7-3

COLLINS, Dale, *Sea-Tracks of the Speejacks*, Doubleday, Page and Company, New York, 1923.

CLARK, Victor, *On the Wind of a Dream*, Hutchinson of London, London, 1960.

CLOUGHEN, Maurice, *A World to the West*, David McKay, Inc., New York, 1979.

COPELAND, Lisa, *Just Cruising*, Romany Enterprises, Vancover, British Columbia, 1993. ISBN 0-9697690-0-8

... *Still Cruising*, Romany Enterprises, Vancover, British Columbia, 1995. ISBN 0-9697690-1-6

CORNELL Jimmy, *World Cruising Routes*, International Marine Publishing Company, Camden, Maine, 1990. ISBN 0-87742-331-8

CROWE, Bill and Phyllis, *Heaven, Hell and Salt Water*, Adlard Coles Ltd., London, 1955.

DARWIN, Charles, *The Voyage of the Beagle*, 1860, Anchor Books, New York, 1962. ISBN 0-385-02767-2

DAVOCK, Marcia, *Cruising Guide to Tahiti and the French Society Islands*, Wescott Cove Publishing Company, Stanford, Connecticut, 1985. ISBN 0-918752-043

DEVINE, Eric, *Midget Magellans*, Harrison Smith & Robert Haas, New York, 1935

FREELY, John, *Classical Turkey*, Chronicle Books, San Francisco, 1990. ISBN 0-87701-729-8

FLEISCHMANN, Julius, *Footsteps in the Sea*, G.P. Putnam's Sons, New York, 1935.

FREUCHEN, Peter, *Book of the Seven Seas*, Julian Messner, New York, 1957.

GRAY, William, *Coral Reef and Islands*; David and Charles; London, 1988. ISBN 0-7153-0077-6

GRAHAM, Robin Lee, *The Boy Who Sailed Around the World Alone*, Golden Press, New York, 1973.

GREENWALD, Michael, *Survivor*, Blue Horizon's Press, San Diego, 1989. ISBN 0-931297-03-6

GRIFFITH, Bob and Nancy, *Blue Water Cruising*,
Sail Books, Inc., Boston, 1979. ISBN 0-914814-19-2

GUZZWELL, John, *Trekka Round the World*,
Adlard Coles, Ltd., London, 1963

HEIKELL, Rod, *Greek Waters Pilot*,
Imray Laurie Norie & Wilson, St. Ives, England, 1992.
ISBN 0-85288-174-6

. . . , *Mediterranean Cruising Handbook*,
Imray Laurie Norie & Wilson, St. Ives, England, 1988.
ISBN 0-85288-112-6

. . . , *Turkish Waters Pilot*, Imray Laurie Norie & Wilson,
St. Ives, England, 1989. ISBN 0-85288-138X

HEYERDAHL, Thor, *Fatu Hiva*,
Doubleday & Company, Inc., New York, 1974.

. . . , *Kon-Tiki*, Rand McNally & Company, Chicago, 1950.

HINZ, Earl, *Landfalls in Paradise*,
Western Marine Enterprises, Marina del Ray,
California, 1986. ISBN 0-930030-46-X

HISCOCK, Eric. C., *Cruising Under Sail*,
Oxford University Press, Oxford U.K., 1981.
ISBN 0-19-217599-8.

HOLM, Donald, *The Circumnavigators*,
Prentice Hall, New York, 1974. ISBN 0-13-134452-8

HUTCHINSON, Hubbard, *Around the World on the
Resolute*, The Knickerbocker Press, New York, 1924.

. . . , *Far Harbors Around the World*,
The Knickerbocker Press, New York, 1924.

JACKSON, M. H., *Galápagos*, The University of Calgary
Press, Calgary, 1989. ISBN 0-919813-10-0

JOHNSON, Irving and Electa, "The Yankee's Wander-
World," *National Geographic Magazine*, January, 1949.

. . . , "Yankee Roams the Orient," *National Geographic
Magazine*, March, 1951.

. . . , *Yankee's Wander World*, W.W. Norton,
New York, 1949.

KARPODINI-DIMITRIADI, E, *The Greek Islands,*
Ekdotke Athenon S.A, Athens, 1992.
ISBN 960-213-064-4
KENNY, K., *Celestial Navigation: A Step-by-Step Procedure for the Complete Idiot,* K. Kenny,
Topanga, California, 1979.
LAFEBER, Walter, *Panama Canal,*
Oxford University Press, New York, 1978.
ISBN 0-19-502360-9
LINKLATER, Erik, *The Voyage of the Challenger,*
1872, Cardinal, New York, 1974.
LUCAS, Alan, *Cruising in Tropical Waters and Coral,*
International Marine Publishing Company,
Camden, Maine, 1987. ISBN 0-87742-954-5
. . . , *Cruising the Coral Coast,* Horwitz Grahame,
Sydney, 1968. ISBN 0-7255-2101-5
. . . , *Red Sea and Indian Ocean Cruising Guide,*
Imray Laurie Norie & Wilson, St. Ives, England, 1985.
ISBN 0-85288-096-0
MARANGON, Lila, *Amorgos; Monastery of the Panayia Khozoviotissa*; Holy Monastery of the Khozoviotissa,
Athens, 1991.
McCULLOUGH, David, *The Path Between the Seas: The Creation of the Panama Canal,* 1870 - 1914,
Simon and Schuster, New York, 1972.
ISBN 0-671-22563-4
MELVILLE, Herman, *Typee,* 1911, Penguin Classics,
New York, 1972.
MICHENER, James A., *Return to Paradise,*
Bantam Books, New York, 1951.
. . . , *Tales of the South Pacific,* Fawcett Publications,
Greenwide, Conn., 1973.
MONSARRAT, Nicholas, *The Kappillan of Malta,*
William Morrow & Company, Inc., New York, 1974.

MOORE, Denton Rickey, *Gentlemen Never Sail to Weather*, Prospector Press, Moore Haven, Florida, 1993. ISBN 0-9628828-3-6

MOORE, Jim, *By Way of the Wind*, Sheridan House Inc., Dobbs Ferry, New York, 1991. ISBN 0-924486-09-0

MORGAN, Dodge, *The Voyage of American Promise*, Houghton Mifflin Company, Boston, 1989. ISBN 0-395-44096-3

MORISON, Samuel Elliot, *The Great Explorers*, Oxford University Press, New York, 1978.

DEPT. OF NAVY HYDROGRAPHER, *Ocean Passages for the World*, 1895, Taunton, U.K., 1973.

NEILSEN, Carl, *The World Is All Islands*, George Allen & Unwin Ltd., London, 1957.

NORDOFF, Charles and James Norman Hall, *The Hurricane*, Triangle Books, New York, 1935.

PARR, Charles McKey, Ferdinand Magellan, *Circumnavigator*, Thomas Y. Crowell Company, New York, 1964.

PANAMA CANAL COMMISSION, *Panama Canal Guide for Yachts*, Panama, 1991.

PATRICK, Noel, *Curtis Coast*, Riverston Holdings Pty. Ltd., Gladstone, Qld, 1986. ISBN 1-86252-737-7

PAYNE, Bob and Nick Ellison, *The International Marine Boat Manager*, International Marine Publishing Co., Camden, Maine, 1992 ISBN 0-87742-301-6

PIDGEON, Harry, *Around the World Single-handed*, D. Appleton and Co., New York, 1932.

REYNOLDS, Earle and Barbara, *All in the Same Boat*, David McKay Inc., New York, 1962.

RIDGEWAY, John and Andy Briggs, *Round the World Non-Stop*, Patrick Stephens, Wellingborough, U.K., 1985 ISBN 0-85059-757-9

ROBERTSON, Dougal, *Survive the Savage Sea*, Granada
 Publishers Ltd., London, 1985. ISBN 0-246-12509-8
ROQUEFEUIL, Camille de, *A Voyage Around the World
 1816 -1819*, Ye Galleon Press,
 Fairfield, Washington, 1981. ISBN 0-87770-258-6
ROSE, Sir Alec, *My Lively Lady*,
 David McKay Company, Inc., New York, 1968.
ROTH, Hal, *Always a Distant Anchorage*,
 W. W. Norton & Company, New York, 1988.
 ISBN 0-393-03312-0
SKENE, Norman L., *Elements of Yacht Design*,
 Dodd, Mead, New York, 1962.
SLOCUM, Joshua, *Sailing Alone Around the World*,
 1900, Sheridan House Inc., Dobbs Ferry, New York,
 1993. ISBN 0-924486-74-0
STUERMER, Gordon and Nina, Starbound,
 David McKay Company, Inc., New York, 1977.
 ISBN 0-679-50778-7
TESTA, Serge, *500 Days*, Trident Press,
 Aspley, Qld. Australia 1988. ISBN 0-7316-48498
VILLIERS, Alan, *Captain James Cook*,
 Charles Scribner's Sons, New York, 1967.
. . . , *Monsoon Seas: The Story of the Indian Ocean*,
 McGraw-Hill, Inc., New York, 1952.
VOSS, John C., *The Venturesome Voyages of Captain Voss*,
 Charles E. Lauriat Co., Boston, 1926.
WOOD, Charlie, *Charlie's Charts of Polynesia*,
 Surrey, British Columbia, 1989. ISBN 0-9691412-6-2
WRIGHT, C. H., *Survival at Sea: The Lifeboat and
 Liferaft,* Sheridan House Inc., Dobbs Ferry,
 New York, 1988. ISBN 0-85174-540-7
ZWEIG, Stefan, *Conqueror of the Seas; The Story of
 Magellan*, Viking Press, New York, 1938.

GLOSSARY

Admeasure To assign a measurement for the purpose of assessing fees.

Aft Towards or near the stern.

Afterguy A line leading aft from the outboard end of the spinnaker pole and used to control the position of the pole.

Aground A vessel is aground when she is stuck on the bottom. She grounds when she just touches the bottom.

Antipodal Points Two points on opposite sides of the earth from each other.

Apparent Wind The wind that appears to a sailor on a vessel. If there is no true wind at all and the vessel is moving North at 7 knots wind would appear to be out of the North at 7 knots. If true wind was 7 knots out of the South and the vessel was moving North at 7 knots apparent wind would be nil. If true wind was 7 knots out of the West and the vessel was moving at 7 knots North, wind would appear to be out of the Northwest.

Awash Water over the deck.

Backstay A cable from the top of the mast to the stern of the vessel to keep the mast from bending forward.

Banjo Fitting	A fitting, looking like a thick washer and hollowed from the inside, to transfer liquids from an orifice on a stud to the outside edge of the fitting and into a tube.
Beam Reach	A point of sail with the wind 90° to 120° aft of the vessel's bow.
Beam Sea	Waves that are coming at 90° to 120° aft of the vessel's bow.
Beating	A point of sail with the wind 40° to 50° aft of the bow. To travel more directly into the wind a vessel must tack or follow a zigzag course.
Bend On	To fasten a sail to the vessel.
Bilge	The lowest point of the inside of the vessel where any water coming aboard will collect.
Bimini	A collapsible sun shield over the cockpit.
Boom	A horizontal spar that holds out the foot of the sail. The boom on the *Lusty Wind II* is attached to the mast and the clew, or aft corner of the main, is attached to the end of the boom. The foot, or the bottom of the sail, is loose. The sheet line is connected to the outboard end of the boom.
Boom Gooseneck	The connection of the boom to the mast.
Bow	The whole forward part of the vessel.
Brightwork	Woodwork on a vessel that is kept varnished.

Broad Reach	A point of sail with the wind 120° to 150° aft of the vessel's bow. The wind is blowing over the aft quarter of the vessel. This the best point of trade wind sailing.
Bruce Anchor	A modern anchor shaped much like a manta ray. These anchors were designed to hold oil rigs in the North Sea. They hold well under most conditions.
Burgee	A triangular flag of a yacht club.
Bung	A tapered dowel usually of soft wood used to drive into broken seacocks or pipes to avoid flooding the vessel.
Capstan	A turning drum for applying pulling force to lines.
Cay	A Spanish word meaning small island.
Centerboard	A board which is designed to be lowered through a slot in the keel of a vessel to provide more lateral resistance and raised to reduce draft.
Chafe	Damage caused by rubbing.
Clew	The after most corner of a sail.
Companionway	A hatch with a ladder or steps to provide access below.
Close Reach	A point of sail with the wind 50° to 90° aft of the vessel's bow.
Cutter	A sailing vessel with one mast and more than one headsail. *Lusty Wind II* is a cutter.
Davit	A crane used for hoisting a dinghy aboard.

Dead Reckoning	Derived from the phrase deduced reckoning. The process of estimating ones position by keeping track of the speed and direction of travel from a known beginning point. In rural Kentucky, many still say "I reckon" instead of "I know."
Deckhead	The underside of the deck assembly and for cabins, the ceiling.
Dhow	A sailing vessel, pronounced d•o•h, with a lanteen sail still found the Indian Ocean and Red Sea.
Dinghy	A small open boat used primarily for transportation from an anchored yacht to shore.
Displacement Hull	A hull that is supported by its buoyancy even when moving as opposed to a planing hull that skims the top of the water.
Dodger	Canvass and clear vinyl assembly looking like a windshield to protect the cockpit from wind and spray.
Drogue or Sea Anchor	An open ended pyramid shaped or woven parachute shaped object used to keep a vessel's bow or stern to the seas in heavy weather.
Flotsam	Generally cargo, wreckage, or items accidentally falling off a vessel into the water.
Flying Dutchman	A ghost vessel that lures ships into shallow water.

Freshen Nip	To alter the position of a line under load so chafe, at points of friction, occur at a different position on the line.
Following Seas	Waves that are moving toward the stern of a vessel.
Foreguy	A line from the outboard end of a spinnaker pole leading forward and used to control the position of the pole.
Forward or Fore	The front part of a vessel.
Furl	To gather up a sail for storage on a stay or spar.
Galley	Kitchen
Gallows	A framework to support the boom. When not sailing the boom is in the gallows to take strain off the rigging and in a storm the boom is lashed to the gallows to prevent it from swinging wildly.
Genoa	The most forward sail attached to the forestay and a foot that runs aft of the mast. Called a jib if its clew is forward of the mast and a genoa if it comes past.
Ground Tackle	All anchoring equipment including the anchor and the rode.
Grounds	A vessel grounds when she touches the bottom. She is aground when she is stuck on the bottom.
Halyard	A line used to pull the sail into position generally by pulling the head of the sail toward the top of the mast. The term comes from hall yard.

Head	Bathroom - more specifically the toilet. Also the front of the vessel; hence heading, headway, heads up etc.
Headstay	A cable going from the top of the mast to the bow to keep the top of the mast from bending aft.
Heel	When the boat leans over on her beam.
Hook	Anchor
Irons	A sailing vessel is in the irons when the apparent wind angle is too close to the bow to be able to sail.
Jetsam	Debris intentionally thrown overboard from a vessel.
Jibe	To turn the boat so that the apparent wind swings from one aft quarter past the stern to the other aft quarter. This can be dangerous in strong winds as much force can be generated as the boom swings around. A jibe puts much strain on the sheet and boom gooseneck.
Knot	A measurement of speed being one nautical mile per hour or 6,076 feet per hour. A knot is 15.1% more than a land mile per hour. Seven knots, our average speed, equals 8.06 statute miles per hour.
Lanteen Rig	A triangular sail of Arab origin set on a long boom running obliquely from the bow at about 45°. Usually found on a dhow.
Lazarette	A below deck area at the stern of a vessel primarily for steering gear, however, also used for other machinery and storage.

Lee	On a boat it is the side opposite to that from which the wind is blowing. On land it is the shore that can be seen from the boat looking over the side opposite from which the wind is blowing. Thus "beware of a lee shore" as this is the shore the wind will blow a boat upon.
Leeway	The amount of sideways movement of a boat as a result of the wind or distance between the lee side of the boat and danger. "She running out of leeway."
Line	Rope that has been taken off a spool and put to a specific use. Such as dock line, anchor line, or sheet.
Mooring	Chain from a harbor seabed usually to a floating ball. A vessel ties to a mooring to be more secure than at anchor.
Motor-sail	Using sails and the engine at the same time.
Motu	A polynesian word meaning small island formed on coral.
Nautical Mile	A unit of measurement used by seamen and being the length of one minute of arc or latitude. By international agreement it is 6,076 feet. This measurement is different from the statute or land mile which is 5,280 feet. A nautical mile is thus 15.1% longer than a statute mile.
Norseman Fitting	A patented fitting that securely attaches to the blunt end of a cable or wire rope then itself is attached to a secure point.

Outhaul	A line used to pull the clew of the mainsail towards the aft end of the boom.
Port	The left side of a vessel when looking forward. (Haw in Kentucky.)
Quay	Masonry or stone dock (pronounced key).
Range Lights	Two lights to indicate a vessel is on the proper course for a channel. The lights are at two different elevations and the shorter is closer to the channel than the taller. When the farthest light is directly over the closest light, the vessel is on the correct course.
Reserve Buoyancy	Additional buoyancy not usually required to maintain floatation. Provides extra buoyancy to prevent the vessel from being swamped in heavy sea.
Rode	The chain, cable, or line attached to an anchor and the vessel called by land lubbers, "The anchor rope."
Rhumb Line	A line crossing all meridians or lines of longitude at the same angle. A rhumb line is a straight when drawn on the Mercator Projection.
Running	The point of sail when the wind is more than 150° aft of the bow. It is very easy to have a jibe while running.

Running Backstay	Stays on the port and starboard only used when the staysail is being used and supports the mast behind the point approximately two-thirds up the mast opposite the top of the staysail. When the wind is on the port side the port running backstay is used. When the wind is on the starboard side, the starboard backstay is used. Failure to use the running backstay when the staysail is in use will cause pumping of the mast and possible fracture.
Running Lights	Lights that must be exhibited by vessels when underway after nautical twilight. Green lights are exhibited on the starboard side, red lights on the port side, and white lights aft. The red and green lights are to show from the bow back and 112.5°. The white stern light should be seen for 135°, or 67.5° either side of the stern. These lights allow other navigators to know the bearing of the vessel.
Scupper	Drains for the deck along the joint of the deck and toerail.
Seacock	A valve at openings in the hull both near and below the waterline.
Sextant	An instrument with mirrors to measure the angular difference of two objects. Used in navigation to measure the angle between the horizon and a celestial body.
Sheet	A line from the clew of a sail.

Shoal	Shallow water where a ship may run aground.
Skeg	A deep part of the keel that for its short length extends well below the rest of the keel.
Snatch Block	A block or pulley that opens so that it may be put on a line for tension when the line is fastened at both ends.
Sole	Floor of a ship's cabin.
Spinnaker	A sail like a parachute made of light cloth to be used in light winds to gain maximum power.
Spinnaker Pole	A pole used to hold the clew of the spinnaker outboard and prevent the sail from collapsing and loosing its drive.
Starboard	The right side of the vessel looking forward. The name comes from steer boards which were on the right side of the ship where the helmsman stood. The name for the portside of the vessel comes from the side normally laid to a quay or dock in order not to damage the steer board. The placement of the red and green running lights are related. The green light is on the starboard side where the helmsman stands and can keep watch. The red light indicating danger is on the port side where the helmsman may not be able to watch as well. (Gee in Kentucky.)
Staysail	The sail hanked to the inner stay. This sail is smaller and closer to the mast.
Stern	The rear of the vessel.

Sternway	The motion of the boat when backing.
Storm Trysail	A small sail of heavy material to be used in severe weather. The sail is designed to be used in place of the main with the boom lashed in the gallows.
Topside	That portion of the hull that is above the waterline.
Traveler	A small car on a thorship's track below the boom used to control the angle of the downward pull of boom by the sheet line.
Trick	A period of duty at the helm.
Tripper Boat	In Greece, small fishing boats often used to ferry passengers.
Wake	A wave caused by a vessel moving through the water.
Way	A vessel makes way when she is moving through the water. Headway is moving bow first; sternway is stern first; leeway is sideways in the opposite direction where the wind is coming from; and steerage way is when she has enough way on to answer to the helm. Legally a vessel is under way when she is not moored, anchored, or aground.
Weigh Anchor	To raise the anchor. Is it way or weigh? Both come to English from the early German *wegh*, to go or to carry. General usage is underway (to go) and weigh anchor (to carry). These words may even be traced back to the Latin *vehere* and Sanskrit *vah* both meaning to carry.

Wildcat (or gypsy)	A wheel often on a windless designed to grab the links of a chain and pull the chain aboard. Some designs will also grab anchor line.
Winch	A mechanized drum for putting tension on lines usually halyards and sheets.
Windless	Mechanism for pulling the anchor line, or rode, and weighing the anchor. The name comes from without wind as sailing ships were often brought into or out of harbors by rowing the anchor ahead, dropping it, and pulling the boat forward with this gear and repeating.
Windward	On a boat it is the side to which the wind is blowing. On land it is the shore that can be seen from the side of the boat to which the wind is blowing.

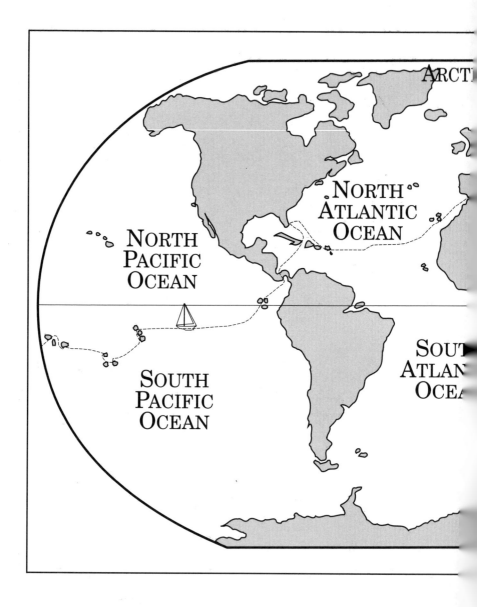